Acknowledgments

We thank the experts who contributed their time for this report, including the members of a 2001 roundtable discussion on ecological riverfront design sponsored by the Urban Land Institute: Steve Apfelbaum, Elizabeth Benson, Uwe Brandis, Ignacio Bunster-Ossa, Patrick Condon, Steve Durrant, Paul Fishman, Carol Franklin, Peter Harnik, Jim Heid, Barry Hersh, Mark Johnson, John Knott, Jr., Ilze Jones, Nan Laurence, James MacBroom, Roy Mann, Brian Reilly, Daniel Redondo, Bill Wenk, and Joe Zehnder. We also thank staff of the National Park Service, Rivers, Trails and Conservation Assistance program for their input: Diana Allen, Chris Brown, Shannon Collier, Charlotte Gillis, Jerry Willis, Dawn Godwin, Steve Morris, Charlie Stockman, and Caroline Wolf. We also thank Sarah Beck, Gary Belan, Ryan Bell, Amy Butler, Naomi Cohn, Portia Cornell, Andres Ferrate, Beth Matthews, Andrea Petzel, Andy Schwartz, Amy Souers, Jason Todd, and Steve Wise for researching and developing case studies, as well as Kathy Dickhut and Nelson Cheung, City of Chicago, for reviewing case study material. We especially wish to thank Ignacio Bunster-Ossa, Donald Brandes, Carol Franklin, Colin Franklin, Ken Kay, Tom Liptan, Bill Thompson, and Bill Wenk for their valuable input. Special thanks to wetlands ecologist Stephen Getlein. Jim Hecimovich and his editorial and design staff at APA did a wonderful job of marshalling this long project through editing and production.

Thanks also to Ralph Sanders of Portland's Bureau of Planning for providing us with the cover photo and other graphic help. Finally, the authors and editors are extremely grateful to Thomas Schueler of the Center for Wetlands Protection for his valuable and insightful review of this manuscript.

This report was funded, in part, through generous contributions from American Rivers, the Beim Foundation, Patrick and Aimee Butler Family Foundation, Carolyn Foundation, The Dibner Fund, Ecolab Foundation, The George Gund Foundation, Marbrook Foundation, The McKnight Foundation, National Park Service Rivers, Trails and Conservation Assistance program, Irwin Andrew Porter Foundation, Surdna Foundation, the American Planning Association's Planning Advisory Service, and contributions from several individual donors.

This publication is a joint production of American Rivers and the American Planning Association.

American Rivers, founded in 1973, leads a nationwide river conservation movement to protect and restore healthy rivers, and the variety of life they sustain, for the benefit of people, fish, and wildlife. It advocates for a national Citizens' Agenda for Rivers, updated every two years based on common sense solutions and the major threats to rivers. It builds and mobilizes grassroots river groups and raises awareness among key decision-makers of threats to rivers and why it matters that we protect and restore them. Headquartered in Washington, D.C., American Rivers operates a Northwest regional office with locations in Seattle and Portland, and eight field offices across the country that work with local communities and river activists. For more information, please see www.AmericanRivers.org.

Ecological Riverfront Design
Restoring Rivers, Connecting Communities

Betsy Otto, Kathleen McCormick, and Michael Leccese

TABLE OF CONTENTS

A New Vision for Urban Riverfronts

Cities are rediscovering their rivers. For at least the past 30 years, cities and towns have been turning back to their rivers, transforming industrial and derelict land into new parks, residences, and commercial space. The trend appears to be continuing and perhaps even accelerating, with major planning and construction efforts underway in cities around the country. After abusing urban rivers through years of hard use and neglect, we have come to realize they are valuable economic and community assets.

This Planning Advisory Service Report promotes the view that we can achieve much greater environmental as well as social and economic success if urban riverfronts are designed with ecological principles in mind.

While this renaissance movement has been overwhelmingly positive, the prevailing view of the urban riverfront is of a blank canvas for "aesthetic enhancements" and economic development initiatives. Too often, the river itself is not considered, an oversight that ignores the possibilities for enhancing the ecological value of the river. Ultimately, these missed possibilities are detrimental to the city and the public, not just the environment. As cities reclaim their rivers, a rare opportunity is offered to repair past damage, to prevent new injury, and to create more sustainable communities. In virtually every case, these cities have a tremendous opportunity to direct riverfront revitalization efforts that will help to bring rivers and the communities that depend on them back to health.

To take advantage of this opportunity, we need to effectively integrate ecological considerations with economic and social goals along the nation's urban rivers. This Planning Advisory Service Report promotes the view that we can achieve much greater environmental as well as social and economic success if urban riverfronts are designed with ecological principles in mind. While we have some mechanisms for protecting our environment, such as water-quality regulations, environmental considerations are often an afterthought in urban riverfront planning. Yet the manner in which these riverfronts are developed can have a tremendous impact on water quality and other environmental concerns.

We firmly believe that communities will find better, more appealing, and more sustainable solutions by integrating ecological considerations upfront in riverfront redevelopment efforts. Indeed, the experience of many communities suggests that treating the river as an equal partner improves environmental quality and quality of life—both of which have significant economic impacts for cities.

This PAS Report aims to put forth a new vision for the nation's urban riverfronts. It provides a set of planning and design principles that can be employed to ensure that, as we reclaim our urban river edges, we do so in the most ecologically sound and economically viable manner possible. The material in this report is intended to help planners, mayors, public works and environmental officials, river advocates, and the general public in their research about effective, ecological riverfront design. The report is structured to provide general information on a number of key topics related to ecological health and human interaction with rivers. It is not intended as a comprehensive list of all issues of concern on riverfronts, but rather as a set of essential ideas that can help communities to achieve more with their riverfront revitalization efforts.

This PAS Report does not address in detail the economic development issues that must also be considered for community riverfronts to be vital and successful. Cities that may want to use the principles described here are likely to be heavily engaged already in economic development activities. Nor does this report address the classic aspects of planning, architectural, and landscape design requirements for successful public spaces (e.g., how to improve the image of a derelict or abandoned urban riverfront area, or how to organize pedestrian pathways to build a sense of liveliness and interest in a place).

The reality in many cities is that significant riverfront development has already happened, and that redevelopment of some kind is now planned or underway. Our report begins from this premise. Further, we assume bringing people to the river often involves providing facilities and services that require buildings and other structures.

This PAS Report, therefore, does not call for removing all buildings or preventing any new structures, but it does espouse a strong view that minimizing impacts and keeping urban riverfronts as natural as possible (i.e., not overburdened with buildings, roads, and other concrete infrastructure) should be a goal for all cities. Indeed, in many instances, it makes better sense, economically and ecologically, to remove old structures and keep new development out of the floodplain and away from sensitive river areas.

In most instances, the ideas and ecological principles put forth in this report can, and should, be applied to river edges being considered for new development. Having said that, we strongly encourage communities to resist extensive new development in the floodplain and along the urban riverfront. Communities should instead seek to maintain a more natural, undeveloped river edge. It is still possible, and often just as desirable, to place housing, commercial space, restaurants, shops, and other amenities near, but not on, the urban riverfront.

Chapter 1 gives some very general background on and history of urban riverfront redevelopment efforts and briefly addresses the benefits of more fully integrating ecological considerations into urban riverfront projects.

Chapter 2 provides background on urban river health, including a basic primer on the key components of river ecosystems that communities should consider as they plan and design riverfront developments. Discussion of any of these components could easily fill a book and is given only a brief overview in this report.

Chapter 3 is the heart of the report. It offers guiding principles for ecologically sound urban riverfront development, including some general perspectives, a set of planning principles, and a set of related, more detailed, design principles.

Chapter 4 gives an overview of the economic benefits of including strong river protection and restoration elements in community riverfront projects.

Finally, Chapters 5 and 6 present two in-depth case studies for the Chicago River and the Willamette River in Portland, Oregon. Both cities have attempted to infuse their urban riverfront revitalization efforts with a stronger ecological focus, and the stories of what they are trying to accomplish and how they are doing it are valuable and vivid reading.

Rebecca R. Wodder
President
American Rivers

CHAPTER 1
A Concise History of
Urban Riverfront Development

Rivers have been hard at work for urban settlements in North America for more than four centuries. The earliest cities were established along the coasts and inland navigable waterways because the movement of people and goods depended heavily on water transportation. As settlers moved west, new river towns served as links between the backwoods and the larger seaport towns. The emerging transport network in North America was a complicated mix of water and overland routes, but rivers were always the most important element: during the early nineteenth century, for example, westward-bound goods were shipped by covered wagon from eastern seaports to Pittsburgh, where barges then carried them along the 1,800-mile length of the Ohio and Mississippi Rivers to New Orleans (Wrenn 1983).

Many cities along coastal rivers from New Jersey to the Carolinas were established at the "fall line"—the geologic meeting point between the flat coastal plain and the Appalachian Piedmont region of inland hills. Because this point represented the limit of navigation for ships, a number of important ports emerged there linking the ocean with inland regions. In some instances, the effective fall line was extended far to the west when canals were dug to bypass non-navigable sections of rivers and to create a more controllable, two-way link between the coast and such inland bodies of water as the Ohio and Mississippi rivers and the Great Lakes. The collision of the Piedmont's harder metamorphic rock with the coastal plain's softer sedimentary rock formed an erosion line that also created waterfalls which powered manufacturing. Both factors were central to the founding of such major port cities as Philadelphia, Baltimore, Washington, D.C., and Richmond, Virginia (USGS 2000).

Throughout the nineteenth and twentieth centuries, river cities—whether smaller inland cities, like Pittsburgh and Cincinnati, or major ports with ocean access, like Philadelphia and Portland, Oregon—have grown in a relatively consistent pattern. Because this pattern has determined today's riverfront land uses and will deeply influence future urban development patterns, uses, and functions, it is important for planners to understand the history of river town expansion. Despite their similarities, however, each town incorporated waterfront uses and development patterns that reflected its unique physical setting as well as the unique needs and commercial interests of its residents.

Throughout the nineteenth and twentieth centuries, river cities...have grown in a relatively consistent pattern. Because this pattern has determined today's riverfront land uses and will deeply influence future urban development patterns, uses, and functions, it is important for planners to understand the history of river town expansion.

THE HISTORY OF A RIVERFRONT CITY

A typical river city was established in the early nineteenth century with a simple wooden jetty, which later grew to include multiple piers and a street network that linked the waterfront to commercial buildings as river traffic increased. Growth occurred whenever this pattern—more piers, followed by more roads and more buildings—was repeated. As a result, growth was centered around transportation, general commerce, shipbuilding, and commercial fishing. Railroads entered most towns and cities by the mid- to late 1800s; accordingly, more river-edge lands were filled in to accommodate rail infrastructure, and warehouse and downtown commercial space increased. As transportation shifted from water to rail, the river edge became less important as a social and retail space, and the city's downtown moved away from the river. Yet the urban riverfront remained active and vital as an economic center. Warehouse, road, and rail infrastructure was expanded, concentrating large-scale commercial and industrial uses along the waterfront. These uses began to dominate many cities' waterfronts by the late nineteenth and early twentieth centuries (Wrenn 1983).

During the first half of the twentieth century, riverfront industry and railroads continued to proliferate. These uses were soon followed by elevated highways that further separated cities from their riverfronts. Urban riverfronts also became popular locations for sewage treatment plants. Even when the plants themselves were not located on the river edge, sewer overflows were commonly found on urban waterfronts discharging untreated sewage during storms directly into rivers. Similarly, urban waterfronts were highly altered by efforts to keep downtown and industrial areas from flooding. The U.S. Army Corps of Engineers had oversight over many of these projects, which typically straightened and deepened channels, removed vegetation, and added bulkheads and floodwalls, completely severing the river from its floodplain.

By the late 1950s, technological changes caused profound shifts in waterfront land use. First, ports were in decline for reasons that included:

- shifts in international travel from passenger ships to transcontinental jet aircraft and in local commuter traffic from ferries and streetcars to private automobiles;

- freight containerization, which shifted cargo unloading from cramped downtown docks to outlying dock sites with larger land areas;

- a shift from port-based commercial fishing to deep-sea trawlers and other methods; and

- a dramatic increase in tanker and freighter sizes that required deep-water ports (Urban Land Institute 2003).

Second, city-based heavy industries abandoned their riverfront locations as business declined or factories became obsolete. As structural shifts occurred in the national and local economies, companies either shut down their industrial and warehouse operations altogether, or moved to suburban and rural sites that offered cheaper labor and land costs and easier highway transportation access.

Third, the highway transportation system was expanding, which coincided with cheap, newly available land along urban riverfronts that could be built on—or over—without displacing existing uses. As a result, many highways were built along urban riverfronts. Philadelphia, Seattle, Louisville, Omaha, and many other cities currently have significant highway barriers built during the 1950s and 1960s that separate their downtowns from the river's edge (Breen and Rigby 1994).

All of these major changes left riverfronts abandoned, often contaminated with industrial waste, and cut off from the cities they had once spawned.

EARLY REDEVELOPMENT EFFORTS

As early as the late 1960s, large and small communities such as San Francisco, San Antonio, Texas, and New Bedford, Massachusetts, decided to turn back to their waterfronts, redeveloping them for public recreation and open space, housing, and office and retail uses to revitalize sagging downtowns (Breen and Rigby 1994). But in other communities, urban riverfronts were stuck for decades in a state of waiting, with land abandoned or used as parking lots, scrap yards, and storage yards. By the 1970s, the changes described above, among others, created a widespread impetus for reuse of the river edge.

Cities realized their downtown riverfronts had fallen into disuse as water-dependent industries declined or moved away. They began to see these areas as valuable untapped resources. Because these waterfronts were the reason for the founding of these cities, local governments worked to reclaim their community's unique heritage by transforming the local waterfront into a new gateway and destination for residents and tourists.

Waterfronts in Baltimore, Boston, and Toronto are often cited as early leaders in this trend. Baltimore's highly successful Inner Harbor redevelopment is a model that has been studied and copied throughout the world: begun in the late 1970s, the project converted former shipbuilding and commercial fishing facilities into public open space, pedestrian ways, an aquarium, shops, restaurants, offices, and housing (see Breen and Rigby 1994, 18–22). Similar urban riverfront redevelopment and restoration efforts have been underway for decades in Chicago, along the Chicago River, and Denver, along the South Platte River, among many others.

We perceive the transformation of urban waterfronts in North America over the last 30 years contributing to, and often playing the major role in, ongoing efforts to restore the centers of our cities and towns to economic and social health.
—ANN BREEN AND DICK RIGBY (1994)

CASE
STUDY

River Issues. In 1938, the U.S. Army Corps of Engineers undertook the cement channelization of the 51-mile Los Angeles River and its tributary streams. Afterwards, Los Angeles turned its back on the river: industrial development soon lined the river and, by the 1980s and 1990s, had left brownfields in its wake. Excessive hardscape and concrete-lined riverbanks have resulted in poor water quality caused by urban runoff and the de-

Peg Henderson

Herongate, by the Los Angeles River in California.

struction of native habitat. The concrete system was designed to move water out to the ocean as quickly as possible, but that objective is being reconsidered given the region's dependence on imported water, the depletion of groundwater, and the impacts of stormwater pollution on state beaches. Despite intense urbanization, Los Angeles remains a hot spot for biodiversity. Much of this rare and threatened habitat is centered in its rapidly disappearing riparian areas.

What Is Being Planned. The Los Angeles River Master Plan was developed in the mid-1990s with assistance from the Rivers, Trails, and Conservation Assistance program of the National Park Service. Its goal is to revitalize the Los Angeles River and create a network of parks, trails, and bikeways by transforming all publicly owned riverside rights-of-way into a continuous greenway. State and local officials, nonprofit organizations, landowners, and the general public support the vision. In 2000, Governor Gray Davis declared his intention to create a linear Los Angeles River State Park that would connect the city's riverfront communities. Since then, two state bond measures have directed more than $140 million toward land acquisition and development.

Three nonprofit organizations—the Trust for Public Land, North East Trees, and The River Project—have created nearly a dozen parks along the river ranging from 100 square feet to several acres in size. Many of these parks are located in the area's most densely populated neighborhoods. This park-building effort has been accomplished with financial assistance from the California Department of Transportation Environmental Enhancement and Mitigation Program, the city and county of Los Angeles, and the state's conservancies.

The heart of the proposed river greenway is a 247-acre brownfield and former railyard near downtown known as Taylor Yard. With more than two miles of river frontage, it presents a wide range of opportunities for environmental restoration and community economic revitalization. In 1999, the state's Coastal Conservancy undertook a multiobjective feasibility study for Taylor Yard and developed a plan that incorporated riparian habitat restoration, runoff remediation, and flood protection with active and passive recreational uses for the land.

Although then-Governor Davis designated the site as a future state park and committed $45 million towards its acquisition in 2000, community groups had to sue to stop a proposed industrial development. In 2001, they prevailed and the state stepped in to purchase the land. A master plan is now being shaped for the site that will balance community services, mixed-use retail, and residential development alongside a 103-acre Los Angeles River State Park. Additional funding for completion will come from both private and public sources, including the city and county of Los Angeles, California Department of Parks and Recreation, Coastal Conservancy, U.S. Army Corps of Engineers, and the U.S. Environmental Protection Agency.

Involving local schools and neighborhood groups in the design and development of the greenway provides an opportunity for Angelenos to discover their cultural, historic, and natural heritage. The Valleyheart Greenway—a quarter-mile stretch of river in Studio City—was recently created through a partnership between The River Project and the fourth graders of Carpenter Avenue Elementary School. A growing awareness of larger watershed issues, crucial to the development of future regional policy changes, has begun to result from just this kind of direct, grassroots involvement.

With funding from the Coastal Conservancy, North East Trees, and The River Project have undertaken comprehensive studies of the Los Angeles River's two major tributaries: the Arroyo Seco and the Tujunga Wash. Their plans include removal of concrete and restoration of the systems' natural processes to enhance water quality, water resources, habitat, community access to bikeways, and open space.

Benefits to the River and Community. The Los Angeles River may be one of the most abused and degraded of American rivers. Most Angelenos are still unaware that there *is* a river in their midst. Los Angeles has less park space per capita than any major city in America, and many of its most underserved communities are located along the river. The Los Angeles River Greenway will enhance the quality of life along the river; connect disparate communities; strengthen local economies; bring awareness to the area's forgotten natural and cultural heritage; improve water quality; increase availability of local water resources; protect and restore native habitats; provide opportunities for public art; increase bicycle commuting; and expand recreational opportunities.

For more information . . .

- See The River Project web site, www.theriverproject.org/lariver.html, the Friends of the Los Angeles River web site, www.folar.org, and the Trust for Public Land web site, www.tpl.org.
- Information about the Los Angeles River Master Plan is available at www.ladpw.org/wmd/watershed/LA/LA_River_Plan.cfm.
- Gustaitus, Rasa. 2001. "Los Angeles River Revivial." *Coast and Ocean*, Autumn, 2–14.
- Morrison, Patt. 2001. *Rio L.A.: Tales from the Los Angeles River*. Santa Monica, Calif.: Angel City Press.
- Price, Jennifer. 2001. "Paradise Reclaimed: A Field Guide to the LA River." *LA Weekly*, August 10–16.
- Sydell, Laura. 2000. "The Politics of Open Space Design." *Weekend All Things Considered*, National Public Radio, September 9. [Accessed January 13, 2004.] Available at www.npr.org/programs/specials/architecture/000909.html.
- Whitaker, Barbara. 2001. "Visions of Parting a Sea of Concrete with a Unifying River Greenbelt." *New York Times*, January 27, A8.

WHAT'S DRIVING URBAN RIVERFRONT DEVELOPMENT TODAY

The renewed attention to waterfronts in the 1970s coincided with a growing interest in historic preservation and with efforts to counteract suburban flight by reviving the urban core. These early urban riverfront initiatives thus sparked a redevelopment trend that accelerated in the late 1970s and boomed in the 1980s and 1990s. The first years of the twenty-first century will likely see as much as $500 million spent on downtown river revitalization projects nationwide (Kratzer 2000).

So what's driving this boom? In addition to the economic shifts that caused industry to move off the riverfront, several other key considerations have prompted urban riverfront redevelopment and, therefore, can help to drive a more environmentally sensitive approach to future redevelopment.

Water Quality Improvements and Brownfield Revitalization

Although some laws enacted before the 1970s helped to stem water pollution, they were primarily aimed at preventing navigation obstructions (e.g., Rivers and Harbors Act of 1899). Beginning in the 1950s, the federal government made some efforts, including grants, to promote basic treatment of raw sewage before it was dumped into rivers and lakes. Industrial and raw sewage discharges, however, had made conditions in the nation's rivers and lakes so abysmal that these conditions galvanized the environmental movement of the 1960s, resulting in the first observation of Earth Day in 1970. Landmark environmental legislation was passed during this period: in 1972 Congress passed the Federal Water Pollution Control Act Amendments, which later became known as the Clean Water Act. This Act created massive spending programs to construct wastewater treatment facilities and reduce the volumes of raw sewage flowing into the nation's waters. The EPA estimates that since the passage of the Clean Water Act more than $1 trillion has been spent to upgrade and expand wastewater treatment facilities (U.S. EPA 2001c). Industry and other municipal dischargers were required to clean up their effluent and obtain permits for the first time.

These efforts have led to enormous improvements in water quality. Previously, industrial pollution, sewage, and decomposing algae fed by the waste had turned many urban rivers into stomach-turning cesspools. Few people were interested in standing near these rivers, much less dining or enjoying an open-air concert on their banks. The cleaner urban rivers that emerged by the 1980s were not just aesthetically appealing; they were healthier and thus able to sustain a wider diversity of fish, birds, and other wildlife. These improvements drew the public to the water's edge to walk, bike, boat, fish, and observe wildlife. As people returned to the river, they expressed a stronger interest in protecting and restoring natural areas and wildlife habitat.

Unfortunately, aging sewers and wastewater treatment systems as well as inadequate investment have begun to reverse past gains. The EPA recently estimated that, between 2000 and 2019, the gap between existing federal, state, and local funding for such infrastructure and the amount of money needed to properly maintain treatment systems would be between $331 billion and $450 billion. "Wastewater treatment efficiencies may be leveling off," the EPA warned, "which, when combined with population and economic growth, could have the effect of reversing hard-won water quality gains. By 2016 pollution levels could be similar to levels observed in the mid-1970s" (U.S. EPA 2002a, 8). Adequate funding is necessary for riverfront revitalization to continue. The Water Infrastructure Network warns that current federal contributions cannot help because they have, in fact, declined by 75 percent in real terms since 1980. In 2000, for example, they represented only about 10 percent of total capital outlays for water and wastewater infrastructure and less than 5 percent of total water outlays (Water Infrastructure Network 2000).

The shift to a service-based national economy has resulted in the abandonment of many riverside industrial warehouses and factories over the past five decades. The problems of cleaning these contaminated sites—so-called brownfields—are especially great when they include urban riverfront lands or urban rivers themselves. Typically, contaminants and wastes were dumped into rivers to "send them away" (i.e., to send them downstream for the next community to deal with). A nationwide drive to clean sites contaminated with toxic pollutants was the impetus for what is commonly referred to as the Superfund Act (or CERCLA, the Comprehensive Environmental Resource Compensation and Liability Act of 1980). Efforts over the past two decades to facilitate toxic cleanups and reclaim brownfield sites have led to more funding and resources for returning these contaminated sites to productive use. The Brownfields Revitalization and Environmental Restoration Act of 2001 (passed in January 2002), for example, is credited with providing "$1.25 billion to states, localities, and Indian tribes over five years" (Government Finance Officers Association 2003), and the EPA has been responsible for "leverag[ing] $3.7 billion in brownfields cleanup" as a result of this new act (U.S. EPA 2002f). Many states and local governments also provide significant funding for brownfield cleanup and redevelopment.

As the U.S. Congress debates the contours of the reauthorization of TEA-21 (the Transportation Equity Act for the Twenty-First Century), there is growing sentiment for making stormwater mitigation part of the federal surface transportation program. The U.S. Senate approved a new provision to dedicate 2 percent of the Surface Transportation Program funding for stormwater improvement projects. Advocates hope that a stormwater mitigation set-aside would do for water quality projects what other transportation programs have accomplished for bike, pedestrian, and trail improvements. During debate on this proposal, a bipartisan group of senators described the impact of transportation projects on water quality and the need to help communities address the problem. As of February 2004, the U.S. House had yet to take action on the idea, but the inclusion of guaranteed funding in the Senate legislation marks significant progress.

Desire for More Park Space and Greenways

Many cities are incorporating open space and park amenities, as well as trails and walkways along their riverfronts. For example, Saint Paul, Minnesota, has developed walkway and trail connections along a section of its downtown riverfront in connection with restoration of an historic park on Harriet Island in the Mississippi River. The recently opened Science Museum of Minnesota, with a new permanent Mississippi River Visitor Center dedicated to the river's natural history, sits across the river from Harriet Island and is a major tourist attraction.

The 1990s brought a surge in interest in outdoor recreation, and many cities are responding to the public's interest in access to nature by combining open space features with more traditional features like shops, cafes, and restaurants (Breen and Rigby 1996). A recent study by the U.S. Fish and Wildlife Service and the U.S. Department of Commerce reported that 31 percent of the U.S. population engaged in wildlife-watching in 2001, increasing their expenditures for trips, equipment, and other items by 16 percent (adjusted for inflation) between 1991 and 2001 (U.S. FWS 2002). For more information on the economic benefits of greenways, open space, and nature-based tourism see Chapter 4 of this Planning Advisory Service Report.

Growing Appreciation of "Green Infrastructure" Benefits

As we learn more about the benefits of protecting our natural resources, there has been a movement toward protecting natural river attributes and restoring areas that have been damaged. In addition to cleaning up past problems, cities are beginning to see the value of guarding against future harm, including obvious and inadvertent impacts. Natural river functions (e.g., flood storage, water purification and supply, wildlife habitat, and safe fishing and recreation) are extremely costly to replace once they are lost or damaged. Federal, state, and local regulations require river water, structures, and functions to be protected. Incorporating river protection into urban riverfront plans, designs, and construction can significantly reduce the costs of meeting these requirements.

SUMMARY

Urban riverfronts are being asked to do many things today. Popular waterfront developments in Baltimore, San Antonio, Chicago, and other cities have awakened the public to the value and potential of reclaiming the river's edge. Rejuvenating city centers by developing vibrant riverfronts can be yet another tool in rejuvenating downtowns and counteracting urban sprawl. Residents and tourists want to enjoy and get close to a river, to learn more about its cultural and natural history, and to see wildlife and engage in various kinds of outdoor recreation.

But while communities are asking more of their rejuvenated rivers, unchecked development elsewhere in the watershed, increases in stormwater runoff, and inadequately treated sewage discharges have become serious challenges. Protecting and recovering river health must be a co-equal goal with efforts to revitalize riverfronts. Without question, the cities that pay careful attention to both the needs of the river and the economic and social needs of their communities will reap the greatest rewards.

CHAPTER 2
Urban River Health

Human activities have had an indelible impact upon rivers. We have come to depend on them for transportation and commerce, to provide food and other substances, and, most problematically, to assimilate and carry away our wastes. Centuries of hard wear have shown their effect most acutely on urban rivers.

Now there is a growing interest in restoring damaged urban rivers and in protecting those river reaches that have not yet been affected by negative impacts from human development. And because rivers are resilient, urban rivers can be remarkably responsive to efforts to protect and improve their physical condition.

If we are going to do a better job of planning and designing riverfront development, we must first understand the history and current state of urban river health. We must also recognize the threats to these rivers, including the essential components of a healthy river, and the prospects for rehabilitating rivers as living ecosystems.

URBAN RIVER HEALTH IN HISTORICAL CONTEXT

Urban river health declined steadily through the first 70 years of the twentieth century due to massive physical alterations of riverbanks, overharvesting of fish and other aquatic animals, and the dumping of larger and larger volumes of sewage and industrial pollutants into rivers.

In general, a river's health is determined by the *chemical* properties of its water as well as the river's *physical* and *biological* properties. All three components are explicitly written into the Clean Water Act, and together are technically considered to constitute "water quality." The Clean Water Act acknowledges that these properties are intricately entwined and often cannot be separated meaningfully, in much the same way that genetics, diet, and exercise are essential and interrelated in human health. For example, stormwater runoff carries contaminants and thus adversely affects water quality by changing the chemical content of river water. But stormwater surges also cause in-stream erosion detrimental to aquatic life. These chemical, physical, and biological effects can be analyzed as separate phenomena; in a river that is inundated by stormwater runoff, however, these effects are never isolated. This Planning Advisory Service Report often addresses aspects of river ecology separately, but planners and other decision makers should keep in mind that each is inextricably linked to the others in the urban river environment.

Water Quality

Before the 1970s, little hard data on water quality were available. Despite the lack of hard evidence, however, urban river water quality and overall health was a growing concern by the 1960s across the United States. Raw sewage was spewing into the Connecticut River, the Potomac River, and the entire Mississippi River, among many other waterways. The Cuyahoga River in downtown Cleveland caught fire at least three times: in 1936, 1952, and, most famously, in 1969. On June 22, 1969, debris and oil floating in the river burned for 20 minutes and caused $50,000 worth of damage. As far back as 1881, the mayor of Cleveland had referred to the Cuyahoga as an "open sewer." This was a common description of many rivers across the United States through the 1960s, yet there was little concerted protest.

By the late 1960s, this had changed. National media coverage of the Cuyahoga burning drew widespread outcry, and the public grew increasingly dissatisfied by the fact that many rivers were devoid of life, dangerous to touch, and unpleasant to smell. Congress responded with strong action.

The 1972 Clean Water Act set an ambitious goal: "To restore and maintain the chemical, physical, and biological integrity of the Nation's waters." Further, it called for the elimination of the discharge of pollutants into navigable waters by 1985 and water quality good enough to allow for fishing, healthy wildlife, and "recreation in and on the water" by 1983.

By 2000, nearly 30 years after passage of the Clean Water Act, the nation's urban rivers and other water bodies were remarkably cleaner. To cite just a few statistics from a retrospective on the Act's 25th anniversary (Schneider 1997):

- The number of waterways safe for fishing and swimming doubled.

- The amount of organic waste released into surface waters between 1972 and 1985 dropped by 46 percent, despite a 30 percent increase in the amount of sewage treated.

- Pollution discharges from factories and municipal treatment plants were reduced by 90 percent.

- The dumping of about 1 billion pounds per year of toxic pollutants was eliminated.

Despite significant progress in cleaning up point sources of water pollution, the Clean Water Act's sweeping goal has not yet been achieved. As the U.S. EPA acknowledges in its 2000 National Water Quality Inventory report to Congress, river and stream quality is still seriously threatened:

- Of the nation's roughly 3.6 million miles of rivers and streams, 39 percent of assessed rivers are "impaired" (and only 19 percent of the river miles in the United States were even assessed). By "impaired," the EPA means that the rivers are not clean enough for fishing, swimming, as a source for drinking water, or other uses for which they are designated.

- The percentage of impaired waters *increased* from 35 percent in 1998 to 39 percent in 2000.

Thus, despite tremendous gains in controlling water pollution, nearly half of U.S. rivers still have poor or declining water quality, and recent trends suggest that earlier gains may be eroding. (See Chapter 1 for discussion on this point.)

Much of the progress over the past 30 years was made in the form of curtailed point pollution, brought about through restrictions on end-of-pipe industrial and sewage discharges and other pollution originating from a single point. Today, the largest sources of water-quality problems come from nonpoint or diffuse sources of contaminated runoff, primarily from urban and agricultural lands. Nonpoint pollution is responsible for 40 percent of impairment in surveyed rivers, lakes, and estuaries (U.S. EPA 2001a). Physical alterations made to river structure and habitat are also a leading cause of damage to rivers. Nationally, the leading pollutants and stressors for rivers are bacteria (affecting 37 percent of impaired rivers), much of which results directly from stormwater runoff, or indirectly when stormwater volumes overwhelm sewers, sending raw sewage into rivers. The next leading cause of impairment to rivers is siltation (tiny particles of soil, also called sedimentation), affecting 31 percent of impaired rivers (U.S. EPA 2002d).

Despite significant progress in cleaning up point sources of water pollution, the Clean Water Act's sweeping goal has not yet been achieved.

FIGURE 2-1. SUMMARY OF QUALITY OF ASSESSED RIVERS, LAKES, AND ESTUARIES

Waterbody Type	Total Size	Amount Assessed* (% of Total)	Good (% of Assessed)	Good but Threatened (% of Assessed)	Polluted (% of Assessed)
Rivers (miles)	3,692,830	699,946 (19%)	367,129 (53%)	59,504 (8%)	269,258 (39%)
Lakes (acres)	40,603,893	17,339,080 (43%)	8,026,988 (47%)	1,348,903 (8%)	7,702,370 (45%)
Estuaries (sq. miles)	87,369	31,072 (36%)	13,850 (45%)	1,023 (<4%)	15,676 (51%)

*Includes waterbodies assessed as not attainable for one or more uses.
Note: Percentages many not add up to 100 percent due to rounding.
Source: U.S. EPA (2002d)

FIGURE 2-2. LEADING CAUSES AND SOURCES* OF IMPAIRMENT IN ASSESSED RIVERS, LAKES, AND ESTUARIES

	Rivers and Streams	Lakes, Ponds, and Reservoirs	Estuaries
Causes	Pathogens (Bacteria)	Nutrients	Metals (Primarily mercury)
	Siltation (Sedimentation)	Metals (Primarily mercury)	Pesticides
	Habitat Alterations	Siltation (Sedimentation)	Oxygen-Depleting Substances
Sources	Agriculture	Agriculture	Municipal Point Sources
	Hydrologic Modifications	Hydrologic Modifications	Urban Runoff/Storm Sewers
	Habitat Modifications	Urban Runoff/Storm Sewers	Industrial Discharges

*Excluding unknown, natural, and "other" sources.
Source: U.S. EPA (2002d)

Over the past 10 years, the U.S. Geological Survey has been conducting in-depth research on the water quality of 40 urban watersheds and has found some startling results. Among its findings:

- Concentrations of fecal coliform bacteria commonly exceed recommended standards for water-contact recreation.

- Nearly 80 percent of urban stream samples contained five or more pesticides. Herbicides were detected in 99 percent of urban stream samples, with the most common being those applied to lawns, golf courses, and road right-of-ways, such as atrazine, simazine, and promenton.

- One or more organochloride compounds were detected in 97 percent of fish tissue samples at urban sites. In 10 percent of these samples, the compound levels exceeded guidelines to protect wildlife.

- Concentrations of total phosphorus are generally as high in urban streams as in agricultural streams. More than 70 percent of sampled urban streams exceeded the EPA's desired goal for preventing nuisance plant growth (such as algae).

- Lead, DDT, and chlordane—all banned in the United States—have shown significant decreases in urban river sediment cores. But zinc and polycyclic aromatic hydrocarbons (PAHs, which result from fossil fuel combustion and tire and pavement wear) are increasing, and both can be toxic to aquatic life in high concentrations. This trend is most likely due to increased motor vehicle traffic and more paved surfaces (Van Metre et al. 2000).

Physical Health

The history of human interaction with rivers since European settlement is one of bending rivers, quite literally, to our will. There were sound economic development reasons for early actions because rivers were essential for transporting goods and powering mills and machinery. As time passed, however, physical alterations to rivers became more widespread and damaging. These alterations include straightening natural river meanders and dredging and deepening channels to move larger vessels; building hydropower and water supply dams; squeezing rivers into narrower channels with dikes, levees, and concrete and steel walls; and separating rivers from their floodplains to manage floods, build highways, and capture more land for farming and development. These alterations are often promoted as economic progress, but together they have had, and continue to have,

FIGURE 2-3. LEADING POLLUTANTS AND SOURCES*
OF RIVER AND STREAM IMPAIRMENT

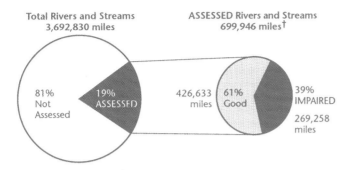

Total Rivers and Streams
3,692,830 miles

81%
Not
Assessed

19%
ASSESSED

ASSESSED Rivers and Streams
699,946 miles†

426,633
miles

61%
Good

39%
IMPAIRED

269,258
miles

The smaller pie chart on the right shows that, for the subset of assessed waters, 61 percent are rated as good and 39 percent as impaired according to U.S. EPA (2002d). When states identify waters that are impaired, they describe the pollutants or processes causing or contributing to the impairment. The bar chart presents the leading causes and the number of river and stream miles impacted. The upper axis shows the percentage of impaired river miles affected by each pollutant/source. The lower axis shows the percentage of assessed river miles affected by each pollutant/source.

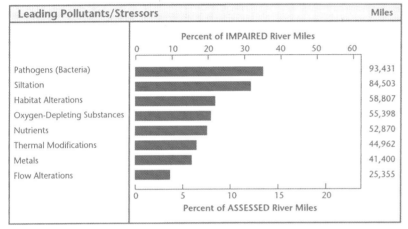

Leading Pollutants/Stressors — **Miles**

Percent of IMPAIRED River Miles

Pollutant/Stressor	Miles
Pathogens (Bacteria)	93,431
Siltation	84,503
Habitat Alterations	58,807
Oxygen-Depleting Substances	55,398
Nutrients	52,870
Thermal Modifications	44,962
Metals	41,400
Flow Alterations	25,355

Percent of ASSESSED River Miles

*Includes miles assessed as not attainable.
Note: Percentages do not add up to 100 percent because more than one pollutant or source may impair a river segment.
Source: U.S. EPA (2002d)

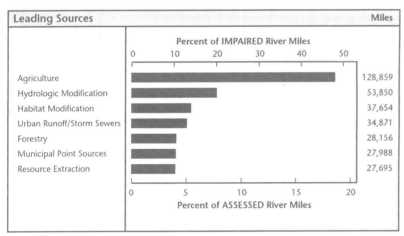

Leading Sources — **Miles**

Percent of IMPAIRED River Miles

Source	Miles
Agriculture	128,859
Hydrologic Modification	53,850
Habitat Modification	37,654
Urban Runoff/Storm Sewers	34,871
Forestry	28,156
Municipal Point Sources	27,988
Resource Extraction	27,695

Percent of ASSESSED River Miles

*Excluding unknown and natural sources.
†Includes miles assessed as not attainable.
Note: Percentages do not add up to 100 percent because more than one pollutant or source may impair a river segment.
Source: U.S. EPA (2002d)

enormous impacts on river ecosystems. They also produce substantial infrastructure and human consequences.

Dams. In the United States, there are an estimated 75,000 dams taller than six feet and at least tens of thousands of smaller dams, according to the U.S. Army Corps of Engineers (American Rivers et al. 1999). Virtually all large rivers of the contiguous 48 states are highly modified by dams, with fewer than 50 rivers free-flowing for more than 120 miles (Cushing and Allan 2001).

Many of these structures are old, in poor condition, and no longer serve a useful function. There is a growing movement to remove unnecessary dams and those whose environmental costs outweigh their economic value, including a number in urban locations (American Rivers 1999). Dam removal has become an important new emphasis in river restoration across the country. At the same time, however, new or larger dams for flood control, water supply, and hydroelectric power are being proposed across the country, despite their huge negative impacts on rivers. (See Chapter 3, Design Principle 3 for more information on the impacts of dams on rivers.)

Channelization, dredging, and other physical alterations. The Army Corps of Engineers—the nation's chief public works agency responsible for modifying rivers—estimates that it has installed, and currently maintains, 10,790 miles of navigation channels and 8,500 miles of levees and countless revetment, dike, and seawall projects. The Army Corps also dredges significant amounts of river material from the nearly 11,000 miles of channels it maintains, with 285 million cubic yards of sediment and other material removed in 2000 alone (U.S. Army Corps of Engineers 2002).

For many years, this was typical treatment for urban streams—channelization. This is Fullerton Creek in California.

Source: Army Corps of Engineers

Headwaters and wetlands destruction. The loss of river headwaters—which generally include wetlands and the smallest continuously flowing, ephemeral, and intermittent streams—to urban development has been another significant negative physical impact for urban rivers. Often wetland loss has gone hand in hand with channelizing rivers and disconnecting them from their floodplains, where many wetlands are located.

Due to more aggressive wetland policies and public education campaigns over the past 15 years, the rate of wetland loss has slowed dramatically since the 1950s, from just under half a million acres per year to a little more than 100,000 acres per year today (Council on Environmental Quality 1998). Despite this slowdown, wetlands are still disappearing rapidly. At the time of European settlement, the area covered today by the contiguous United States had an estimated 221 million acres of wetlands. As wetlands have been drained, dredged, filled, leveled, and flooded, less than half that acreage now exists (U.S. FWS 2001). Since the late 1700s, nearly every state has lost a significant proportion of its original wetlands, with some states—California, Illinois, Indiana, Iowa, Missouri, and Ohio—losing more than 85 percent (Council on Environmental Quality 1998, 304–6).

FIGURE 2-4. PERCENTAGE OF WETLAND ACREAGE LOST, 1970s–1980s

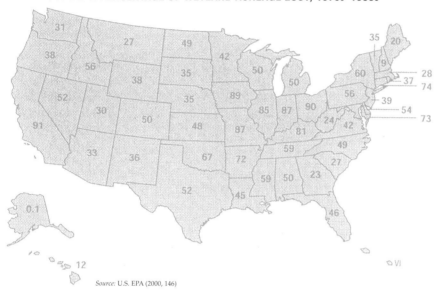

Source: U.S. EPA (2000, 146)

Small streams also continue to be lost—filled in or forced underground into pipes—at an alarming rate. Studies in metropolitan Atlanta in the Upper Chattahochee River watershed show that one-third of all small streams were destroyed by filling and piping during a period of transition from forest to urban land use (Atlanta Regional Commission 2003).

Biological Health

Despite significant impacts, U.S. rivers still contain an astonishing diversity of life. The United States is ranked first in worldwide species diversity in crayfishes, freshwater mussels and snails, and the aquatic insects that form the base of the food web. Ten percent of the world's fish species reside in U.S. rivers, streams, lakes, and other bodies of fresh water.

Yet there have been many documented extinctions of aquatic fish, mollusks, and other aquatic life: since 1900, 123 freshwater animal species and subspecies have been recorded as extinct in North America, including 35 mussel species and 40 fish species (Cushing and Allan 2001). Many other species have likely vanished without our knowledge. Many species of amphibians, reptiles, insects, plants, mammals, and birds depend on healthy rivers and are now at risk. The Nature Conservancy estimates that two-thirds of freshwater mussels and crayfishes are rare or imperiled and more than one-third of freshwater fishes and amphibians dependent on aquatic and wetland habitats are at risk. Forty-six percent of the threatened and endangered species listed by the U.S. Fish and Wildlife Service rely directly or indirectly on wetlands for their survival (U.S. EPA 1998).

In urban environments, once-common aquatic species are no longer present because their physical habitat has been altered, water quality is too poor (e.g., high sediment loads, low oxygen, and increased temperatures and toxics), and invasive species have overwhelmed them. Fish and other aquatic life can rebound when river conditions improve, however. In the past, little more than carp lived in the Chicago River. Today, with significant water-quality improvements, the river sustains 50 species of fish (City of Chicago Department of Environment 2003).

Many urban wetlands have been damaged to the point that once-common aquatic species are extinct.

U.S. Fish and Wildlife Service

COMPONENTS OF A RIVER ECOSYSTEM

River ecosystems are complex, with many interacting components. In order to understand how an *urban* river functions, it is first essential to understand the basic components of a *natural* river ecosystem. To do so requires information from many scientific disciplines and an appreciation of the ways in which various river components are deeply interwoven.

To make informed decisions regarding riverfront development, planners and riverfront decision makers should be aware of the fundamentals of river ecosystems. Each component of a river ecosystem is the subject of many books, articles, and much scientific study. The following section is adapted largely from material in the Federal Interagency Stream Restoration Working Group's extensive handbook, *Stream Corridor Restoration: Principles, Processes, and Practices* (2001), and an excellent general resource, *The River Book* (1998) by James MacBroom, a publication of the Connecticut Department of Environmental Protection.

It is important to note that the character of rivers differs greatly by geography and climate. These differences have a critical bearing on how rivers function, but space limitations restrict us to a very broad discussion here. We strongly recommend that planners consult local natural resource publications when they reach the detailed planning stage of any specific riverfront development for more specific information about the physical structure, function, and ecology of local river types.

Presented below is a basic primer on the component parts of a river ecosystem—watersheds and the hydrologic cycle, sediment cycles, headwaters, floodplains, and river channels—and the impacts of urbanization on each.

Watersheds and the Hydrologic Cycle

A watershed is the area of land that drains into a given stream, river, lake, or wetland. Water movement through a watershed begins with rain or snow-melt or groundwater that wells up to the surface of the land. It moves down-hill (even in seemingly flat terrain, water will move in one direction or the other depending on the gradient of the land) over the ground as a sheet of water, then collects in small rivulets that erode shallow channels in the soil and feed small streams. These streams receive more runoff and groundwater discharge as they descend, eventually merging where their valleys inter-sect. In large watersheds, they join to form major rivers that ultimately empty into the oceans.

Watersheds, the hydrologic cycle, and rivers are all closely intertwined. The natural system by which water circulates through the Earth's atmo-sphere, over its surface, and beneath the ground is called the hydrologic cycle. Water vapor enters the atmosphere when the sun's heat causes it to evaporate from oceans, lakes, and streams, as well as directly from snow, ice, and soil, and through transpiration, which is the release of water vapor by plants during photosynthesis. It is returned to the Earth as precipita-tion, which soaks into the ground or runs over the surface and into streams as described above.

When a stream's water level is lower than the water table, groundwater seeps into the channel, replenishing the flow. (See Figure 2-5.) The U.S. Geological Survey estimates that, on average, 40 percent of annual streamflow comes from such groundwater discharges, also known as baseflows (Alley et al. 1999). In dry seasons and arid climates, groundwater may constitute nearly all the flow in a river. Groundwater from springs and seeps is also important to water quality and aquatic life, because it is usually cool, clean, and rich in dissolved oxygen.

FIGURE 2-5. THE HYDROLOGIC CYCLE

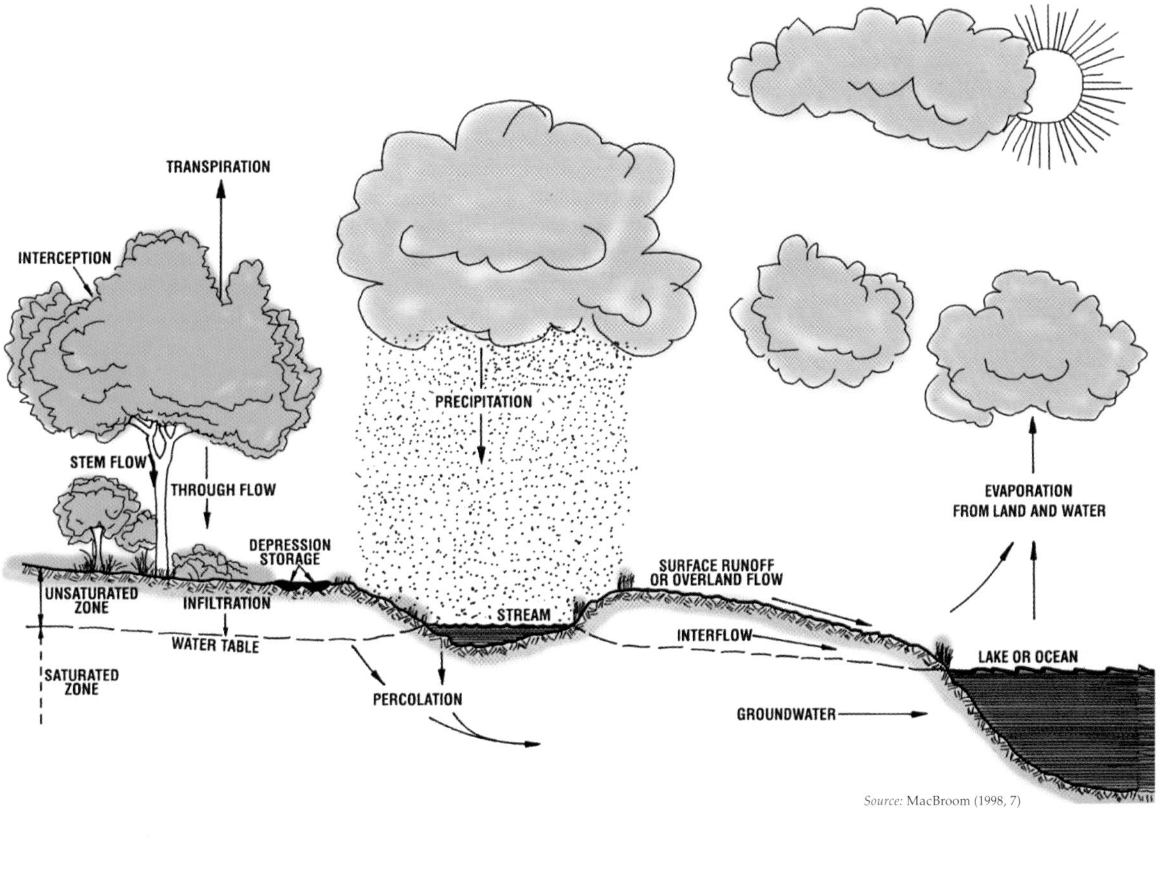

Source: MacBroom (1998, 7)

What occurs on the land in watersheds has a profound impact on the hydrologic cycle, and thus on rivers—from water quality to water-flow volumes and timing. For example, in undeveloped watersheds, rain and melting snow are intercepted by the leaves of trees and other vegetation; what does not evaporate is absorbed into the soil. In urban watersheds, precipitation hits hard surfaces, such as roofs, roads, and parking lots (all are called impervious surfaces), and rushes into storm sewers without being absorbed, thereby short-circuiting natural hydrologic processes. (See Figure 2-6.) As a result, larger amounts of water surge through streams and rivers in shorter periods of time. Studies have repeatedly shown that the percentage of impervious cover in a watershed has a direct impact on the physical integrity and aquatic life of rivers and streams (Schueler 1995a).

Increased runoff causes significant negative impacts on streams and rivers. It often carries sediment and other pollutants that change the physical and chemical qualities of a body of water. In addition, when runoff flushes into rivers with greater velocity than under natural conditions, physical damage to rivers is typically the result: banks erode, causing additional sedimentation and damaging riverbeds and other river habitats and structures. Similarly, runoff that would gradually rise and recede in natural settings peaks and recedes much more quickly in urban environments. The total volume of urban runoff is also much higher. More paved surfaces means less water can infiltrate into the ground; as a result, groundwater baseflows to rivers can be severely depleted, which is particularly damaging in dry seasons and arid climates.

Increased temperatures in urban streams also are a threat. Thermal loading disrupts aquatic organisms that have finely tuned temperature limits (U.S. EPA 1993). Water temperature varies primarily with air temperature and stream size (because larger streams have more water that acts as a thermal buffer) (Cushing and Allan 2001). But water temperature is also substantially affected by shading, groundwater flows, flow obstructions, and runoff from impervious surfaces. Temperature can change significantly when streamside vegetation is removed since more solar energy reaches the water surface. In some streams and seasons, groundwater is a substantial component of river flows: it remains at a relatively constant temperature—roughly the average annual air temperature—and is generally cooler in summer and warmer in winter than surface waters (Cushing and Allan 2001). Thus when groundwater flow is disrupted by urbanization, river temperature can also be disrupted. Dams and other structures that impede natural flows can cause water temperatures to warm when pools of still water absorb significant amounts of solar energy. Impervious surfaces act as heat collectors, heating urban runoff as it passes over paved surfaces. Studies indicate that intensive urbanization can increase stream temperature as much as five to 10 degrees Celsius during storm events (Galli and Dubose 1990).

Changes in water flow cause serious problems not only for rivers; they also increase costs of flood damage, costs to maintain bridges and other infrastructure, as well as costs to meet drinking water and water-quality standards. For example, river water levels are often unnaturally low during periods of little rainfall because paved and other impervious surfaces disrupt the natural processes that absorb precipitation into the soil, transform it into groundwater, and then slowly discharge it as baseflow into rivers. Low water levels also make it much more difficult for wastewater treatment plants to meet water-quality standards for their discharges since there is less flow in the river to dilute the effluent. These indirect effects of urbanization have very real price tags for communities.

Increased runoff causes significant negative impacts on streams and rivers. It often carries sediment and other pollutants that change the physical and chemical qualities of a body of water.

FIGURE 2-6. HYDROLOGIC CHANGES RESULTING FROM URBANIZATION

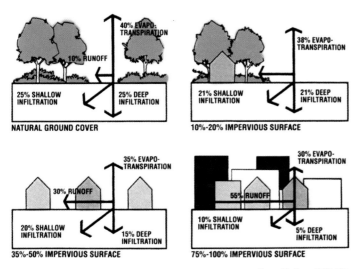

Source: MacBroom (1998, 141)

Sediment Cycles

The sediment cycle starts as soils in the watershed erode and are transported by surface runoff that washes into rivers. Subsequent movement of sediments through river systems is a complex and extremely important aspect of how rivers function. Heavy sediment particles, such as gravel and cobbles (loose rock smaller than boulders), usually originate in the channel itself. Lighter, suspended particles of silt, clay, or sand may originate on the land or be scoured from the channel itself. The overall composition of sediments varies widely among regions of the country and can vary significantly along the same river (MacBroom 1998).

Most sediment is transported during periods of high-water flows and high velocities. Heavier sediments, such as gravel and cobbles, are pushed, dragged, and bounced downstream along the bed of the channel. Lighter sediments, such as clay and silt, can remain suspended in a river for a significant period of time—giving it a muddy appearance after a rainstorm—until water flows and velocities decrease sufficiently for the sediment to settle out and deposit on the river bed, bank, or floodplain. Sediment movement in streams is a natural process that can be significantly altered by human changes to channels, such as dams and flood-control structures, as well as changes in amounts and timing of urban runoff (MacBroom 1998).

Changes to sediment cycles in urbanizing rivers occur first during active construction phases, when natural groundcover or agricultural crop vegetation is removed for site grading and preparation. This releases tremendous amounts of sediment into nearby streams and rivers. Runoff from construction sites is by far the largest source of sediment in urban areas under development. Uncontrolled construction site sediment loads have been reported to be on the order of 35 to 45 tons per acre per year (U.S. EPA 1993).

As urbanization progresses and natural surfaces are paved over, runoff increases and surges more rapidly into receiving waters (Riley 1998). These altered urban flows carry strong erosive force and cause significant channel erosion. Researchers have documented that channel erosion constitutes as much as 75 percent of the total sediment in urban streams, particularly during periods of urbanization when the channel is still enlarging (FISRWG 2001).

State environmental protection agencies report that siltation, comprising tiny sediment particles, remains one of the most widespread pollutants affecting rivers and streams. Siltation affected 31 percent of "impaired" river and

HOW URBANIZATION AFFECTS STREAMS

Changes in stream hydrology resulting from urbanization include the following (Caraco 2000):

- Increased peak discharges compared to predevelopment levels

- Increased volume of urban runoff produced by each storm

- Decreased time needed for runoff to reach the stream, particularly if extensive drainage improvements are made

- Increased frequency and severity of flooding

- Reduced streamflow during prolonged periods of dry weather due to reduced level of infiltration in the watershed

- Greater runoff velocity during storms due to the combined effects of higher peak discharges, rapid time of concentration, and the smoother hydraulic surfaces that occur as a result of development

Siltation is one of the leading pollution problems in the nation's rivers and streams. Over the long term, unchecked siltation can alter habitat with profound adverse effects on adequate life. In the short term, silt can kill fish directly, destroy spawing beds, and increase water turbidity resulting in depressed photosynthetic rates.

FIGURE 2-7. THE EFFECTS OF SILTATION IN RIVERS AND STREAMS

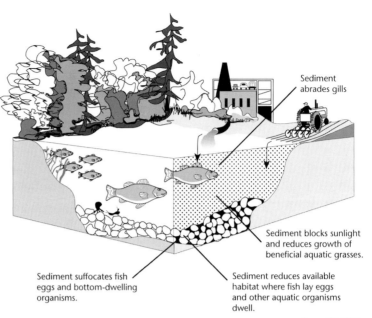

Sediment abrades gills

Sediment blocks sunlight and reduces growth of beneficial aquatic grasses.

Sediment suffocates fish eggs and bottom-dwelling organisms.

Sediment reduces available habitat where fish lay eggs and other aquatic organisms dwell.

Source: EPA (2000d)

stream miles, according to the U.S. EPA. Siltation alters aquatic habitat, suffocates fish eggs and bottom-dwelling organisms, and can interfere with drinking water treatment processes and recreational use of a river (U.S. EPA 2002d).

Urban rivers with dams—and few rivers do not have some kind of engineered structures for flood control, water supply, hydropower, or other industrial uses—block or seriously constrict normal river flows and, paradoxically, exacerbate downstream erosion. The reason is that healthy rivers carry and deposit sediments as a normal function. Because sediments settle in the still waters of a dam reservoir, the river may actually exert more erosive power downstream of the dam on the river's bed and banks because it has almost no sediment to deposit. As a result, the river may erode and scour its downstream channel until it achieves equilibrium by reducing its slope and sediment transport capacity (MacBroom 1998). The loss of natural sediment loads downstream of a dam also causes scouring of the stream channel, lowering the streambed and eroding streambanks and floodplain, vital habitat for many species. Additionally, as the stream channel becomes incised, the water table underlying the riparian zone also lowers. Thus, channel incision can lead to adverse changes in the composition of vegetation within the stream corridor (FISRWG 2001).

The phenomenon of sediment being trapped upstream by human alterations to rivers causes particularly severe problems in ecosystems that depend on high sediment flows. For example, coastal beaches often depend for their replenishment on sand flowing from river mouths, and large rivers with significant sandbar and island habitats require certain sediment flows to sustain these structures.

Headwaters

The term "headwaters" may bring to mind a small, clear, icy-cold, heavily shaded stream that tumbles down a steep, boulder-filled channel. Indeed, there are thousands of miles of such shaded, mountainous headwater streams in the United States. But the term encompasses many other types of small streams. Headwaters can be intermittent streams that flow briefly when snow melts or after rain, but shrink in dry times to become individual pools filled with water. Desert headwater streams can arise from a spring and run above ground only a few hundred yards before disappearing into the sand. Other spring-fed headwaters contain clear water with steady temperature and flow. Yet other headwaters originate in marshy meadows filled with sluggish tea-colored water.

Headwaters arise from different sources depending on the landscape. In mountainous regions, headwaters occur as snowmelt and rain, which flow in channels down slopes. Where the water table intersects the surface of the land, headwaters appear as springs and seeps, which form the headwaters of many small streams and wetlands (MacBroom 1998).

The majority of America's river miles—more than 85 percent—are small headwater streams, also known as first-order through third-order streams (Leopold et al. 1992). Even urban areas often have small streams feeding into major rivers, either directly or through a tributary into which the smaller stream feeds.

FIGURE 2-8. THE STREAM ORDER SYSTEM

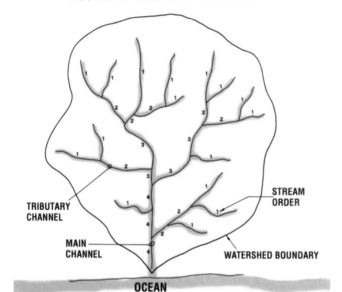

Source: MacBroom (1998, 25–26)

THE VALUE OF HEADWATERS

Because of their small size, headwater streams in some locations have been treated as mere water "conveyances" and have been ditched, channelized, moved, or even buried in pipes. Historically they have not been appreciated for their contribution to water quality. By their sheer numbers, however, they have important ecological and economic functions. They affect the ecological and economic viability of downstream rivers through the regulation of floodwaters, the maintenance of safe and high quality drinking water, pollution prevention, and numerous other ecosystem services.

—Ohio Environmental Protection Agency (2001)

First-order to third-order streams can be considered headwaters streams. When two first-order streams merge, they create a second-order stream; when two second-order streams merge, they create a third-order stream; and so on.

Because they occupy the entire range of climatic and geological conditions found in the United States, headwater ecosystems collectively contain an enormous diversity of riparian and wetland plants and animals, with many unique species and communities. Individual headwater streams support hundreds to thousands of organisms, ranging from bacteria to bats. The species in a typical headwater stream include fungi, algae, higher plants, invertebrates, fish, amphibians, birds, and mammals. Some of these animals become food for predators such as fish, salamanders, crayfish, and birds, which, in turn, become prey for larger animals, including herons, raccoons, and otters. Many widespread species also use headwaters as spawning sites, nursery areas, feeding areas, and travel corridors.

Urban watersheds often have significantly altered headwaters. Headwater streams and wetlands are often drained or filled for development or other human activity. For example, suburban development around Rock Creek in suburban Maryland near Washington, D.C., has reduced the miles of headwaters streams within the watershed by 58 percent (Leopold 1994). Many headwaters streams are buried in pipes under roads, buildings, and other structures. Burying streams in underground pipes still allows water to be conveyed but destroys the stream as a living system.

Headwaters influence downstream conditions in a number of ways. Because of their intimate connection to the surrounding landscape, headwater streams deliver nutrients and organic material to downstream regions, providing an important base for aquatic life downstream (FISRWG 2001). Headwaters are also highly effective at capturing and filtering out sediments, as well as organic material and excess nutrients (Meyer et al. 2003).

Small streams provide much of the freshwater flow into downstream rivers, lakes, and estuaries. In the Great Lakes Basin, for example, the U.S. Geological Survey estimates that over 31 percent of the water entering Lake Michigan comes from indirect groundwater discharges to streams that then flow into the lake (Grannemann et al. 2000). In the Chesapeake Bay Basin, nearly 100,000 miles of interconnected streams, rivers, wetlands, and their riparian areas serve as a "circulatory system" for the Chesapeake Bay. Collectively, this network of small streams supplies 90 percent of the freshwater flow that drives the health of the nation's largest estuary (Center for Watershed Protection et al. 2002).

Floodplains

The riverside land that is periodically inundated by a river's floodwaters is called the floodplain. Floodplains serve important purposes. They:

- temporarily store floodwaters;

- improve water quality;

- provide important habitat for river wildlife; and

- create opportunities for recreation.

Natural floodplains help reduce the heights of floods. During periods of high water, floodplains serve as natural sponges, storing and slowly releasing floodwaters. Floodplains therefore provide additional "storage,"

FIGURE 2-9. FLOODPLAIN WATER STORAGE

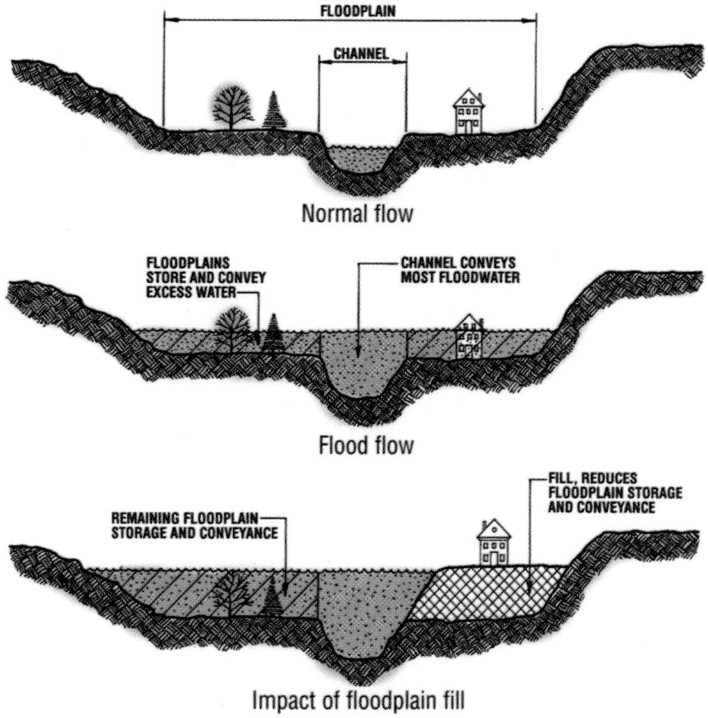

Normal flow

Flood flow

Impact of floodplain fill

Source: MacBroom (1998, 144)

FIGURE 2-10. URBAN RIVER FORMATION

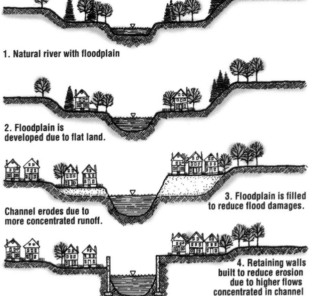

Source: MacBroom (1998, 148)

reducing the velocity of the river and increasing the capacity of the river channel to move floodwaters downstream.

Many floodplain plants help to improve water quality by capturing excess nitrogen and phosphorous carried in floodwaters before these pollutants can reach the river. In addition to filtering out pollutants, floodplain trees and plants also anchor the river's banks, preventing bank erosion and providing shade, which reduces water temperatures.

Floodplains also provide fish and wildlife the places they need to feed and reproduce. Nearly 70 percent of all vertebrate species rely upon the land along the river's edge—called the riparian zone—during their life cycle. Healthy riparian zones create a vegetated transition zone between rivers and upland habitats, providing shelter, food, and migration corridors for river wildlife. Riparian areas in the western United States, where water and wildlife habitat are scarce, are especially important sources of food, shelter, water, shade, forage, and cover for aquatic and terrestrial animals alike.

Despite the wide array of benefits provided by undeveloped floodplains, many communities continue to allow building in floodplains or to build flood control structures to protect floodplain development. In many cities, a significant amount of development is already present in the floodplain.

CASE STUDY

River Issues. The Guadalupe River has a long history of winter flooding that has repeatedly damaged adjacent homes and businesses in downtown San Jose, California. As the economic investment there has increased dramatically in recent years, the impetus for flood protection, coupled with the community's desire for open space, has grown.

Guadalupe River flood in downtown San Jose, California.

What Is Planned. Guadalupe River Park, being developed by the city of San Jose in conjunction with a federal flood control project, is a three-mile stretch of parkland along the river on the edge of downtown San Jose. While a substantial amount of the park is already in place, the remaining elements will be built as part of a flood control project to be completed in 2004. In addition to providing recreational amenities to the local community, the project will provide an ecologically sound system of flood control and habitat restoration.

The U.S. Army Corps of Engineers, the Santa Clara Valley Water District, and the city of San Jose are developing an underground system of box culverts to create a flood control mechanism

But even in these situations, it is often cheaper and certainly more environmentally beneficial to relocate structures to higher ground.

When the river is cut off from its floodplain by levees and dikes, flood heights are often increased. The construction of levees along the Lower Missouri River, for example, has increased flood heights by as much as 12 feet. By contrast, protected floodplain wetlands along the Charles River in Massachusetts store and slowly release floodwaters, providing as much floodwater storage as a medium-size reservoir.

Despite significant spending on federal levees and dams, national flood losses continue to rise. The reasons are clear: at the same time more people are building their homes and businesses in floodplains, farmers and home developers are increasing the rate and volume at which water moves off the landscape and floods local streams and riverside communities. Poor land-use decisions have put more people at risk by allowing development in harm's way and by eliminating the natural flood control functions of wetlands and floodplains (American Rivers 1999). (For more information on reducing development impacts in floodplains, see Planning Principle 3 in Chapter 3 of this PAS Report.)

Channels

Nearly all channels are formed, maintained, and altered by the water and sediment they carry.

The dimensions of a channel cross section define the amount of water that can pass through without spilling over the banks. Two attributes of the channel are of particular importance—

without destroying the streamside vegetation and trees. Maintaining the natural channel is critical to providing water temperatures cool enough to sustain the chinook salmon and steelhead populations in the river. While protecting the ecological integrity of the river, the system will have the capacity to divert significant amounts of floodwater to an existing floodplain.

Extensive mitigation planting also is part of the project, with many plants propagated from seeds gathered within the Guadalupe watershed. An extensive system of recreational trails will extend the length of the park and link to surrounding neighborhoods.

Playgrounds, picnic areas, and plazas for community celebrations will make the park a center of active urban life. Integrated into the plazas and along the trails will be interpretive information on the history, ecology, and hydrology of the project.

Benefits to the River and Community. The Downtown Guadalupe River Flood Control Project, the foundation of the Guadalupe River Park plan, has been extensively refined over the past 15 years to meet the ecological needs of the river and to preserve native fish habitat. These revisions have been a result of changing regulatory requirements, new legislation, protected species listings, threats of citizen lawsuits, and, most recently, a collaborative process launched to seek consensus among all parties involved. Rather than using traditional flood control mechanisms, such as channel widening and armoring, the partners have been able to maintain a more natural riparian corridor along most of the river that complements the recreational amenities offered by the park.

For more information . . .

- See the Guadalupe River Park and Gardens and Guadalupe River Park and Flood Protection Project web site, www.grpg.org.

channel equilibrium and stream-flow. If one variable changes, one or more of the other variables must increase or decrease proportionally if equilibrium is to be maintained. For example, if slope is increased and streamflow remains the same, either the sediment load or the size of the particles must also increase. Likewise, if flow is increased (e.g., by stormwater surges) and the slope stays the same, sediment load or sediment particle size has to increase to maintain channel equilibrium. A stream seeking a new equilibrium tends to erode more sediment and of larger particle size. Streams that are free to adjust to changes in four variables—streamflow, sediment size, sediment load, and stream slope—generally do so and reestablish new equilibrium conditions. Streams with bedrock or artificial streambeds, such as concrete channels, are unable to adjust as they would naturally, which may cause more erosion or damage downstream (FISRWG 2001). In urban areas, artificial channels can often cause a chain reaction of more channel armoring downstream to protect against the energy of the artificial disequilibrium upstream.

In some rivers, particularly large Western rivers with heavy sediment loads, the river naturally moves across a wide meander plain depending on floods and other stream-flow events that change the previous stream channel equilibrium. In these cases, the best policy is to keep development out of the floodplain, allowing rivers to meander and the channel to realign (Committee on Riparian Zone Functioning and Strategies for Management et al. 2002).

Urbanization changes stream channels directly and indirectly. To accommodate buildings and infrastructure, urban stream channels are often straightened or moved altogether.

To move rainwater down these channels more efficiently, vegetation, meanders, backwaters, boulders, dead trees, and other natural structures are removed or "improved" for maximum speed of floodwater conveyance. In many instances, channels are dredged and deepened to facilitate commercial and recreational boat traffic. All of these direct alterations can have significant negative impacts on river habitat and health.

But at the same time, urbanization indirectly causes rivers to widen their channels or cut deeply into their streambeds (downcutting)—or both—to accommodate more frequent, higher-volume flows. Exactly how channels change through urbanization depends on such factors as channel slope, bed materials, the nature of the impervious landscape, and the degree to which the surrounding watershed is sewered (FISRWG 2001). Urban stream channels often enlarge their cross-sectional areas by a factor of two to five times, depending on these factors. In addition, streams can adjust to urbanization by changing their gradient (channel slope) and meander pattern, making it difficult to plan activities along the river corridor and downstream from urbanized areas (Riley 1998).

Like direct interventions, indirect channel alterations cause ecological damage, including in-stream sediment loading as channels become less stable and more susceptible to erosion. Significant changes to bed and bank habitats for insects, fish, amphibian, and other river animals soon follow. When channel downcutting occurs, the river and its natural floodplain and riparian area are separated with the surface of the river far below the top of the streambank, effectively disconnecting the river from its floodplain. Damage is not limited to natural resources, however. Ever-widening and deepening channels cause a loss of property as the river chews into riverside lands, flood damages increase, and infrastructure—culverts, sewer and water lines, bridges—placed near, alongside, or under the river channel is threatened.

Although urban river channels have usually been highly altered, it is worth understanding what the river's natural condition would have been without human intervention. In some cases, a relatively natural channel and environment still prevail and can be enhanced or restored to more closely approximate natural conditions.

CHAPTER 3
Principles for Ecologically Sound Riverfront Design

Renewing urban riverfronts entails restoring natural river systems, redeveloping riverfront sites, or both. Restoring ecological systems such as riverbanks and stream buffers contributes to a healthier environment and improves conditions for activities such as fishing, boating, swimming, and wildlife watching. Environmentally sensitive redevelopment of riverfronts to include public amenities such as parks and trails, cultural attractions, commercial buildings, and housing can draw new investments to a city and improve the quality of life for its residents.

Urban riverfront planning must reconcile development, flood control, and recreation with environmental designs and strategies that enhance the river's ecological systems. As a consequence, every riverfront requires a unique combination of environmental strategies that reflect:

- the intensity of current development,

- the nature and intensity of planned development or redevelopment,

- the geometry and constraints of the riverfront, and

- the intended riverfront purposes and management, preferably defined as an outcome of a community planning process (Schueler 2003).

The development intensity of a riverfront corridor can be classified according to the degree or percentage of impervious cover— hard surfaces such as buildings, streets, parking lots, and sidewalks— found within the corridor.

TAILORING THE PLAN TO THE RIVERFRONT CORRIDOR AND ITS WATERSHED

Too many urban riverfront plans suffer from a "me-too" mentality. Politicians and planners mistakenly want their urban riverfront to become just like the San Antonio Riverwalk or Baltimore's Inner Harbor. They soon find that attempts to transplant ideas from other places often don't work.

Every urban riverfront is different and requires planning solutions appropriate to its unique conditions. Before considering how to apply these principles, planners must carefully define their urban riverfront, including its characteristics, measurements, and boundaries. Factors to consider are described in the following sections.

River Size and Geometry

Each riverfront corridor has its own geometry, including length, width, and high-water mark, established by common site constraints such as floodplain, public infrastructure, municipal landownership, and historical development patterns. The riverfront corridor can be delineated and mapped on the basis of such factors.

River Classification

An urban river is a specific entity that is quite different from rural rivers or streams. In an urban river corridor, a fourth-order or higher stream or river intersects with areas that have been developed as neighborhoods or for commerce. (See Figure 2-9 on page 24 for a description of stream hierarchies.) A fourth-order stream or river is on average 12 miles long and has a mean watershed size of 109 miles (Riley 1998). Rivers can be classified as high as tenth-order, the size of the world's largest rivers. By contrast, the Allegheny River in the eastern United States is a seventh-order river, the average length of which is 147 miles with a mean drainage area of 11,700 square miles. Accurately classifying a river is essential to developing a suitable riverfront plan: what works for a fourth-order river will be unsuitable for a seventh-order one.

Intensity of Development

The development intensity of a riverfront corridor can be classified according to the degree or percentage of impervious cover—hard surfaces such as buildings, streets, parking lots, and sidewalks—found within the corridor. A basic classification system might be:

- ultra-urban (80 to 100 percent impervious cover),
- urban (40 to 79 percent impervious cover), and
- suburban (10 to 39 percent impervious cover) (Schueler 2003).

A riverfront may have sections within each classification, from densely developed downtown-commercial riverbanks to stretches of more naturalized riverbanks in suburban-residential areas. Planners whose goal is restoring ecological systems and developing or redeveloping land parcels therefore should create a classification system that responds to the specific site conditions, as well as to the overall master plan or mission of riverfront redevelopment.

Infrastructure

Every urban riverfront is crisscrossed by a unique network of roads, bridges, sewers, and storm-drain pipes, all of which can present significant challenges to the environmental restoration of the riverfront and the river itself. Planners must be sure to identify all infrastructure features and incorporate them fully into any riverfront plan. Infrastructure can also play an important role in revitalizing a river: water quality, wildlife habitat, and public access can all benefit, for example, from reconfigured sewers and stormwater systems that reduce combined sewer overflows (CSOs).

Watershed Planning

Riverfront corridor planning must also consider the river's watershed, or the land area drained by a river and its tributaries. The health and vitality of a river cannot be improved without the comprehensive treatment of stormwater and other erosion and pollution sources across the whole watershed (Schueler 2003).

OVERVIEW OF ECOLOGICAL PRINCIPLES

This chapter provides an overview for planning and designing riverfront renewal and discusses the comprehensive, holistic, and regionally specific approaches needed to improve the ecological and economic health of urban riverfronts. It makes a strong case for a regional planning approach that begins at the scale of the watershed and prescribes small, incremental changes.

The following three major sections in this chapter offer concrete examples of planning and design principles put into action.

The first section presents **five general principles** for ecologically sound riverfront design. It states that economic and ecological goals can work in concert, although compromises may be necessary, and the public always must be engaged.

The second section offers **five planning principles** that emphasize regional planning, the celebration of natural and cultural history, and broad public access for riverfront recreation.

Eight design principles in the third section suggest how to implement the general and planning principles. These include an overview of zoning measures that preserve riverbanks and buffers, river restoration techniques, and innovative programs to interpret the natural resources and cultural history of rivers.

Many techniques described in this chapter have succeeded in a variety of settings. After the description of each principle, a brief case study illustrates a specific instance of implementation of that principle.

The most important principle of this chapter, however, is to reject the conventional wisdom of the past that accepted dams, stream culverts, and floodplain development as inevitable. There is no substitute for a healthy, intact river or stream ecosystem where no portion of the system is impaired. Thus, when faced with a healthy, intact river or stream, planners must strive to preserve water quality, hydrology, riverbanks, and riparian vegetation with buffers that will protect the river or stream from the damaging effects of new development.

Yet this is a somewhat rare scenario. Most cities founded before 1900 were built close to the riverfront in the floodplain to provide access to shipping and water sources. River valleys are logical conduits for highways and railroads, which can easily follow their contours. Decisions made for ease of commerce and engineering have degraded many riverfronts and made them difficult to access and enjoy.

As this chapter will show, some municipalities have reclaimed their floodplains by removing buildings and other structures. This encouraging trend is not going to be repeated everywhere; nor, as we acknowledged in the preface to this report, is it feasible for all riverfronts. Some dams, levees, highways, rail yards, and floodwalls may be removed, but others will stay in place for generations. As General Principle 4 explains, there is still much room for improvement.

This PAS Report makes a strong case for a regional planning approach that begins at the scale of the watershed and prescribes small, incremental changes.

GENERAL PRINCIPLES

Riverfront reclamation has begun to transform some of the nation's most polluted, neglected, and forlorn waterfronts. Five general principles set the stage for planning success.

GENERAL PRINCIPLES

General Principle 1: Ecological goals and economic development goals are mutually beneficial

General Principle 2: Protect and restore natural river features and functions

General Principle 3: Regenerate the riverfront as a human realm

General Principle 4: Compromises are necessary to achieve multiple objectives

General Principle 5: Make the process of planning and designing riverfronts broadly participatory

---

GENERAL PRINCIPLE 1:
Ecological goals and economic development goals are mutually beneficial

Public and private development that brings people to the waterfront to live, eat, shop, relax, recreate, and participate in cultural events builds a sense of connection and stewardship for the river.

Healthy, functioning rivers are appealing and attractive to residents and businesses. An engaged public that enjoys riverfront features and activities also cares about the river's long-term health. Communities are beginning to understand the allure of a more natural riverfront to residents and visitors. Beyond supporting tourism, these benefits include cost-effective flood control, improved water quality, reduced infrastructure costs, and increased property values and tax base.

For example, a generation ago, the South Platte River in Denver was little more than an urban ditch, filled with abandoned cars, sewage, and other debris. But after the river's devastating flooding in 1965—when communities from Denver to the Nebraska border suffered $540 million of damage and 28 deaths—the city launched efforts to clean and improve it (Massengill 1998). By the mid-1970s, a coalition of citizens and governments started planning and building greenway trails, which soon became one of Denver's most popular recreation facilities.

The scene of Denver's worst flood now teems with life. Since the mid-1970s, some 150 miles of hiker/biker trails, boat launches, whitewater chutes, and parks have been built in four counties and nine municipalities. Even transportation infrastructure has been modified. The city negotiated with railroads to consolidate 16 freight tracks along the riverfront into one line. Hundreds of downtown acres were freed up. This land has been transformed into city parks, reclaimed wetlands for natural flood control, and new riverfront neighborhoods. A $2 million initial investment in the project has been parlayed many times over.

As access to the river improved, citizens viewed their polluted river with new eyes. From 1995 through 2003, Mayor Wellington Webb launched programs to build a string of parks, many of which incorporated flood control into wetlands and included native plants for wildlife habitat. Water-rights

Healthy, functioning rivers are appealing and attractive to residents and businesses. An engaged public that enjoys riverfront features and activities also cares about the river's long-term health.

agreements have ensured minimum flows to support wildlife habitat, fishing, and boating. Rafting chutes were built to span check dams and other river obstacles. In 2001, the city of Denver built the $30-million Commons Park in Lower Downtown on a 20-acre tract that had been a rail yard.

As a direct result of municipal investments, the Central Platte Valley, some 650 acres of once-derelict industrial land just above the floodplain, has become valuable urban property and a prime spot for private investment. About 1,100 people now live in 1,600 condos and apartments in eight residential projects, and 1,600 people work in this once-barren area. All told, the revitalized Central Platte Valley has attracted $1.24 billion of public and private investment in the last 10 years.

Since 1995, the Central Platte Valley has become the setting for a new baseball stadium, a Six Flags amusement park, a sports arena, a skateboard park, an aquarium, and the first half of a planned 6-million-square-foot mixed-use neighborhood built on abandoned rail yards. Historic buildings also have been refurbished, including a former trolley powerhouse that has become the nation's largest REI store. The adventure-sports equipment store celebrates its location at the confluence of Cherry Creek and the South Platte with river access that features a kayak course. A new light-rail line connects all these amenities (Welty 2003).

Other river-based development has accelerated along the South Platte. In north Denver, the 14-acre, $4.1-million Northside Park was built in 2001 on the reclaimed site of an abandoned wastewater plant. Featuring a wetland pond and grasslands where local children can take camping trips, the park is designed to attract "clean" industries to adjacent lands zoned for redevelopment, bringing new jobs to the working-class Globeville and Swansea neighborhoods. In 2001, the project also was awarded the U.S. Environmental Protection Agency's Region 8 Phoenix Award, presented annually to recognize innovative brownfield redevelopment (Wenk 2002).

Confluence Park is one of a string of parks that Denver has built since 1995 to combat flooding and promote wildlife habitat on the South Platte River.

GENERAL PRINCIPLE 2:
Protect and restore natural river features and functions

Rivers provide vital natural benefits that must be protected. Natural river features such as meanders, backwaters, wetlands, and gradually sloped banks serve essential ecological functions. They also provide human benefits such as cleaner water and flood storage. In many urban settings, it may not be possible to restore these features, but even small efforts can have a positive impact. Environmental improvements can be made along even the most heavily impacted rivers.

For example, the Anacostia River—Washington, D.C.'s "other" river—has often been viewed as the district's dumping ground and a dividing line between rich and poor neighborhoods. By the Civil War, the river had already been silted-in by deforestation and poor agricultural practices and was no longer navigable by ocean-going vessels. Today's problems range from overflowing sewers that carry raw sewage into the river to limited access from adjacent neighborhoods, which are among the city's poorest. More than 70 percent of the Anacostia watershed is urbanized. The Anacostia is one of the Chesapeake region's most polluted rivers (Anacostia Waterfront Initiative 2002).

The Anacostia Waterfront Initiative envisions an energized waterfront. AWI seeks to revitalize neighborhoods, enhance and protect parks, improve water quality, and increase access to waterfront destinations.

Anacostia Waterfront Initiative

Despite its poor water quality, the Anacostia offers rich wildlife habitat for bald eagles, heron, and osprey. Since 2000, the members of the Anacostia Waterfront Initiative (AWI)—a partnership between the District of Columbia and 17 federal agencies, who together own 90 percent of the Anacostia shoreline—has worked to improve the river by coordinating the rebuilding of ecological settings, wildlife habitats, parklands, and neighborhoods on both sides of the river. Since 2000, these partners have developed a master plan for seven miles of river, covering 2,830 shoreline acres, or 4.4 square miles.

To enhance the floodplain with a broader, more natural edge, the AWI plan proposes creating a major riverfront park system by stitching 900 acres of public lands owned by different agencies together with reclaimed brownfields. In some places, the plan proposes bioengineering banks to create a 150-foot-wide floodplain. These banks will aid flood control while providing natural filtration of runoff. All of the river's tributary creeks will be "daylighted" and naturalized with wetland edges and buffers of native plantings.

By 2002, the U.S. Army Corps of Engineers had already reclaimed 42 acres of wetlands by regrading portions of the Anacostia's bank. To provide access to new park lands, the U.S. EPA and the District of Columbia have committed $8 million toward environmental restoration of Poplar Point, a former nursery site contaminated by remnant fertilizers, herbicides, and pesticides. Washington's mayor, Anthony Williams (2002), has set a goal of swimming and fishing in the Anacostia "within our lifetime."

Key elements of the plan are currently moving ahead. In 2003, the U.S. Congress approved $10 million toward design and construction of a 12-mile riverfront trail system. To remove major barriers to the waterfront, infrastructure such as bridges, highways, and sewers have been reconstructed. Canoe trails are planned through restored wetlands.

Environmental restoration is being closely tied to economic redevelopment, which included $1.1 billion committed in private funds and $600 million in public funds by June 2003 (Berger 2003). At that time more than a dozen riverfront projects were completed or underway with a goal of revitalizing commercial areas, preserving historic buildings and homes, and adding 10,000 new homes near the river for people of different income levels. For example, the U.S. Navy has invested $200 million to restore historic structures at the Navy Yard, which has also brought 5,000 new jobs to the riverfront. The U.S. Department of Housing and Urban Development has committed $35 million toward redevelopment of the Arthur Capper and Carrollsburg Dwellings public housing project as a mixed-income neighborhood. These projects are being carefully coordinated with efforts to protect and improve the river's buffers, floodplains, and wetlands (AWI 2002).

GENERAL PRINCIPLE 3: Regenerate the riverfront as a human realm

A riverfront project may have to overcome physical, political, social, and economic barriers to increase public use and enjoyment of this public resource.

Many successful projects are designed to include spaces that specifically accommodate parks, walkways, docks, and special events such as concerts and festivals. Good riverfront designs consider the needs of all neighborhoods, ages, and cultures in the community. They allow community members to experience the river up close. In turn, this physical and visual access helps create lively, diverse places that encourage a sense of community and an appreciation for nature.

Consider Hartford, Connecticut. A highway once severed downtown Hartford from the Connecticut River. Now the $22-million Riverfront Plaza spans Interstate 91 and floodwalls, both of which formerly were barriers to the river. The plaza connects downtown to a riverfront promenade, terraces, trails, docks, and an evolving four-mile riverfront park system. The new 1.5-acre plaza encourages residents to see and enjoy the river for the first time in a generation.

By bridging barriers to waterfront access—made possible by $200 million in highway improvements to the interchange of I-84 and I-91—and creating comfortable, attractive, and versatile gathering spaces, this riverfront project has become a popular venue for concerts, boating, and fishing.

In 2001, Riverfront Plaza, programmed by the nonprofit group Riverfront Recapture, attracted 850,000 visitors and pumped $17 million into the local economy. The revitalized riverfront is generating investment through redevelopment in a city that badly needs new economic vitality. The foremost example is Adriaen's Landing, a 30-acre, $770-million mixed-use develop-

Good riverfront designs consider the needs of all neighborhoods, ages, and cultures in the community. They allow community members to experience the river up close.

Riverfront Plaza spans Interstate 91, removing barriers to riverfront access in Hartford.

Greg Kriss, Riverfront Recapture

ment scheduled to be completed by 2005 and connected to the river by Riverfront Plaza (Dillon 2000; Riverfront Recapture 2002).

GENERAL PRINCIPLE 4:
Compromises are necessary to achieve multiple objectives

Urban waterfronts are meeting grounds for sometimes-competing interests. Recreational trails and wetlands are often interwoven with waterfront condos and port facilities. It is not possible or even desirable to focus exclusively on economic development or environmental concerns along most urban rivers. Because of existing development, few cities could re-create a completely natural river environment. But riverfront redevelopment aimed at boosting a city's economic vitality need not eliminate natural features, compound riverfront damage, or limit public access. Riverfront communities will benefit from integrating and balancing ecological, social, and economic concerns.

The Big Rivers Partnership in Minnesota is a team of nonprofit and government agencies that seeks to protect and improve river valley habitat along three major rivers in the seven-county Twin Cities metropolitan area. Recognizing that complete restoration of a natural river environment often is impossible, the Big Rivers Partnership uses the term "conversion" for efforts such as replanting native species or replacing impervious ground with porous cover. These measures will not restore the complex and fully functioning ecosystem of presettlement times. But they will enhance and create habitat and improve water quality (Karasov 2002, 2003).

At the heart of this watershed, in downtown Saint Paul, the continuing revitalization of the Mississippi River seeks to insert natural values alongside intensive redevelopment. Since 1984, this effort has been led by the Saint Paul Riverfront Corporation (SPRC), a nonprofit organization chartered by the city to coordinate revitalization. This effort accelerated in 1992 when a large private employer left downtown. City leaders recognized they needed a comprehensive strategy to fill the economic gap. The SPRC commissioned architect Ben Thompson—a Saint Paul native who designed Boston's Fanueil Hall Market and other successful "festival marketplaces"— to forge this new vision for downtown based on riverfront revitalization. That effort led to development of the *Saint Paul on the Mississippi Development Framework* (Urban Design Strategies 1997), which was fleshed out by the *Saint Paul River Corridor Urban Design Guidelines* (Close Landscape Architecture et al. 2000).

The *Saint Paul River Corridor Urban Design Guidelines* divided this urban section of river into seven types of landforms. It identified areas suitable for development and opportunities for natural restoration and enhanced water quality through wetlands, ponds, improved tributary streams, and underground sand filters (Martin 2001).

As a result of these planning efforts, since the mid-1990s the city's riverfront has seen the construction of new cultural facilities, businesses, and thousands of homes. Meanwhile, shipping continues to thrive on this working waterfront. Roads have been moved to increase access to the river through five miles of new trails and 92 acres of new parks, including a newly revitalized historic park on Harriet Island (SPRC 2003).

Although these efforts have included construction of some concrete banks and a U.S. Army Corps of Engineers levee, the revitalization planning also has reclaimed seven miles of industrial lands along the river. Here the non-

FIGURE 3-1. SAINT PAUL NORTH QUADRANT PRECINCT PLAN

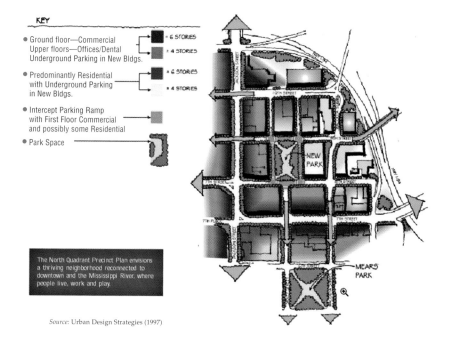

Source: Urban Design Strategies (1997)

profit organization Great River Greening (GRG), which works on Mississippi restoration in the Twin Cities region, has leveraged $1 million in funding and the work of 10,000 volunteers to clear weeds and plant 35,000 native trees. Volunteer projects also are being harnessed to restore native vegetation to two eroded river bluffs in Saint Paul (Karasov 2002).

GRG and the city's Department of Parks and Recreation are collaborating on a master plan for ecological management of 16 city parks along Saint Paul's 17 miles of riverfront. These will be managed as complementary ecosystems rather than as discrete, stand-alone parks. One of these park units, the 500-acre Crosby Natural Area, a rare riverfront ecosystem that

Nearly 200 volunteers helped plant native trees, shrubs, prairie grasses, and wildflowers along Saint Paul's Smith Avenue High Bridge on the banks of the Mississippi.

Great River Greening

hosts endangered species such as the Blandings turtle, will have its own management plan to balance preservation, restoration, and human use (BRW, Inc. et al. 1999; Karasov 2003).

GENERAL PRINCIPLE 5:
Make the process of planning and designing riverfronts broadly participatory

Riverfront planning and design must include the participation of a wide variety of community members. The process must extend beyond identifying traditional stakeholder groups and reach out to neighborhoods that historically may not have used the riverfront. The needs of various neighborhoods and constituencies may differ. Riverfront designs will be more vibrant, inclusive, and successful when they consider these different priorities. Local officials and developers, as well as planning staff, must participate in public meetings to ensure that everyone works toward the same vision, and that all important considerations are made known.

The Schuylkill River Development Council (SRDC) put this principle in practice. In 2001, SRDC, armed with nearly $3 million in foundation and state grants, launched a nine-month process to create a master plan for 8.5 miles of the Schuylkill, a tidal river flowing through Philadelphia. SRDC made concerted outreach efforts to involve residents of river neighborhoods, which included both gentrified and low-income areas. Rather than simply scheduling public meetings, SRDC interviewed city officials to identify target audiences and then made special presentations to church, community, and school groups. A measure of success emerged when Vare Middle School, a public school in South Philadelphia, integrated Schuylkill River projects into its curriculum.

Recognizing that not everyone uses e-mail or the Internet, the SRDC informed residents about meetings by placing posters around neighborhoods and buying ads in community papers. Those who attended meetings were given large, easy-to-read worksheets that allowed them to locate their own homes on a map and trace preferred routes for river access.

Residents were also invited to tour the Schuylkill on a flat-bottom boat. Many had never been out on the river before. The residents' ideas were charted on "idea maps" folded into the final plan. In all, 25 to 30 community groups and hundreds of residents from both sides of the river participated in the process. The final plan envisions a new Schuykill River Park with related greenways (Hodge 2002).

In 2002, a critical first phase of this park was constructed: a $6.7 million, 1.8-mile greenway stretching from the historic Fairmount Waterworks to Locust Street. This greenway provides many residents with their first-ever safe access to the riverfront. The project incorporates plans for many other river improvements, such as retrofits of auto bridges with ramps and stairs to allow pedestrian access to the waterfront, ramps over railroad tracks, $600,000 of new docks at Fairmount Waterworks, and fish ladders on dams (Torres 2003).

PLANNING PRINCIPLES

Planning for riverfront revival must consider regional development patterns, natural and cultural history, flood control, public access, recreation, and education. The following five principles should be integrated into master plans and implemented through zoning and building codes, engineering standards, and site plans and designs.

PLANNING PRINCIPLES

Planning Principle 1: Demonstrate characteristics of the city's unique relationship to the river in the riverfront design

Planning Principle 2: Know the river ecosystem and plan for a scale larger than the riverfront

Planning Principle 3: Because rivers are dynamic, minimize new floodplain development

Planning Principle 4: Provide for public access, connections, and recreational uses

Planning Principle 5: Celebrate the river's environmental and cultural history through public education programs, riverfront signage, and events

PLANNING PRINCIPLE 1:
Demonstrate characteristics of the city's unique relationship to the river

Every river city has a unique relationship and history interwoven with its river. San Antonio and Chicago, for example, have very different riverscapes, scales of development, and historic uses along their rivers. Riverfronts should have a look and feel that evokes and celebrates their city's special character and relates directly to their natural history.

Citizens must understand that their city's river is a place that grants their region its identity, one that provides wildlife habitat, recreation, drinking water, and jobs. When citizens value these factors, they become advocates for protecting and restoring their riverfronts.

The St. Louis region, for example, plans a 40-mile Confluence Greenway and Conservation Area linking cities and towns to the spot where Lewis and Clark launched their 1804 expedition. The project will knit together cultural and natural resources into a 200-square-mile park system in Missouri and Illinois. Stretching from downtown St. Louis at the Gateway Arch to the confluence of the Missouri and Mississippi Rivers, the greenway system will encompass natural and restored wildlife and conservation

The Confluence Greenway and Conservation Area links cities and towns in Missouri and Illinois and makes it possible for cyclists and others to visit the spot where Lewis and Clark launched their 1804 expedition.

Trailnet

areas, parks, neighborhoods, river towns, agriculture, and commerce. The Confluence Greenway will stimulate recreation and tourism dollars by offering extensive waterfront access.

At the confluence, the new Edward "Ted" and Pat Jones-Confluence State Park is being developed in St. Charles County, Missouri. The state's Department of Natural Resources is creating access through entry roads and trails that lead to the confluence while providing opportunities for wildlife observation and river recreation. The park will also interpret the historical significance of the rivers. Park development will be linked to the Lewis and Clark bicentennial celebration of 2004.

The project aims to restore and protect environmentally sensitive land, plants, and wildlife, while assisting flood control and reducing stormwater runoff. Community members will be trained as trail rangers to provide information about the river.

In January 2003, this project took a major step forward. A partnership of 13 local, state, and federal agencies and private organizations collaborated to expand Confluence State Park from 253 acres to 1,118 acres. For example, a $1 million federal grant made under the North American Wetlands Conservation Act allowed the Missouri Department of Natural Resources to add 350 acres of protected wetlands to the park. Using an interest-free loan from a local foundation, private nonprofit conservation organizations acquired and held another 515 acres until public agencies could raise funds to purchase this parkland.

PLANNING PRINCIPLE 2:
Know the river ecosystem and plan for a scale larger than the riverfront

Planners should consider riverfront development in the context of the river's natural structure, including:

- characteristics of the watershed (the land area drained by a river and its tributaries);

- the floodplain and the river channel with the structure of its bed and banks;

- hydrology (water flows and timing);
- water chemistry; and
- the biological needs of wildlife, including insects, fish, amphibians, reptiles, birds, and mammals.

It is also important to understand how a river's structure has been altered and how it may change in the future. Rivers are affected by what happens in their watersheds, and riverfront activity, in turn, affects areas beyond the river's edge. Planners must keep in mind the consequences of riverfront design and activities on *all* areas of the watershed. Each river has a watershed that is nearly always much greater in area that the riverfront corridor. One cannot improve the health of the river without comprehensively addressing stormwater and other pollution sources across the entire watershed. Thus, riverfront corridor planning is best performed within the context of sound watershed planning, which is conducted at a much greater scale (Schueler 2003).

In Minnesota's Twin Cities region, the nonprofit group Great River Greening (GRG) is refurbishing natural functions in the Mississippi, Minnesota, and St. Croix River valleys. To determine priorities for a series of ecological "conversion" projects, GRG created a geographic information system (GIS) database of the 54,000-acre Mississippi National River and Recreation Area (MNRRA), designated as part of the National Park System in 1988. However, less than 10 percent (about 4,600 acres) of the MNRRA is currently preserved as public parkland (National Park Service 2003; Overson 2002). The rest is the commercial, institutional, and residential land of a metropolitan area—from airports to landfills to subdivisions. GRG and its partners seek to increase public lands, trail access, and ecological function along with the region's commerce and culture.

FIGURE 3-2. GREAT RIVER GREENING PROJECTS

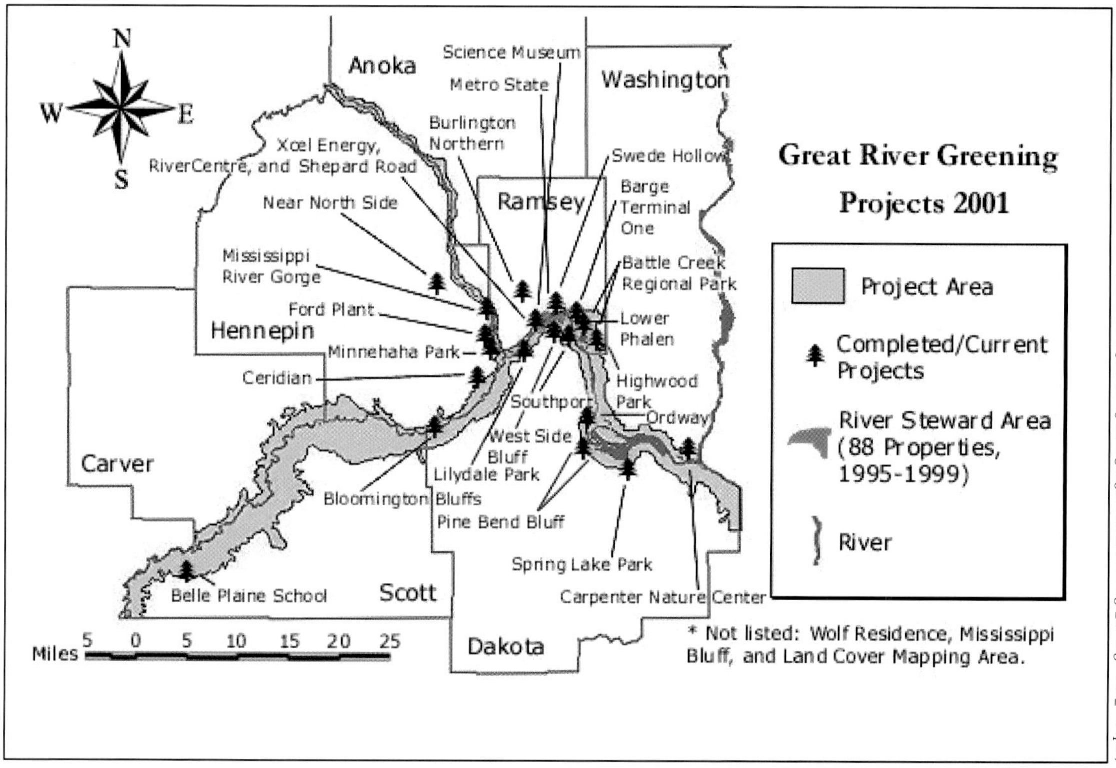

Source: www.greatrivergreening.org/downloads/Gorge_Management_Plan.pdf,

Throughout the region, the GIS database records such elements as land use, tree canopy, slopes, soil conditions, water quality, and areas with invasive plant species. The data is used to create benchmarks for factors such as tree cover, impervious surface, and stormwater filtration for different types of urban, suburban, and natural landscapes (Karasov 2002, 2003).

Completed in December 2002, this database is available for free on CD-ROM to Twin Cities communities through the Trails and Open Space Partnership, a project of the MNRRA. Established in 1996, the partnership works with more than 50 government agencies, institutions, nonprofits, and private landowners toward the goal of a continuous 72-mile greenway within the MNRRA. The GIS database allows communities to earmark funds to acquire the most sensitive natural areas and build the most critical trail connections. Communities also can download this information as PDFs and zoom in on individual parcels for detailed information. The information allows communities to evaluate development proposals based on their potential to damage or to enhance sensitive natural areas.

By 2003, nearly 50 miles of public trail were built in the MNRRA corridor, with plans to acquire another 2,000 acres of public parklands. By thinking regionally, the Trails and Open Space Partnership has attracted $7 million from government agencies and nonprofit organizations to help realize these projects (Overson 2002).

PLANNING PRINCIPLE 3:
Because rivers are dynamic, minimize new floodplain development

Rivers by nature change continually. For example, on some rivers, spring flood elevations exceed nonflood levels by 20 feet or more. Some rivers freeze in winter. Others experience little seasonal change. The effects of changes upstream and in the surrounding watershed can significantly alter these natural variations, often with disastrous results. Extreme cases of flooding—often made worse by floodplain development—constitute the nation's most destructive natural disasters.

Undeveloped, connected floodplains are essential to river health. New development on the riverfront, including trails and parks, should be designed to minimize floodplain intrusions. Where new development must occur, structures or facilities should be designed to:

* ensure that contaminants will not be released during flooding;

* cause no net decrease in flood storage capacity; and

* cause no flooding or other downstream impacts.

Large permanent structures should not be built within the 100-year floodplain because they increase the amount of impervious surface, exacerbate runoff problems, and increase the risk of costly flood damage.

Habitat diversity and water quality become severely compromised when as little as 10 percent of a floodplain is paved or covered with an impervious surface. A floodplain that is more than 50 percent paved will result in a waterway with little wildlife habitat and few natural features (MacBroom 1998).

Structural flood-control approaches—such as dams, levees, and channelization—do not necessarily prevent floods, but they do destroy habitat, recreation, and other river values. These engineering techniques should be used sparingly, if at all, to protect new floodplain development.

Located along the Mississippi River, Davenport, Iowa, is one of the largest river cities in the United States without hard-engineered flood structures. In 1984, Davenport (pop. 100,000) rejected a U.S. Army Corps of Engineers proposal to build a $50 million levee. The city believed the cost of the levee would far outstrip the cost of potential damage from flooding. Since then,

Davenport has moved to expand its floodplain and to "flood proof" its downtown. (The city owns and controls six of its nine riverfront miles, which signficantly enables these efforts.)

Numerous downtown businesses have been moved to higher ground, with the abandoned sites converted to open parkland that enhances recreation and tourism. The city has bought and removed 65 residences and retrofitted another 20 historic buildings in the floodplain with waterproof gates and sump pumps (Lloyd 2002).

In addition, River Action, Inc., a nonprofit group that addresses riverside beautification and flood control, is participating with the U.S. Environmental Protection Agency to cleanse the 513-acre Nahant Marsh within city limits on the riverfront. Under a 1998 master plan adopted by the city council, River Action has acquired 252 acres of the flood-absorbing marsh with plans to open this riverfront area to the public with a boardwalk, interpretive areas, and staging areas for field trips (Wine 2002, 2003).

The city realizes flooding is a riverwide problem that it cannot solve alone. Thus River Action is working with 12 riverfront communities in Illinois and Iowa to encourage healthy river designs that will enhance flood control (Wine 2002).

Despite these efforts, Davenport has not been exempt from flood damage. In July 2001, the river rose seven feet above normal, causing the second-worst flooding in the city's history. Cleanup costs were $3.1 million, with the federal government picking up 90 percent of the costs. Yet Davenport's share of $310,000 still compares favorably to the $250,000 annual cost of maintaining a levee. After this flood, the city revisited a levee proposal and is now designing a small levee to protect the municipal water supply (Wine 2003).

Davenport's approach has been highly controversial. During the 2001 floods, the director of the Federal Emergency Management Agency attacked the city for refusing to build a floodwall. River advocates remain steadfast that flood engineering generally doesn't work, and that floodwaters can no more be prevented than earthquakes or hurricanes. Moreover, cities with levees were also threatened and damaged by the rising waters in the flood years of 1993 and 2001. River advocates maintain that Davenport's approach of protecting the floodplain and expanding wetlands—where a single acre can absorb 1.5 million gallons—will benefit other Mississippi River communities as well as other watersheds (Wine 2002).

Physical contact with a river is important. New developments along a river should always provide direct access to the river.

PLANNING PRINCIPLE 4:
Provide for public access, connections, and recreational uses

Easy access is vital to draw people to a riverfront. Visual connections to the river from nearby commercial and residential areas also are important. Physical and visual access should not be reserved only for select neighborhoods or businesses along the redeveloped river. Riverfronts can include many recreational uses, from bicycling to bird watching. Riverfront communities should provide areas or facilities for as many of these uses as possible.

People should be able to touch and interact with the river in appropriate locations, whether through wading, fishing, launching a boat, or sitting on the riverbank. Economic revitalization along riverfronts, such as new mixed-use development with housing, restaurants or cafes, and open space, is more successful when it includes visual and physical access to the water.

In Norwalk, Connecticut, for example, a capped 13-acre landfill on the tidal Norwalk River has become the platform for a new $6.5 million, 20-acre riverfront park and riverwalk, started in 1991 and still evolving. Oyster Shell Park features stormwater channels that cut diagonally across the landfill cap and drain into a five-acre pond on the riverfront. A riverwalk located three feet above the 100-year floodplain provides access to the pond, which freezes for winter ice-skating. A west-facing slope is expected to become a popular sledding hill. An adjacent 80-acre site above the floodplain is being redeveloped with a hotel, shops and restaurants, and office space.

The riverbanks have been regraded to encourage intertidal wetlands, which are expected to regenerate oyster beds in an area that already rivals the Chesapeake Bay for productivity. Increases in heron and river otter population have already been reported, while the water-quality commission plans to monitor the return of oysters (MacBroom 2002; Overton 2002).

PLANNING PRINCIPLE 5:
Celebrate the river's environmental and cultural history

Riverfronts are rich in both human and natural history. Interpretive and path-finding systems can describe the river, its environment, and how river and city history are intertwined. Educational and cultural programs, performances, and public art entice people to the riverfront.

Ecological education is especially meaningful along urban rivers because so much of the original ecosystem has been erased. As active, visually rich environments, rivers can be powerful tools for science and nature education. Educating the public about the river and its natural systems will generate a sense of stewardship and a connection to the river's history.

On New Jersey's Hackensack River, artist and environmentalist Richard Mills created low-cost "signworks" that illustrate the river's natural and cultural history. Arrayed along a 3.5-mile greenway in Teaneck, the signs combine text with images created by schoolchildren and other local residents, maps, historical photos, satellite images, postcards, and interviews with local historians. The artist hopes to "get people to fall in love with the river" so they will want to see it protected and restored (Mills 2002).

This is one of 16 signs created along the Hackensack River illustrating the river's natural and cultural history.

A walk along the greenway encompassing all the 16 signworks begins with the era of Native American villages, includes the age of schooner traffic and the industrial pollution of the 1950s, and ends with today's restoration efforts. Printed digitally and mounted on aluminum, the two-by-three-foot signworks cost only $75 each to produce. Low-cost printing makes it practical to revise and update signs. The costs of the construction and installation of stanchions ($1,000 each) have been donated by local governments and the utility company PSE&G. The artist also donated 3,500 hours of work. Erected in 1998, the Hackensack River Stories Project has given residents a new perspective on the potential to regenerate one of the nation's most polluted and threatened rivers (Mills 2000, 2002).

DESIGN PRINCIPLES

"First, do no harm" summarizes the ethic of the Hippocratic Oath. Planners for riverfront revival must also follow this dictum. The best way to ensure the health of an urban waterway is, first, to protect its healthiest features, whether they are water quality, wetlands, or urban forests. Allowing development to disturb these features and then attempting to reconstruct them—even using best management practices—is no substitute for protecting the intact elements of a healthy ecosystem.

DESIGN PRINCIPLES

Design Principle 1: Preserve natural river features and functions

Design Principle 2: Buffer sensitive natural areas

Design Principle 3: Restore riparian and in-stream habitats

Design Principle 4: Use nonstructural alternatives to manage water resources

Design Principle 5: Reduce hardscapes

Design Principle 6: Manage stormwater on site and use nonstructural approaches

Design Principle 7: Balance recreational and public access goals with river protection

Design Principle 8: Incorporate information about a river's natural resources and cultural history into the design of riverfront features, public art, and interpretive signs

This section provides an overview of some of the most effective preservation techniques, including protective zoning, buffer conservation, and open space preservation programs. It also describes the best practices for reconstructing the ecological features of urban rivers, including efforts to remove dams, reduce pollution from runoff, rebuild in-stream habitat, and restore healthy, natural riverbanks.

DESIGN PRINCIPLE 1:
Preserve natural river features and functions

Preserving the natural features and functions of America's 3.6 million miles of streams and rivers contributes greatly to urban riverfronts. Through zoning, land preservation practices, and careful site design, communities can protect sensitive areas of rivers and streams from development. As part of the preservation process, communities should determine ecological goals for urban riverfronts and identify missing or altered natural features.

RIVER PRESERVATION TOOLS FROM THE PLANNER'S TOOLBOX

Growth Management

In recent years, Maryland, New Jersey, Oregon, and Washington have enacted smart growth legislation to encourage revitalization of cities and towns while preventing sprawl. Municipalities such as Portland, Oregon, and Boulder, Colorado, have established urban growth boundaries.

Some municipalities offer incentives for development in higher-density areas. Others refuse to subsidize development in "greenfield" areas through public construction of sewers or roads. Or they may impose development moratoria or limitations on the number of building permits issued.

The most successful programs combine incentives for infill or brownfield redevelopment with strategies to protect or enhance natural areas and open space.

Comprehensive regional planning helps mitigate the environmental and economic impacts of urbanization. Especially when combined with effective stormwater management, concentrating development within a metropolitan region can reduce the region's overall impervious surface. The most heavily urbanized sites with the greatest concentration of impervious surface, however, may still require substantial structural stormwater measures. But as long as these measures are carefully designed, a compact metropolitan area guided by smart-growth principles will generate fewer negative impacts and preserve more of a river's natural features than an area dominated by sprawl (Lehner et al. 2001).

Transit-Oriented Development

Transit-oriented development (TOD) concentrates development around public transit, bike and pedestrian routes, and carpooling facilities. Commercial uses located near transportation nodes can reduce vehicle miles traveled as well as the number and land area of roads and parking lots. TOD thus produces less impervious cover, stormwater runoff, and pollution discharge. Transportation-related hard surfaces account for more than 60 percent of the total imperviousness in many suburban areas (May et al. 1997).

Traditional Neighborhood Design

Traditional neighborhood design minimizes the impervious footprint of a neighborhood through compact development patterns that feature narrower roads, smaller lots, shorter front setbacks, shared alleys, and protected open space. New Urbanist developments go a step further by varying housing types and densities and featuring mixed uses. Stores, offices, schools, daycare centers, recreation facilities, and mass transit are included on site or within walking distance, which reduces reliance on automobiles and thus reduces the impervious cover generated by streets and driveways.

Clustering and Conservation Subdivision Design

Clustering concentrates homes on a limited portion of a site and leaves the rest for open space and wildlife habitat. This approach also includes narrower roads, shared driveways, and shorter setbacks from residential streets. Conservation subdivision design reduces the amount of impervious road surface for residential

(continued)

In stable streams and rivers, natural equilibrium controls the water flow and sediment supply. Yet many urban rivers have been greatly altered by dams and flood-control structures. Preserving natural river features and functions means avoiding the use of new dams and other engineering solutions,

RIVER PRESERVATION TOOLS
FROM THE PLANNER'S TOOLBOX *(continued)*

developments. Some municipalities expand the concept to treat native landscapes as functional elements of a development. In such cases, open space, often through restoration and management practices, is used to treat stormwater, enhance biodiversity and wildlife habitat, and provide an enjoyable environment for residents (Lehner et al. 2001).

Land Purchases by Environmental Trusts

The Land Trust Alliance's 2002 census recorded 6.2 million acres of natural lands in the United States protected by 1,263 local and regional land trusts. These lands are in addition to those protected by the nation's top land conservation organizations: the Trust for Public Land (TPL), the Nature Conservancy, the Conservation Fund, and Ducks Unlimited (Aldrich 2003; Land Trust Alliance 2003a). Since 1972, TPL alone has helped protect more than 1.4 million acres in 45 states, from recreation areas to small city parks. In June 2002, the Conservation Fund helped transfer 860 acres worth $4.5 million along Plum Creek in Louviers, Colorado, from the DuPont corporation to Douglas County's open space program. These lands, featuring mature cottonwoods and undisturbed riparian areas, preserve a key wildlife corridor for the region, and create a greenbelt for Louviers, a historic company town formerly owned by DuPont (Macy 2002).

Conservation Easements

Conservation easements are legal agreements between a landowner and a land trust or a government agency that permanently prohibit or limit land uses to protect conservation values. Conservation easements allow landowners to continue to own and use the land and to sell it or pass it on to heirs. By removing the land's development potential, the easement lowers its market value, which in turns lowers estate tax. If the landowner donates the easement, and the donation benefits the public by permanently protecting important conservation resources while also meeting other federal tax code requirements, it can qualify as a tax-deductible charitable donation. The amount of the donation is the difference between the land's value with the easement and its value without the easement.

Conservation easements are popular and commonly used. From 1990 to 2000, local and regional land trusts in the U.S. protected 2.6 million acres through easements (Land Trust Alliance 2003a; Palone and Todd 1998).

Transfer of Development Rights

Transfer of development rights (TDR) programs allow municipalities to preserve unique and environmentally sensitive natural areas. A form of overlay zoning, TDRs protect landowner property values because landowners are permitted to transfer their right to develop, based on the underlying zoning district, to an area designated for more intense development. TDRs therefore allow riparian corridors and other sensitive areas to be permanently deed-restricted from development without diminishing the land's value. TDRs are also used to encourage higher-density development within urban growth boundaries or other specified areas. However, TDRs are complex to negotiate and thus are less frequently used.

such as straightening, channelizing, or placing streams in underground pipes and culverts.

Fully restoring the ecological features and functions of most urban rivers and streams may be impossible. Yet communities have numerous opportunities to preserve critical areas that support a more natural riverfront. Many urban rivers retain surprisingly rich and extensive predevelopment features, such as forested banks, fish and bird habitat, and wetlands. Preservation of these natural watershed features also can save money.

The U.S. Army Corps of Engineers, for example, found that buying land or easements to preserve a network of natural wetlands in the Charles River Valley outside of Boston cost $8 million, compared to the estimated $100 million cost of building a dam. Maintaining these natural wetlands benefited the aesthetic and ecological qualities of the floodplain and increased the value of adjacent properties (Lehner et al. 2001).

FIGURE 3-3. THE CHARLES RIVER NATURAL VALLEY STORAGE AREA

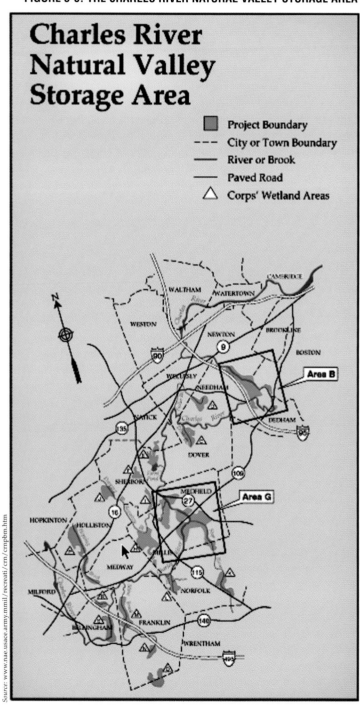

Working with the Charles River Watershed Association, the Corps studied marshes, swamps, and meadows throughout the upper watershed. These wetlands act like huge sponges, storing floodwaters and slowly letting them go over several weeks. The Corps determined that, compared to constructing a dam or levees, preserving the wetlands would not only cost less but would also result in greater storage capacity. These wetlands could temporarily store 10 vertical feet of water.

In 1974, Congress authorized the Charles River Natural Valley Storage Area to acquire and protect 17 wetlands throughout the watershed. By 1979, the Corps had purchased 8,103 acres and today maintains the wetlands. The Massachusetts Division of Fisheries and Wildlife manages some of the acres as open space (Zimmerman 2003).

Development and River Degradation

Poorly conceived urban development can degrade a river's natural processes and destroy or fragment wildlife habitat. Development generally increases impervious surfaces, which in turn increases stormwater runoff. The greater volume and velocity of stormwater runoff erodes riverbanks and enlarges river and stream channels. The combination of erosion and channelization increases sediments, destroys aquatic habitats, and creates an unstable channel that can increase flooding downstream.

Damage can also occur when infrastructure—including water and sewer mains and transmission lines—is installed in the hyporheic zone, the area below and surrounding the stream channel where critical chemical, biological, and habitat functions occur (see Chapter 2). Digging in these sensitive areas causes severe long-term damage. Riverfront development plans should be especially careful to preserve these less-visible natural features.

Low impact development (LID) is a stormwater management approach that seeks to integrate the built environment with a functioning part of the ecosystem. LID mimics a site's predevelopment hydrology through design techniques that infiltrate, filter, store, evaporate, and detain runoff close to its source. This approach relies on engineering technologies to maintain or restore a watershed's hydrologic and ecological functions. Such techniques include permeable pavers, bioswales, and maintaining buffer zones. The results control pollutants, reduce runoff volume, and manage runoff timing (Low Impact Development Center 2003).

Land Protection Strategies

Communities can help determine the quality of urban streams and rivers through their land-use decisions. The following strategies for land protection can be a part of a program to maintain the ecological integrity of urban rivers and riverfronts.

Watershed planning. Watershed planning considers all resources in the watershed as a single, interrelated system. A watershed is an area of land that drains water, sediment, and other materials downslope to the lowest point. The water moves through a network of drainage pathways, both underground and on the surface. Generally, these pathways converge into streams and rivers, which become progressively larger as the water moves on downstream, eventually reaching an estuary and the ocean (adapted from Watershed Professionals Network 1999). Watersheds can occur at multiple scales, from the multistate watersheds of the Mississippi and Columbia Rivers to the watersheds of small streams that measure only a few acres.

Watershed boundaries—the land area or catchment that contributes water to a specific river or stream—are the basic unit of management, rather than political boundaries. The premise of watershed planning is that impervious

Watershed planning considers all resources in the watershed as a single, interrelated system.

SMART-GROWTH DEVELOPMENT

Smart-growth development features:

- Mixed land uses

- Compact site design that uses less land than conventional suburban development

- A range of housing opportunities and choices

- Walkable neighborhoods

- Distinctive, attractive communities with a strong sense of place

- Open space, farmland, and critical environmental areas

- Development or redevelopment of existing communities

- Transportation choices

- Predictable, fair, and cost-effective development decisions

- Community and stakeholder collaboration in development decisions

Source: Adapted from Smart Growth Online (2003).

cover, rather than population density, is the best measure of growth impact and future stream quality.

Watershed planning begins with an evaluation of current and ideal conditions for each body of water in the watershed, as well as comprehensive mapping of land-use practices. Planners then determine land uses that promote healthier rivers, streams, wetlands, and lakes. Public officials, residents, and other stakeholders create a watershed plan and land-use ordinances that designate the locations, levels, and types for new development or redevelopment that will protect or enhance the watershed (Lehner et al. 2001).

Infill and brownfield development. Infill and brownfield development recycles urban infrastructure. Reuse and renovation of these urban and suburban sites provide opportunities for economic development and can reduce impervious surfaces, depending on the site design (old parking lots can be replaced by mixed-use buildings and open space, for example). Like other smart growth strategies, infill development may present challenges to communities and developers, but the benefits to local watersheds can be significant (Northeast-Midwest Institute and Congress for the New Urbanism 2001).

Open space and buffer preservation. In many communities, zoning ordinances protect open space and buffers around streams, steep slopes, and other sensitive areas. Many municipalities also purchase land as a cost-effective way to reduce stormwater runoff and control flooding while adding natural areas. This strategy has attracted strong public support. Through LandVote 2002, the Trust for Public Land and the Land Trust Alliance found that voters approved a total of 139 of 188 measures in 2002, generating about $10 billion in conservation and conservation-related funding, including land acquisition (Trust for Public Land 2003b; Land Trust Alliance 2003b).

Protective zoning. Many communities write watershed preservation into zoning codes. Examples of protective zoning include:

- *Overlay zones.* Overlay zones superimpose natural resource protection zoning on traditional zoning to protect riparian buffers and other critical areas while still allowing underlying uses in suitable forms. This strategy gives municipalities legal control of an area without having to own the property (Palone and Todd 1998).

- *Performance standards.* Rather than specifying land uses, municipalities may create performance standards for open-space preservation, impervious surface area, maximum pollution emissions, or other criteria. Some performance zoning ordinances rank proposed developments on a point scale based on the degree to which they achieve objectives, such as reducing potential pollutant runoff. Only projects that exceed a minimum threshold are approved. Performance standards may also include incentives, such as density bonuses for projects that exceed standards or provide additional natural amenities such as natural restoration within the development (Lehner et al. 2001).

- *Resource protection zoning.* Municipalities can protect riparian areas through resource protection zoning that establishes a natural resource right-of-way similar to a utility right-of-way. Setback width is then determined before construction begins. When applied to streams and rivers, resource protection zoning ordinances typically establish either

THE FOCUS OF SMART GROWTH

Smart growth focuses on:

- *Community quality of life*, helping create community and a sense of place through housing and transportation choices, urban green spaces, recreational and cultural attractions, and policies and incentives that promote mixed-use neighborhoods.

- *Design*, promoting resource-efficient building and community designs, green building practices, low-impact development, and mixed-use and walkable neighborhoods with health, social, economic, and environmental benefits.

- *Economics*, encouraging community-based small businesses, local employment opportunities, and new businesses and industries, with efficient government services and public and private investments aimed at quality-of-life improvements.

- *Environment and health*, conserving energy and reducing threats from air and water pollution and indoor air contaminants through resource-efficient building design. Transportation options such as mass transit, bike lanes, and pedestrian walkways also engage residents and workers in a more active, healthy lifestyle.

- *Housing*, combining diversity of lifestyles and socio-economic levels with mixed-use, affordable housing, and compact development.

- *Transportation*, promoting new transportation choices and transit-oriented development that offers alternatives to automobile-dependent communities.

Source: Adapted from Smart Growth Online (2003)

(1) a fixed buffer, which prohibits development within a certain distance of the high-water line of a perennial stream, or (2) a floating buffer, which varies in width depending on site, soil, and runoff characteristics (Palone and Todd 1998).

- *Large-lot zoning.* Large-lot zoning is low-density zoning. In some areas, this reduces density to one home per two acres; in other areas, it reduces density to one home per 35 acres. Ostensibly created to disperse the impact of development and reduce stormwater runoff, large-lot zoning actually contributes to sprawl by requiring longer road networks that, in turn, increase impervious cover (Schueler 1995c).

Suburban sprawl also contributes to water scarcity and increased stormwater runoff and pollution by promoting more and larger lawns. According to a study conducted in the Seattle metropolitan area, large suburban "estate" properties consumed up to 16 times more water than homes on smaller lots within a traditional urban grid. Suburban soils beneath lawns are often as impervious as roads and parking lots because they have been compacted by heavy grading equipment used to create subdivisions. Stormwater runoff from turf areas also is more likely to contain pollutants such as pesticides and fertilizers (American Rivers et al. 2002; Schueler 1995b).

DESIGN PRINCIPLE 2:
Buffer sensitive natural areas

Buffers are areas next to a shoreline, wetland, or stream where development is restricted or prohibited. They protect a river's ecological integrity, enhance connections between wildlife habitats, and allow rivers to function more naturally. A network of buffers acts as the right-of-way for a river or stream and functions as an integral part of the stream ecosystem. Buffers of varying widths protect natural areas around rivers and streams, especially fragile areas such as steep slopes and wetlands.

Buffers also reduce a site's overall imperviousness, and they filter sediments and such stormwater pollutants as fertilizer and pesticide runoff. In their role as filters, buffers can reduce water treatment costs by preventing pollutants from entering drinking water sources. Preserving open spaces as buffers along the river provides a cost-effective means of stormwater and flood control. Buffers also reduce erosion caused by uncontrolled runoff and stabilize riverbanks with vegetation.

Well-designed buffers protect water quality and plant and wildlife habitats. Buffers provide shade that lowers water temperature and protects fish habitat.

Well-designed buffers protect water quality and plant and wildlife habitats. Buffers provide shade that lowers water temperature and protects fish habitat. Trees, shrubs, grasses, and other native plants provide cover and food for birds, mammals, and other animals that live along the river. Humans can also benefit: flourishing buffers are visually appealing and often double as greenbelts, parks, and recreation areas.

Creating buffers that benefit the river ecosystem can mean giving up some traditional notions of what is "attractive." Manicured lawns, formal landscape designs, and pruned shrubs, for example, do not encourage biodiversity, often require harmful pesticides, and do not provide the food and shelter that wildlife needs.

Identifying Buffer Areas

Locations in need of a buffer can be easily identified: a walk along any riverfront will reveal the areas where erosion, channelization, and other signs of degradation are greatest. Generally, the most critical areas to buffer possess steep slopes, wetlands, erodible soils, and endangered or threatened animal or plant species. Geographical information systems (GIS) and aerial photos are the most effective tools for identifying buffer sites of more than several miles. Buffers should be recorded on official maps and protected through conservation easements, regulations, and signs.

In the Twin Cities region, Great River Greening (GRG) is working to identify, protect, and restore buffers. With the help of a staff landscape ecologist, aerial photos, and GIS technology, the organization has identified the highest-quality buffers along a seven-county stretch of the Mississippi River. Using this information, GRG formulates priorities for ecological restoration, protecting and buffering natural areas, and preserving and creating wildlife habitat, especially for songbirds (Karasov 2002).

GRG also has worked with the Friends of the Mississippi River and more than 100 landowners to protect and enhance buffers. A prime example is their plan to create the 1,300-acre Pine Bend Bluffs Natural Area overlooking the Mississippi. This area includes 700 acres owned by Flint Hills Resources, an operator of local oil fields and refineries that is participating in restoration efforts. Although largely untouched since the nineteenth century, the area was choked by nonnative plants when efforts began in 2000 to restore original oak savanna, oak forest, and prairie habitats. Volunteers cleared invasive plants from 78 acres and identified native species. By late 2001, the area had been replanted with native prairie wildflowers and grasses.

With financial support from Flint Hills, the National Fish and Wildlife Foundation, the Trust for Public Land, the Minnesota Department of Natural Resources' Metro Greenways program, and other public and private organizations, the multistage project has enhanced the river buffer with native plants and porous cover. Ultimately GRG hopes to protect all 1,300 acres in this important river corridor (Friends of the Mississippi River 2003; Great River Greening 2003; Karasov 2002, 2003).

Laws, Ordinances, Design Guidelines, and Standards

State laws and local planning ordinances can help preserve buffers through development regulations. For example, the Georgia Planning Act of 1990 limits land-disturbing activities within a 100-foot buffer on all protected rivers. Georgia's Metropolitan Rivers Protection Act goes further, establishing a 2,000-foot stream corridor on both sides of the Chattahoochee River and its impoundments for the 84 miles between Buford Dam and the downstream limits of Atlanta. Within this corridor, the law, administered by the Atlanta Regional Commission, specifies a 150-foot setback for impervious surfaces (Atlanta Regional Commission 2003).

A collection of planning practices known as "better site design" can conserve natural areas, reduce watershed pollution, save money, and increase property values. Better site design is a fundamentally different approach from typical subdivision design for residential and commercial development. These practices seek to accomplish three goals: reduce impervious cover, conserve more natural lands, and use porous areas for effective stormwater treatment.

In 1996, the Center for Watershed Protection convened a national site-planning roundtable composed of experts in planning, design, development, and environmental sciences, as well as representatives of local governments. The roundtable created 22 model development principles, organized into three areas: residential streets and parking lots, lot development, and conservation of natural areas (see sidebars on pp. 54 and 76–77).

A collection of planning practices known as "better site design" can conserve natural areas, reduce watershed pollution, save money, and increase property values.

BETTER SITE DESIGN
FOR CONSERVATION OF NATURAL AREAS

The following six principles related to natural areas conservation in new suburban development are based on the roundtable's work and are adapted with permission from CWP (2003b). They are intended to help local governments modify their ordinances rather than to serve as national design standards.

1. Create along all perennial streams a variable-width, naturally vegetated buffer system that encompasses critical environmental features such as the 100-year floodplain, steep slopes, and freshwater wetlands.

2. Preserve or restore riparian stream buffers with native vegetation. Maintain the buffer system through the plan review, delineation, construction, and post-development stages.

3. Limit clearing and grading of a site to the minimum needed to build lots, allow access, and provide fire protection. Manage a consolidated portion of the community open space as protected green space.

4. Conserve vegetation at each site by preserving and planting native plants, clustering tree areas, and incorporating trees into community open space, street rights-of-way, parking lot islands, and other landscaped areas.

5. Encourage incentives and flexibility to conserve stream buffers, forests, meadows, and other areas of environmental value. Encourage off-site mitigation where it is consistent with locally adopted watershed plans.

6. Prevent new discharges of stormwater runoff into wetlands, sole-source aquifers, or sensitive areas.

If filtering pollutants is the goal, the buffer should be at least 100 feet wide. To protect wildlife habitat, a generally accepted minimum buffer width is 300 feet, though that varies with animal species.

Buffer Size

How big should a buffer be? To protect stream quality and aquatic habitat a minimum stream buffer of at least 100 feet is recommended (Stormwater Manager's Resource Center 2003). Often even that is too narrow to protect ecological values, depending on the size and topography of the river, nearby land uses, and the purpose of the buffer.

The Federal Interagency Stream Restoration Working Group (2001, 8-12) notes that "most local buffer criteria require that development be set back a fixed and uniform distance from the stream channel." Standards vary widely. Urban stream buffers range from 20 to 200 feet from each side of the stream, with a median of 100 feet, according to a national survey of 36 stream buffer programs by the Metropolitan Washington Council of Governments (MacBroom 1998).

If filtering pollutants is the goal, the buffer should be at least 100 feet wide. To protect wildlife habitat, a generally accepted minimum buffer width is 300 feet, though that varies with animal species. For large rivers, buffers should cover a significant portion of the floodplain to prevent flood damage.

The most important section of a stream buffer is the first 25 feet of land from the edge of the water. This zone—the streamside zone, which includes the stream bank, canopy trees that overhang the stream, and aquatic vegetation along the water's edge—should always be kept free from development. Next, the outer (or supplemental) buffer zone is located 100 to 200 feet from the water's edge. This outer zone provides additional river protection but can also accommodate low-impact human activities (MacBroom 1998; University of Georgia Institute of Ecology 2003; Washington County Soil and Water Conservation District 1999).

Planning ordinances specify either fixed or variable buffer widths. Fixed-width buffers typically express a political compromise between protecting a natural resource and minimizing the impact on development and private-property rights. Variable buffers, which become wider in critical natural areas and narrower in stretches of more urbanized development, can be more ecologically sound, but are often more difficult for jurisdictions to administer.

The steeper the buffer's slope, the wider the buffer must be to absorb runoff that gains speed and force as it rushes downhill. An urban buffer's ability to treat stormwater depends in part on how much the flow has been channelized before it enters the buffer. Channelization—the degree to which the flow is concentrated into a single stream, often fast, narrow, and straight—in turn determines how long stormwater will be detained in the buffer, another measure of a buffer's ability to treat runoff. If a buffer receives large amounts of runoff from a street, flow-spreading devices like multiple curb cuts and spacers can redistribute the flow and thus improve the buffer's treatment performance.

Restoring Buffers in Industrial Floodplains

Increasingly, local governments are purchasing brownfields to restore key buffers. In downtown Saint Paul, the Bruce Vento Nature Sanctuary provides an example of this type of reclamation. Named after the late Congressman Bruce Vento, an environmental advocate, this 26-acre floodplain site is wedged between railroad tracks, I-94, and the Mississippi River. The land was abandoned 30 years ago by its owner, the Burlington Northern-Santa Fe railroad. A tributary, Phalen Creek, had been filled in and the floodplain was polluted from years of railroad and industrial use.

When the land was put up for sale, the Lower Phalen Creek partners—more than 20 organizations representing neighbors and river advocates—began a "visioning" process. Realizing that the land could link three neighborhoods to downtown along the river valley, the partners developed the Lower Phalen Creek Project, outlining plans for a nature sanctuary with a riverfront park, trail, and wetlands. Backed by $1.3 million appropriated by Congress through the National Park Service, and additional local, state, and private funding, the Trust for Public Land led acquisition negotiations and purchased the property from Burlington Northern in November 2002. It then transferred ownership to the city of Saint Paul, which is overseeing an environmental cleanup (City of Saint Paul 2003; Embrace Open Space 2002).

In another example, Toronto launched ambitious efforts in the 1980s to revitalize the city's industrial waterfront through a network of parks and open-space corridors where the Don River meets Lake Ontario (Hough et al. 1997). Known as the Port Lands, this area near downtown is well connected by highways, rail lines, and marine transportation routes. However, run-down buildings, junkyards, storage areas, tanneries, and chain-link fences made it seem derelict and unsafe. At the same time, the Port Lands' open spaces include spectacular examples of natural regeneration, such as Tommy Thompson Park, a world-renowned site for migratory birds and other wildlife.

In 2000, Toronto's Waterfront Revitalization Corporation, a nonprofit corporation, began creating a 10-year business revitalization plan for the

The steeper the buffer's slope, the wider the buffer must be to absorb runoff that gains speed and force as it rushes downhill. An urban buffer's ability to treat stormwater depends in part on how much the flow has been channelized before it enters the buffer.

DESIGNING STREAM BUFFERS

Riverfronts are exceptionally difficult areas in which to create vegetated buffers because of the need for water views and access, recreation, hardscape, park management, safety, crime prevention, and flood protection. Little if any research exists on creating riverfront buffers in highly developed urban areas. In cities, buffer-sizing criteria may be based on site conditions as well as economic, legal, and ecological factors.

Thomas Schueler of the Center for Watershed Protection offers eight performance criteria to determine the size, management, and crossings of stream buffers. These criteria were developed for creating buffers in developing watersheds with new development on private land. They are offered here as a starting point for thinking about urban riverfront buffers:

1. Three-zone buffer system: Effective urban stream buffers have three lateral zones—streamside, middle, and outer. Each performs a different function and has a different width, vegetation goal, and management scheme.

The *streamside zone*, ideally mature riparian forest, protects the physical and ecological integrity of the stream ecosystem.

The *middle zone*, mature forest with some clearing for stormwater management, access, and recreational uses, extends from the streamside zone across the 100-year floodplain, adjacent steep slopes, and protected wetlands, and provides distance between the stream and upland development.

The *outer zone* is the buffer's buffer, an additional 25-foot setback from the outer edge of the middle zone to the nearest permanent structure. In parks or backyards, this buffer zone can be expanded by replacing lawns with native trees and shrubs.

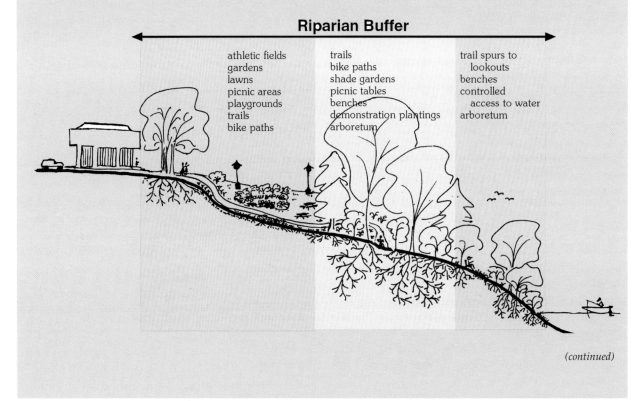

Riparian Buffer

athletic fields	trails	trail spurs to
gardens	bike paths	lookouts
lawns	shade gardens	benches
picnic areas	picnic tables	controlled
playgrounds	benches	access to water
trails	demonstration plantings	arboretum
bike paths	arboretum	

(continued)

riverfront on both sides of the Don, which is owned by the city and the province of Ontario. The plan focuses on cleaning up toxic land and water, instituting a $15-million flood-management plan, and selling some suitable adjacent lands for mixed-use redevelopment. As part of the process, the Metropolitan Toronto and Region Conservation Authority, a regional government agency, has begun an environmental assessment of the riverfront land (Freeman 2002).

Throughout the Port Lands, "green infrastructure" will provide a framework for redevelopment, restore biodiversity, create linkages for wildlife

DESIGNING STREAM BUFFERS *(continued)*

2. Restoring buffers to predevelopment vegetation: The model for converting urban stream buffers is the riparian plant community that existed in the floodplain before development. This may include mature forest in many regions, prairie grasses in the Midwest, and indigenous shrubs such as willows and dogwoods in the arid West.

3. Buffer expansion and contraction: Many communities require expansion of the buffer's minimum width as needed. The middle zone's average width can be expanded to include the full 100-year floodplain; undevelopable steep slopes (greater than 25 percent); steep slopes (5 to 25 percent); or nearby wetlands and wildlife habitat.

4. Buffer delineation: Develop criteria for three issues: At what mapping scale will streams be defined? Where does the stream begin and the buffer end? From what point should the inner edge of the buffer be measured? Define limits and uses of the stream buffer system during each stage of development.

5. Buffer crossings: Stream buffers should maintain a corridor of riparian forest (or other appropriate native vegetation) and allow for fish passage. However, provisions must be made for roads, bridges, underground utilities, and enclosed storm drains that cross streams and rivers.

6. Stormwater runoff: Although buffers are an important component of stormwater treatment systems for developed sites, they generally treat runoff from less than 10 percent of the watershed. The remaining 90 percent must be managed by using different approaches known as best management practices elsewhere in the watershed.

7. Buffer education and enforcement: Educate the public and enforce protection by making buffers "visible." Encouraging awareness and stewardship among adjacent property owners by:

- marking buffer boundaries with signs that describe allowable activities;

- publishing educational pamphlets;

- conducting stream walks and meetings with property owners;

- ensuring new owners are informed about buffer limits and uses when property is sold or transferred;

- guiding a stewardship program, including reforestation and backyard "bufferscaping" programs; and

- conducting annual buffer walks to check on encroachment.

8. Buffer flexibility: In most regions, a 100-foot buffer will take about 5 percent of the total land area of a watershed out of use or production. This may represent a hardship for landowners. Communities concerned that buffer requirements may constitute an uncompensated "taking" of private property should make it clear that buffer programs modify the location of development, but not its overall intensity. Buffer ordinances can include such flexible measures as: maintaining buffers in private ownership, buffer averaging, transferring density to other locations, variances, and conservation easements.

Source: Adapted from Schueler (1996, 155–163)

and humans, and improve the area's image and sense of place. This effort includes proposed trails connecting major parks, including new open space at the mouth of the Don, where the river will be moved from a channel into a more natural setting with wetland buffers.

So far Toronto has commitments of $1.5 billion for waterfront renewal from the municipal, provincial, and federal governments, including $300 million for the first four projects. One of the first projects underway is a $2 million environmental assessment to renaturalize the mouth of the Don and provide flood control for the West Don Lands area. Other projects will

FIGURE 3-4. VIEW OF BRUCE VENTO NATURE SANCTUARY FROM KELLOGG BRIDGE

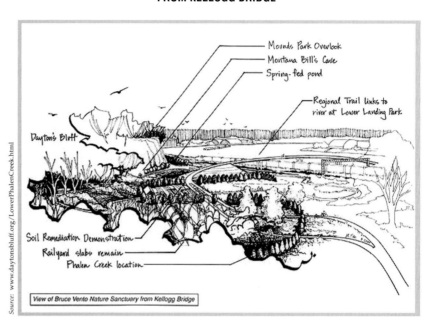

Source: www.daytonsbluff.org/LowerPhalenCreek.html

prepare the Port Lands' underused and contaminated land for redevelopment and construct a subway platform and a street to connect the waterfront with transit. In summer 2004, the revitalization of Cherry Beach in the Port Lands' Central Waterfront will debut. The Toronto Waterfront Revitalization Corporation is investing $1.5 million to clean up the beach and install a tree-lined grand entrance and parking, which will become part of a planned waterfront regional park (City of Toronto 2003; Toronto Waterfront Revitalization Corporation 2003).

FIGURE 3-5. TORONTO'S CHERRY BEACH REVITALIZATION PLAN

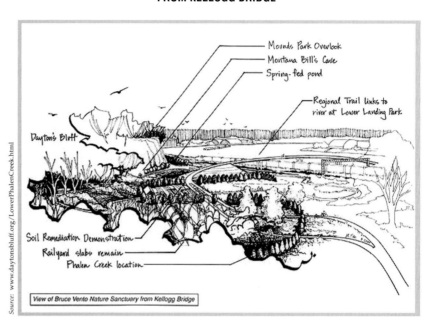

Beyond the Port Lands, decade-long efforts have been underway to revitalize other parts of the Don watershed, which is more than 80 percent developed and home to more than 800,000 people. In 1992, the Metropolitan Toronto and Region Conservation Authority formed a task force (later called the Don Watershed Regeneration Council), which published 40 recommendations on restoring water quality, natural areas, and community access to the river. The Council issues a report card every three years that charts the region's progress (Don Watershed Regeneration Council 1994, 2000).

DESIGN PRINCIPLE 3:
Restore riparian and in-stream habitats

Restoring riparian habitat requires action far beyond simply replanting indigenous plants. First, planners must address watershed and regional factors to establish healthy hydrological cycles and water quality. For example, planted buffer zones must be created and maintained, stormwater controlled and cleansed, and new dams and reservoirs avoided or removed where possible. Likewise, in-stream flows from reservoirs and dams must be managed to protect wildlife habitat.

It is also necessary to conduct research on upstream and downstream natural communities to identify likely restoration areas and habitat types for fish, birds, and other animals. Planners should consider these areas in the context of the larger river system (for example, the relationship of smaller feeding or nursery areas to larger upstream or downstream habitats). After water quality and habitat are improved, native fish and other species dependent on healthy aquatic ecosystems can be reintroduced.

Successful habitat restoration projects should combine at least four major elements:

1. *Natural channel design:* A rebuilt channel should closely resemble its original, natural shape. The reconfiguration and reconstruction of a degraded channel should allow for meanders and other elements of a naturally flowing river or stream.

2. *In-stream habitat structures:* New boulders, gravel, logs, and other natural materials can be deposited to create river features such as riffles, pools, and rapids.

3. *Vegetation management:* Vegetation management includes removing exotic plants and replanting native species, enforcing no-mow zones in riparian buffers, and working with businesses, homeowners, and public agencies to remove impervious surfaces and to promote native plantings in watershed landscapes.

4. *Bioengineering:* Native plants and other natural materials can stabilize and rebuild eroded banks. Live woody cuttings or poles of readily sprouting species can be inserted deep into the soil of a bank or anchored by other means. Bioengineering is discussed as part of Principle 4.

This section addresses natural channel design, daylighting creeks, in-stream habitat structures, dam removal, and vegetation management.

Natural Channel Design

In the 1950s, Luna Leopold, then a senior research hydrologist for the U.S. Geological Survey, led a comprehensive research project that measured streams across the United States. He found that natural features such as oxbows, floodplains, and eddies helped slow floodwaters and prevented river channels from clogging with sediments—problems that plague hard-

**CASE
STUDY**

River Issues. After three centuries of development and industrialization, the Bronx River was considered an "open sewer." More recently, abandoned industrial areas, neglected parklands, channelization, and riverbank erosion have only added to the stresses on the river. Few tidal wetlands remain, and riparian habitats have been destroyed. In addition, excessive stormwater runoff, flooding, and non-point source pollution have contributed to the ecological damage to the river.

Bronx River, New York, New York.

What Has Been Accomplished. The Bronx River is the only freshwater river in New York City. For much of the twentieth century, the reality of a river flowing through the Bronx was ignored and forgotten as the city grew up around it. More often, the waterway was perceived as an open dumping ground for trash, abandoned cars, and appliances. The last quarter century, however, has seen a revitalization and transformation of the Bronx waterfront to a place where people in the city can go for recreation, education, and enjoyment of nature. To redress current threats to the river, local groups have developed joint strategies to mobilize greater community involvement in the restoration of the river and the city's parks.

The Bronx River Alliance serves as the new voice in restoring and protecting the Bronx River. Starting with the Bronx River Restoration Project in 1974, there is a rich history of restoration work in the area. The goal of the Alliance is to: "serve as a coordinated voice for the river and work in harmonious partnership to protect, improve, and restore the Bronx River corridor and greenway so that they can be healthy ecological, recreational, educational, and economic resources for the communities through which the river flows."

Emphasizing the focus of public participation and community involvement, the Bronx River Alliance serves as the coordinated voice for the river. The Alliance is made up of more than 75 community groups, government agencies, schools, and businesses. Among the major partners are the Bronx River Working Group; Partnerships for Parks, Waterways, and Trailways; Bronx Riverkeeper Program; and New York City Department of Parks and Recreation.

engineered flood control projects. Leopold, possibly the leading hydrologist in the past century, inspired later research by scores of scientists, who determined that these natural features also maintain water quality and create wildlife habitat, especially for fish.

In Leopold's wake, many other projects have revived the benefits of natural river and stream channels. For example, a 2001 U.S. Forest Service handbook on stream corridor restoration catalogues techniques to reconstruct a waterway's "profile" to create optimal habitat for fish, plants, insects, birds, and mammals. In assessing conditions for restoration projects, the handbook emphasizes the importance—and suggests careful measurement—of such factors as bank slope, the ratio of the stream length compared to the length of its valley, and even the size of pebbles and other materials in the streambed (FISRWG 2001).

Natural channel reconstruction should include the following steps (adapted from FISRWG 2001, 8-28–8-31):

Cleanup of the waterfront, which began in the late 1970s, continues to this day. Trash piled upwards of 20 feet high along the banks is being removed along with the multitude of items in the riverway itself. Over the years, the Bronx River Working Group has worked tirelessly to reclaim sections of the river and replant them with greenery. With funds secured from federal, state, and local sources, the Working Group has a grand vision for the restoration of the Bronx River. Included in this vision are greenways and parkways along both sides of the river, hiking and biking trails, construction and restoration of wetlands, and projects to contain the overflow of sewage and stormwater. At the heart of this cleanup project is community involvement. Special events such as the Bronx River Golden Ball, where a 36-inch golden orb symbolizing the "sun, energy and spirit of the river" is floated down the river, serve to unite the community and draw attention to the wide variety of areas the river traverses.

Benefits to River and Community. These efforts have increased public awareness of the ecological value of Bronx River habitats in supporting commercially and recreationally important fish species. Also, the river is recognized as a valuable natural resource that is central to the well-being of local communities.

For more information . . .

- See the Bronx River Alliance web site, www.bronxriver.org
- The Bioengineering Group, Inc. 2000. "Bronx River Preliminary Restoration Plan." [Accessed February 26, 2004.] Available at www.bioengineering.com/tbg_website.htm.
- Clean Water Action Plan. 2000. "The Bronx River Watershed: Community Cooperation in Urban Watershed Restoration." *Watershed Success Stories: Applying the Principles and Spirit of the Clean Water Action Plan, 1998-2000.* [Accessed February 26, 2004.] Available at www.cleanwater.gov/success/bronx.html
- "A River Rises," *New York Times*, December 3, 2000, Section 14, pp. 1, 26.

- *Study physical aspects of the watershed.* Reconstruction should emulate the channel's natural width and depth, hydrology, size of bed sediments, and riparian vegetation.

- *Reference the reaches.* Find another stable and ecologically healthy reach of the same waterway to use as a reference point for the dimensions of natural channel design. Ensure that the information captured includes the chemical, physical, and biological make-up of the healthy reach—not just the habitat structure, but also the mix of creatures in it.

- *Determine the size and placement of bed materials such as sand, pebbles, river stones, boulders, and tree stumps.* These will create habitat and "armor" the waterway against erosion.

- *Analyze hydrology.* Natural channel designs must be able to handle flood control. Analyze flows and adjacent land uses to help select the channel location, alignment, width, depth, and floodplain size.

In Montgomery County, Maryland, near Washington, D.C, the 13.3-square-mile Sligo Creek watershed, in poor condition before 1990, has benefitted from a reconstruction effort. More than 60 percent of the watershed was paved or impervious surface. The creek was polluted by combined sewer overflows (CSOs) during storms. As a result, only a few fish species—none of them native—survived in Sligo Creek.

From 1991 to 1994, Sligo Creek received one of the nation's most extensive watershedwide restorations—one that combined many techniques described in this section. The creek and its tributaries were improved by separating storm and sanitary sewers to eliminate CSOs and through revegetation, bank stabilization, and reconfiguration of in-stream flows. Upstream, three connected ponds were built to detain runoff for up to 36 hours, which

FIGURE 3-6. SLIGO CREEK TRAIL (NORTHERN PORTION)

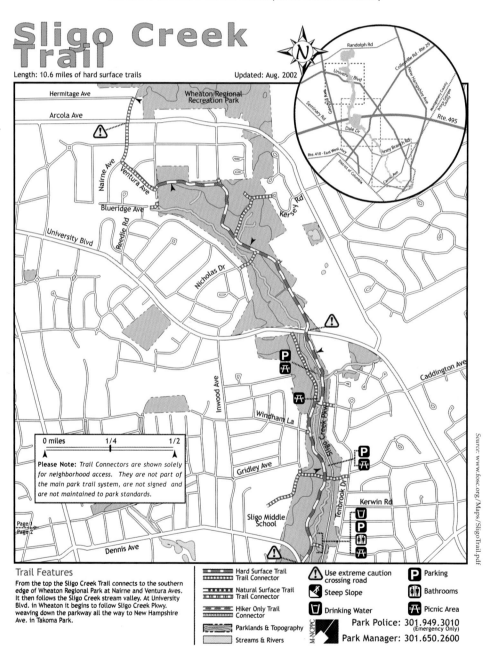

allowed pollutants and sediments to settle out. The downstream channel was completely rebuilt with 19 native shrub species reintroduced to the riparian zone. Volunteers then reintroduced native fish by the bucketful. By 1996, fish species had increased from three to 16, including native and pollution-sensitive fish. Fish deformities, lesions, and tumors dropped 75 percent. New greenway trails provide access to this revitalized resource (Thompson 1996).

Daylighting Creeks

Creeks channeled into underground culvert pipes destroy a healthy natural environment. Small streams are highly efficient in scrubbing pollution from runoff and auto emissions and thus are critical to the health of the entire watershed (Peterson et al. 2001). Piped creeks lose this capacity to clean runoff. They can dump polluted water into rivers at high velocity, also causing erosion. Culverts often create bottlenecks in stormwater conveyance systems that lead to flooding. Piped creeks also have no value for wildlife.

Creeks that have been encased in pipes or hidden beneath decks can be "daylighted." A daylighted creek is one whose channel has been excavated and restored. Daylighting seeks to restore creeks to their original channel or to thread them in a new, open channel between buildings, parking lots, and ballfields. Stormwater pipes also can be daylighted or replaced with naturalized swales, constructed wetlands, or rehabilitated estuaries (Pinkham 2000).

California, for example, which has lost 95 percent of its riparian habitat since presettlement times, is now reclaiming hundreds of culverted and piped streams. One of the first was Berkeley's Strawberry Creek. In 1984, a 200-foot-section of Strawberry Creek buried beneath an abandoned rail yard was re-exposed. As an 80-year-old culvert was dug out, the rehabilitated channel was modeled on the width, depth, and meander pattern of a healthier creek section several blocks upstream. Banks were replanted with native willows, cottonwoods, pines, manzanitas, and other species that require little maintenance or irrigation once established. The creek became the centerpiece for a four-acre, $580,000 city park. Daylighting represented less than 10 percent of that cost (Pinkham 2000).

Strawberry Creek has been an ecological, social, and economic success. While the native riparian vegetation thrives, Strawberry Creek has withstood numerous major storms that would have overwhelmed the culvert. Hundreds of people visit the park and its natural areas daily. Neighborhood property values have risen, and nearby buildings have been redeveloped. The Strawberry Creek project's success has led to several spin-offs of other creeks in Berkeley.

In Pittsburgh, the daylighting of Nine Mile Run has created an attractive and ecologically diverse new setting on the Monongahela River. For 60 years, Nine Mile Run was buried under a growing 20-million-ton slag heap that covered 238 acres at the stream's confluence with the Monongahela. In 2001 and 2002, this slag heap was regraded to create a platform for a new residential community called Summerset at Frick Park. The regrading of the slag (an inert byproduct of steel production) also uncovered Nine Mile Run, which is now undergoing an $8 million restoration.

More than 200,000 tons of topsoil have been layered over the regraded slag to sustain newly naturalized landscapes. These will be connected to Frick Park, a 455-acre forest preserve, and to new riverfront trails. Nine Mile Run is also becoming a major amenity for Summerset, which represents a $210 million investment into a formerly underused riverfront site (Bonci 2001, 2002; Ermann 2003).

The daylighting of Nine Mile Run along the Monongahela River in Pittsburgh has created an attractive and ecologically diverse setting. Here, people take a guided stream tour.

Nine Mile Run Greenway Project

In-Stream Habitat Structures

Within the river channel, in-stream habitat structures include rocks, gravel beds, snags (downed trees), roots and other naturally rough spots in the stream channel, and fabricated structures like dams and weirs. These can be manipulated to change the river dynamics—in other words, to speed or slow the flow of water, create rapids and pools, and reintroduce riverbends into a waterway that has been straightened. In general, dams should be avoided as they can severely alter natural flows, raise water temperatures, trap beneficial sediment and other materials, and create impassable barriers to fish (American Rivers 2003a).

In-stream habitat structures alone do not substitute for good riparian and upland management. Yet in-stream habitat structures can improve water quality and provide shelter and breeding areas that encourage insects and fish to thrive. In turn, insects and fish attract birds like dippers, herons, and kingfishers, and mammals such as beavers, raccoons, and river otters.

When restoration is required, the design process should follow several basic steps (adapted from FISRWG 2001, 8-71–8-76):

1. *Diagnose problems in advance.* Survey the stream or river to determine habitat and water-quality problems related to hydrology.

2. *Design a habitat improvement plan.* The plan should include in-stream habitat structures, bank restoration through bioengineering, and revegetation. Identify goals for wildlife population increases.

3. *Plan layout.* Each structure must be carefully located, avoiding conflicts with bridges and riparian vegetation. Customize placement for the hydrology and morphology of each individual waterway.

4. *Select types of structures.* The most commonly used structures are weirs, dikes, boulders, and bank covers (also called lunkers, these resemble a child's set of jacks).

5. *Size the structures.* Structures should produce aquatic habitats at a wide range of flows. Generally structures should be low enough so they are almost submerged during high waters.

6. *Investigate hydraulic effects.* Structures should not contribute to flooding by creating barriers to water conveyance.

7. *Consider effects on sediment transport.* Model the effects of structures on erosion and sedimentation.

8. *Select materials.* Materials may include stone, fencing wire, posts, and felled trees. Use natural materials when possible, especially stone or trees from the site.

9. *Monitor and evaluate results.* Track changes in wildlife populations, water temperature and quality, and percentage of area covered with native plants, including tree canopy.

10. *Plan to maintain in-stream structures.* Incorporate a management plan with funding into the design.

In Redmond, Washington, the Sammamish River lost much of its riparian vegetation when it was engineered into a deep trapezoidal channel in the 1960s. In the 1990s, a stretch of river was refurbished through downtown. The project combined bioengineering, in-stream habitat construction, and weed removal. The floodplain was enlarged by 50 feet through sculpted riverbank "benches" planted with native vegetation.

Behind City Hall, the river's meanders and curves have been revived by adding boulders, root wads, and gravel bars to the once-uniform channel. The restored riverfront has become the centerpiece of a new 16-mile trail that connects to a regional greenway system. Salmon, steelhead, native trout, and upland riparian species have returned to the river and its banks (Holt 2002).

Dam Removal

Dams block fish migration, disrupt water flow, change water temperature, and generally wreak havoc on the food chain in rivers. They limit public access to rivers and harm the natural and aesthetic quality of their settings.

(Left) Before trail construction, the west bank of the Sammamish River was cut off visually and overrun with invasive non-native species. (Right) The constructed trail recreated river meanders and provides river access to cyclists, joggers, equestrians, and walkers.

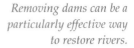
Removing dams can be a particularly effective way to restore rivers.

Bill Hubbard, U.S. Army Corps of Engineers

Efforts to remove unneeded, unsafe, or obsolete dams have been gaining momentum. Of the 75,000 dams identified in a U.S. Army Corps of Engineers inventory, about 66,000 are on rivers. Studies indicate that about 1 percent of these dams are obsolete or unsafe and might be considered for removal. Many communities have low-head dams that no longer serve a purpose, but block fish migration and cause hazards for boating and other recreation. As operating licenses expire and more dams become obsolete, the opportunities to remove dams will increase. By 2020, about 85 percent of all dams will exceed their life expectancy of 50 years.

In recent years, more than 465 dams have been removed across the country. Removing dams where the benefits of removal outweigh the benefits of repair or replacement is the most effective way to restore rivers, save taxpayer money, revitalize riverside communities, and improve public safety.

Removing dams can dramatically regenerate river ecosystems, often in a matter of months. In Hampden, Maine, a dam built to power a grist mill had blocked fish migration along the Souadabscook River since the eighteenth century. Within months of the dam's removal in October 1998, Atlantic salmon established upstream spawning areas for the first time in 200 years. Brook trout, American shad, smelt, and alewife also quickly repopulated the river.

Dam removal also saves money. In 1988, West Bend, Wisconsin, was faced with removing or replacing the deteriorated Woolen Mills Dam from the Milwaukee River. The city spent $86,000 to remove the dam instead of an estimated $3.3 million to replace it (American Rivers et al. 1999).

When it was built in 1837, the Edwards Dam destroyed thriving commercial fisheries along the Kennebec River in Maine. As the first dam from the sea on the Kennebec, the Edwards Dam was literally a cork that, if unplugged, would allow miles of the river to be restored as a natural ecosystem and as prime habitat for migratory fish.

When removal of the Edwards Dam began in July 1999, it signaled a turning point for the Kennebec—and for rivers nationwide. Removal of the dam improved water quality and fish passage while creating new public open space bounded by a free-flowing river.

The most important environmental benefit has been the reopening to sea-run fish of a significant stretch of spawning ground north of the Hudson River. At least 10 migratory fish species, including Atlantic sturgeon, American shad, and Atlantic salmon, are now found in this newly accessible 17-mile stretch of river. During the spring following dam removal, ocean-migrating fish were caught in the river above Augusta for the first time since 1837 (American Rivers et al. 1999).

Downtown Augusta also experienced an economic resurgence following dam removal. Working cooperatively with the state, the city formed the Capital Riverfront Improvement District (CRID) to protect the scenic character of the river, provide public access, and bring additional economic development to a one-square-mile historic riverfront district. Since 1999, the CRID has attracted nearly $10 million in public and private investment, including the award-winning conversion of historic City Hall, vacant for 15 years, into 28 apartments for seniors. The CRID also has raised $3 million for the first phase of an eventual $8 million riverfront park. The park will recycle a remaining brick building from the Edwards Mill as an interpretive center. It will also interpret nine areas of natural and cultural history.

In 2002, the city dedicated the first two miles of a riverfront rail-to-trail conversion through downtown. Already popular, the trail will soon be extended another seven miles toward an eventual 20-mile loop covering both sides of the river and connecting Augusta to neighboring communities (Bridgeo 2003).

Vegetation Management

Native vegetation helps filter runoff, controls flooding, and reduces or eliminates erosion. Native plants provide shelter and food for wildlife. Canopy trees shading creeks help lower the water temperature and therefore create more favorable conditions for native fish.

Nine Mile Run Greenway Project

REVEGETATION TECHNIQUES

The following techniques can be combined to revegetate conditions that suit a particular stretch of river (Riley 1998):

- Create the conditions for native plants to "reinvade" a site. For example, remove invasive species through weeding programs, dredging, or controlled burns. Remove levees or regrade to allow for natural reseeding.

- Layer dead brush, trees, or tree stumps to stabilize the bank and capture sediment that will become a growing medium for native plant communities. Plant live cuttings from native species such as willows and dogwoods that regenerate readily. These "pioneer" species stabilize banks and create habitat for other riparian vegetation.

- Transplant native vegetation from areas being altered by development.

- Plant nursery-grown natives to emulate the number, density, and relationships of plant species within a riparian community.

- Preserve and enhance existing vegetation, including snags and dead trees, through purchase, conservation easements, floodplain zoning, and ecological management.

- In extremely urban situations with a narrow floodplain and channel, use hybrid engineering methods such as riprap and gabion walls that are packed with soil and planted.

Weeds and other nonnative plants generally provide little or no habitat compared to natives. They can create monocultures with no ecological diversity. The most visible example may be the exotic phragmites reeds that choke and provide many urban wetlands almost no wildlife habitat.

Along the river's edge and in the floodplain, native vegetation can be reestablished through a number of methods. Effective riparian restoration provides wildlife habitat, improves water quality, and anchors soil to control erosion and flooding. Yet even the best projects will not replicate a natural, presettlement river. Replanting "pure" native landscapes next to urban areas may be difficult because native plant communities may not survive urban runoff and pollution. In urban areas, native planting schemes must be installed in specially prepared environments and adapted to the site's water levels, contaminated soils, and levels of runoff.

Revegetation requires a complex process of analysis, planning, design, installation, monitoring, and maintenance. It should be undertaken by an experienced team that includes aquatic and plant ecologists, civil engineers, and landscape architects. The team should first identify, survey, and inventory a stream reference corridor—a healthy riparian habitat with similar hydrology, ecosystems, and climate. Often this corridor will be located on a different reach of the same waterway. Studying the stream reference corridor creates benchmarks for plant density, diversity, and placement.

Once study is complete, revegetation projects can pursue several different strategies. Some begin with canopy tree planting; others with understory plantings; others with grasses and other nonwoody plants that allow a natural succession into mature woodland.

Weed removal and control is equally important. Weeds may be removed by hand pulling (a good volunteer project), cutting, burning, or selective use of herbicides (Pinkham 2000).

Revegetation requires analysis, planning, design, implementation, monitoring, and maintenance. Here volunteers work along the banks of the Rouge River in Detroit.

Sally Petrella, Friends of the Rouge River

With proper planning, design, and leadership, volunteers can play a key role in revegetation efforts. In the Twin Cities region, Great River Greening gets citizens involved in reclaiming their riverfronts. Since 1995, the organization has trained 460 volunteer "restoration leaders" who have directed another 10,700 volunteers to plant more than 35,000 native trees and shrubs and 16,500 prairie grasses and wildflowers in Mississippi River valleys (Karasov 2002).

In Salinas, California, a group called Return of the Natives built six greenhouses that produced 30,000 native plants. Local schoolchildren seeded, cared for, and replanted native grasses, shrubs, and trees along Natividad Creek, which was also restored through natural channel design (Return of the Natives 2003).

In Murray City, Utah, residents and government officials are restoring habitat along the channelized Jordan River through replanting, hydrological engineering, and natural lands preservation. Under this pragmatic approach, the city is restoring natural riparian areas where possible while also identifying areas too disturbed to be restored.

Stream banks have been replanted with native grass, shrubs, and trees. Two newly constructed wetland ponds treat urban runoff before discharging it into the river. Dried wetlands were recharged with returned irrigation water. At the upper end of the wetland, sediment basins filter out phosphates and nitrates from stormwater before releasing into wetlands. Some 350 acres have been preserved as natural habitat.

Since the project began in 1990, water-quality testing has shown decreasing concentrations of arsenic, zinc, total suspended sediment, dissolved oxygen, nitrate, and phosphorous. Native birds are returning to the river, along with species not found in Murray City before, including orioles and cinnamon teals. Water-dependent plants are flourishing in the wetland ponds, and wildflowers line the river (U.S. EPA 2002e).

DESIGN PRINCIPLE 4:
Use nonstructural alternatives to manage water resources

For years our rivers and tributaries suffered from their own version of the Four Horsemen of the Apocalypse. These were the infamous "Four Ds." Rivers and creeks were ditched, dammed, and diverted, while associated wetlands were drained. This "hard" engineering approach harmed water quality, caused flooding, and destroyed wildlife habitat. Indeed, despite billions of dollars spent for structural and nonstructural flood control measures, flood damages continue to escalate in part because of intensified floodplain development and engineered river corridors.

A Sustainable Future

In recent years, newer and "softer" approaches have emerged that offer flood protection combined with the benefits of restoring natural river functions. In a landmark report, *National Flood Programs in Review 2000,* the Association of State Floodplain Managers called for a fundamental shift in national policies and programs. ASFPM (2000, i) envisions "a sustainable future—one in which floodplains throughout the nation are used only in ways that protect their integrity as enduring ecological systems."

The organization recommends policy changes at the national, state, and local levels that would promote sustainable natural systems, including purchasing permanent easements, preserving open space, restoring habitat, and adapting watershed-based planning and management (ASFPM 2002).

ASFPM notes that current floodplain management systems are costly and often allow development that fails to evaluate or mitigate damage to other properties. "We continue to intensify development within floodplains," the organization observes in a policy statement, "and do it in a manner where flood prone or marginally protected structures are suddenly prone to damages because of the actions of others in the floodplain" (ASFPM 2003).

In response to this problem, ASFPM developed its No Adverse Impact policy, which states that "the action of one property owner should not adversely impact the rights of other property owners" (ASFPM 2003). The policy aims to counteract the belief, held by many local governments, that hard-engineered federal flood-control approaches are acceptable, not realizing that those approaches may cause more flooding and damage. No

The Napa River Flood Protection Plan is restoring the river's natural characteristics and moving buildings and people out of harm's way in Napa, California.

Chris Malan

Adverse Impact promotes responsible floodplain development through community-based decision making.

California's Napa River is one of the largest rivers to undergo reconstruction guided by nonstructural engineering principles. Although the Napa is the state's last major undammed river, it did not escape from dikes, levees, and channelization, which only increased flooding. In the last 40 years, property damage from six major floods totaled $542 million. Hundreds of acres of wildlife habitat were destroyed.

In 1998, Napa County residents approved a tax increase to remove much of the Napa River's flood control system. The Napa River Flood Protection Plan is restoring the river's natural characteristics by freeing it as much as possible from artificial controls. To move buildings and people out of harm's way, the Napa Flood and Conservation District bought 50 parcels from which buildings have been removed, with plans to remove structures on another 45 properties. Businesses and residents are being moved within

FIGURE 3-7. PLANTING EXISTING RIP RAP

HYDROSEED MIX (USE COIR OR JUTE NETTING ON SLOPES STEEPER THAN 3:1)

6" TOPSOIL BACKFILL ON SLOPES 2:1 AND FLATTER

EXISTING RIP RAP

LIVE WILLOW/DOGWOOD STAKES (PENETRATE THROUGH TO SUBSOIL)

+23
10 YR. FLOOD ELEVATION

+18
ORDINARY HIGH WATER

+10
LEVEL OF PERSISTENT WOODY VEGETATION

Application Requirements:
1. *Stable, existing rip rap*
2. *2:1 slopes or flatter*
3. *Rip rap depth less than five feet.*

0   5   10   20

Source: City of Portland (2001)

the town of Napa. A major bridge has been replaced by a longer bridge with footings removed from the floodplain. Another similar bridge replacement is scheduled.

Levees have been removed to allow the river to recapture 400 acres of natural floodplain. Floodwalls and other structures are being removed, bridges altered, and levees pulled back to give the river room to expand during floods. Trees and other vegetation have been restored to the riverbank. Marshy terraces and wetlands will replace cement terraces. No reseeding is needed since tides on this estuary are reestablishing native wetland plantings. On the river's edge, programs to replant native oaks and buckeyes are underway.

Through downtown, the district has pursued a compromise approach. One riverbank remains engineered with a floodwall. The opposite bank is being naturalized and widened by several hundred feet. Redevelopment on this riverfront is being encouraged with design guidelines for suitable setbacks, limited impervious surfaces, and native plantings.

Developers are also being encouraged to embrace the river by providing visual and physical access. As pelicans and other native shorebirds return to the area, residents are excited about seeing the renewal of the Pacific Flyway's vast ecological richness (American Rivers 2003b; Malan 2002).

Few projects approach the comprehensive scope of the Napa River effort, but all rivers can benefit from nonstructural solutions used there.

Clark County, Washington, is implementing bank protection techniques sensitive to fish and wildlife habitat and long-term bank stability.

Bioengineering

One alternative to hard engineering—bioengineering (also known as soft engineering)—has gained acceptance among civil engineers and public works departments. Bioengineering uses plants to stabilize watershed slopes, a practice that may date as far back as ancient Roman times (Riley 1998).

While held to the same performance standards as hard engineering, bioengineering uses plants and other natural materials to simulate natural forces that, in turn, control floods, maintain water quality, provide access to recreation, reduce erosion, and create wildlife habitat.

Bioengineering minimizes structures like levees in favor of natural floodplain storage through riparian and wetlands restoration. Instead of riprap, concrete, or steel walls, a bioengineering approach uses naturalized bank slopes, broad floodplains, riverbends, and floodplain forests and wetlands to stabilize riverbanks and prevent erosion. Wetlands can be enhanced or created to filter stormwater and reduce flooding. Natural riverbanks often feature gently sloped banks with access for boating and fishing.

Successful bioengineering requires the cooperation of an interdisciplinary team that includes engineers, ecologists, hydrologists, planners, landscape architects, landscape contractors, and an engaged public. Bioengineering must begin with planning at the watershed level. Elements such as the percentage of impervious surface and nonpoint pollution sources should be analyzed, cataloged, and addressed. Once study has been completed, bioengineering projects can be scheduled throughout the watershed, much as public improvements are staged for urban infrastructure through an annual capital improvements budget. Areas receiving attention first might be those with the greatest potential to engage public interest and support, such as public parks, urban waterfronts, and the edges of schoolyards. Or priorities may be based on the need to control floods or to halt and repair erosion.

Bioengineering reverses the degradation of creeks, streams, and rivers. For example, unstable or eroded banks can be bioengineered to simulate the slope, vegetation, appearance, and ecological function of a natural

Bioengineering minimizes structures like levees in favor of natural floodplain storage through riparian and wetlands restoration.

bank. Bioengineering is generally less expensive to construct than hard engineering, which can cost $1,400 per linear foot for a technique like steel sheet piling (Hartig et al. 2001). An Ontario study found consistently lower costs for bioengineering compared to riprap or concrete walls (Patterson 2000).

Long-term maintenance costs of soft engineering can also be lower because over time these "living structures" mature and stabilize, rather than deteriorate. For example, a stable, naturalized riverfront—unlike a channelized river with floodwalls and other hard features—will need almost no bank repairs, will suffer less damage from flooding, and will not collect sediments that must be dredged (Wenk 2002).

Biotechnical engineering presents a hybrid approach to bioengineering. In biotechnical engineering, native plants are interspersed with an engineered erosion-control system, such as geotextile fabrics. Plantings are not expected to hold the soil, but they do provide habitat. For example, riprap can be naturalized by interplanting live stakes of willows or other native species at an angle on the slope. Within a year, live staking can provide shade, habitat, and erosion control (Sotir and Nunnally 1995).

Streambank repairs at Black Ash Creek in Collingwood, Ontario, offer a striking example of the durability of soft engineering. In 1993, one bank of the creek was repaired using bioengineering, specifically a planted cribwall. In 1995, the opposite bank was armored with concrete. Four years later the bioengineered bank matured into a stable, vegetated environment, while the concrete wall was failing (Grillmayer 2000).

Bioengineering approaches and specific techniques should be considered carefully in ultra-urban settings where some structural components such as stone or rock may be necessary due to current velocities, channel alterations for navigation, and adjacent infrastructure, such as bridges (Schueler 2003).

The Willamette River is encased by a seawall as it runs through Portland, Oregon. Efforts to "soften" the seawall and other hardscape features are included in the Willamette Riverbank Design Notebook.

Bioengineering Techniques

Bioengineering systems comprise bundled plant materials, including brush, branches, and live cuttings, that are layered on banks to reduce or eliminate erosion. Bioengineering generally seeks to reestablish native riparian plantings that stabilize banks. Benefits include slowing and filtering stormwater, anchoring soils, and providing wildlife habitat.

The following techniques can be combined as appropriate within the same riverbank (adapted from Riley 1998, 374–84):

- *Fascines* are oblong bundles of cuttings planted on angle to stabilize a slope and slow runoff as it enters a stream. Bundles are staked in rows parallel to the waterline. The cuttings (often native cottonwoods, dogwoods, and willows) will sprout and fill in to cover the bank.

- *Brush layers* are live cuttings laid on terraces that will take root in the banks.

- *Brush mats* consist of live cuttings held in place by a staked mat.

- *Branch packing* involves stuffing clusters of live stakes to stabilize gullies.

- *Live plant materials* can be used in conjunction with synthetic geotextile mats or natural cotton, jute, sisal, and coir mats that will biodegrade.

Bioengineering works best in concert with channel designs that restore natural floodplains and bank grades. Yet urban riverfronts are more difficult to restore with nonstructural alternatives because virtually no urban rivers flow through their original floodplains. Tributaries and creeks, on the other hand, generally are easier to adapt for nonstructural alternatives, including bioengineering and natural floodplain design.

Throughout the United States, efforts are underway to add natural features to urban rivers, even in extreme circumstances. For example, the Willamette River is encased in a huge seawall as it flows through Portland, Oregon. Most of the former natural floodplain is now built up as downtown Portland.

Reconstructing the river's natural features in this highly altered environment is impossible. Yet the city's *Willamette Riverbank Design Notebook* suggests numerous strategies to "soften" the seawall and other hardscape features (City of Portland 2001). Given to property owners who submit plans for waterfront development to a design review board, the *Notebook* provides alternative designs intended to improve conditions for fish (including endangered stocks of Pacific salmon), other wildlife, and people.

The *Notebook* suggests several techniques to add native plantings to the seawall. One calls for the installation of a "timber grid," a latticework that extends beneath the waterline on the seawall and supports aquatic plant species. The grid creates new habitat by providing cover for young fish. Other strategies include attaching root wads to timber pier pilings and creating "floating planters" for native upper-shore plants. These relatively low-tech methods may cost tens of thousands of dollars rather than the millions required for large-scale engineering. Property owners who implement the *Notebook*'s ideas benefit from streamlined review and may have a better chance of complying with the Endangered Species Act (Fishman 2002).

Throughout the United States, efforts are underway to add natural features to urban rivers, even in extreme circumstances.

DESIGN PRINCIPLE 5:
Reduce hardscapes

Hardscapes are roads, parking lots, sidewalks, driveways, paved paths, rooftops, and other impervious surfaces that prevent rainwater from filtering through soil and replenishing rivers and streams as groundwater. Groundwater—the water that moves through the subsurface soil and rocks—generally supplies about half of all stream flows. During droughts, the percentage can rise much higher (Alley et al. 1999).

The impervious surfaces of hardscapes degrade urban rivers because they do not absorb stormwater. In fact, they significantly increase the volume, velocity, and temperature of rainwater runoff. Paved surfaces also

FIGURE 3-10. RELATIONSHIP BETWEEN IMPERVIOUS COVER AND SURFACE RUNOFF

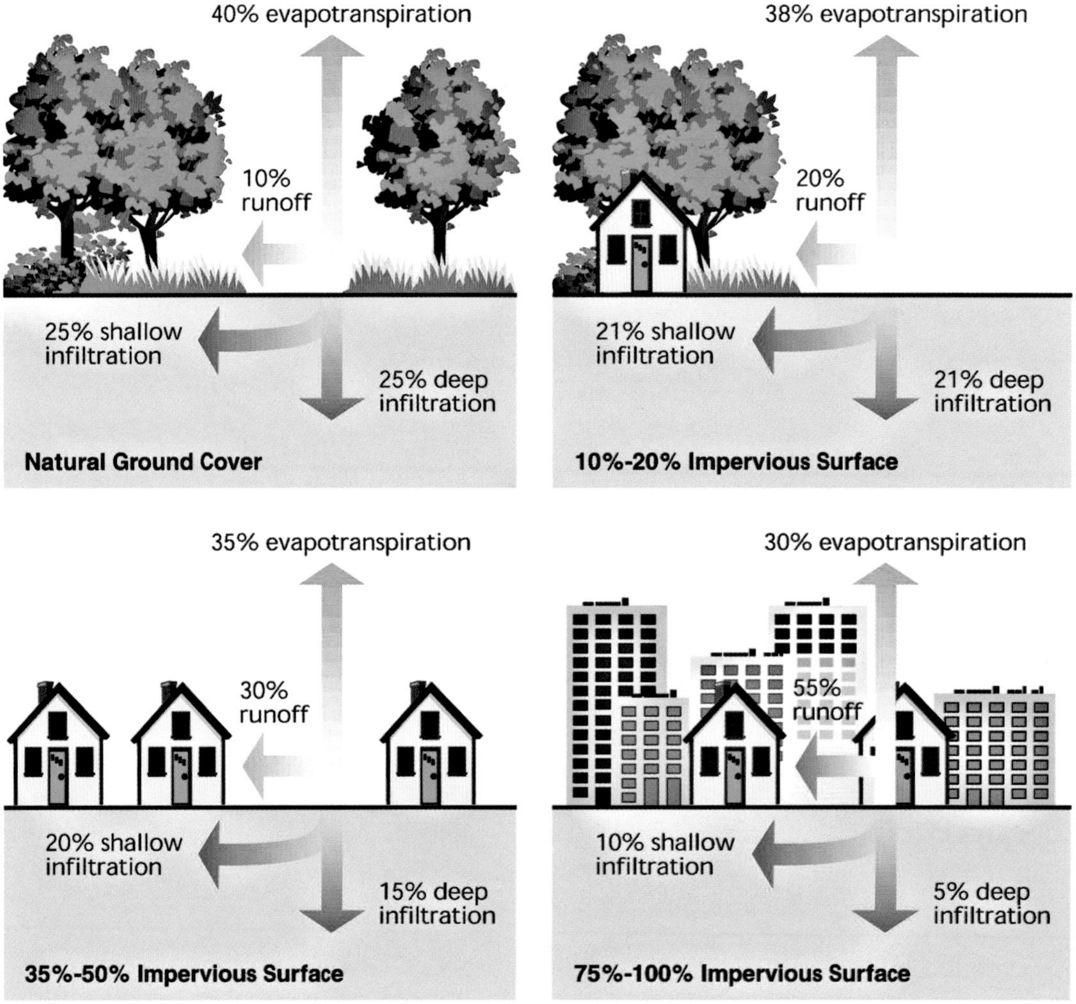

40% evapotranspiration

10% runoff

25% shallow infiltration

25% deep infiltration

Natural Ground Cover

38% evapotranspiration

20% runoff

21% shallow infiltration

21% deep infiltration

10%-20% Impervious Surface

35% evapotranspiration

30% runoff

20% shallow infiltration

15% deep infiltration

35%-50% Impervious Surface

30% evapotranspiration

55% runoff

10% shallow infiltration

5% deep infiltration

75%-100% Impervious Surface

Source: FIRSRWG (2001)

Impervious cover in a watershed results in increased surface runoff. As little as 10 percent impervious cover in a watershed can result in stream degradation.

contribute to pollution when stormwater washes surface oils, fertilizers, heavy metals, bacteria, and other contaminants into rivers and streams.

Watershed experts generally divide impervious surfaces into two categories: habitats for people, such as buildings and sidewalks, and habitats for cars, such as roads, parking lots, and driveways. In suburban areas with big-box stores and sprawl, parking lots and other car habitats represent most paving. In urban areas with structured parking and multilevel garages, human and car habitats are about equal as hardscape factors (Brown 2002). A third category is impaired pervious surfaces, or urban soils such as suburban lawns, which are natural surfaces that have become compacted through human action (Lehner et al. 2001).

Imperviousness is one of the most useful measures of the impacts of land development. Research studies conducted in many geographic areas, concentrating on many variables and employing a wide range of methods, have reached a similar conclusion: at a relatively low level of imperviousness—around 10 percent of cover in a watershed—streams become ecologically stressed. Stream stability is reduced, habitat is lost, water quality degrades, and biological diversity decreases. Imperviousness of 25 percent significantly impairs the stream. At 40 percent, it becomes damaged, and at 60 percent, a stream is severely damaged (Schueler 1995a; Center for Watershed Protection 2003a).

At 35 percent watershed imperviousness, the runoff rate can be 55 percent higher than predevelopment volumes. Depending on the percentage of watershed impervious cover, the annual volume of stormwater runoff can increase by two to 16 times its predevelopment rate, while the groundwater recharge rate (the amount soaking into the ground) reduces by equivalent proportions (Schueler 1995a; Center for Watershed Protection 2003).

Facts bear out that we have indeed paved over much of our metropolitan areas. Total imperviousness in medium-density, single-family residential areas typically ranges from 25 percent to nearly 60 percent (Schueler 1995c). Total imperviousness at strip malls or other commercial sites can approach 100 percent (Lehner et al. 2001).

The problems of erosion and pollution are related. Runoff from hard surfaces is loaded with concentrations of contaminants such as gasoline, antifreeze, and oils that collect on paved surfaces. Runoff also causes spikes of flows into streams. The resulting increased volume and velocity of water erodes streambeds and banks. This produces excessive sediment, the leading pollutant impairing the nation's rivers. Channel erosion constitutes as much as 75 percent of sediment in urban streams, particularly during periods of urbanization when the channel is still enlarging (FISRWG 2001).

As a partial but significant solution, riverfront designs should minimize the total impervious area and use permeable materials wherever possible, including on trail surfaces. Hard surfaces should be interspersed with softscapes where rain and snowmelt can collect and infiltrate into the soil.

Benefits of Reducing Hardscapes

Reducing hardscapes and installing natural landscapes can help restore natural watershed functions, filter pollutants, and prevent erosion of banks and channelization of streambeds. In older, industrial, or derelict riverfront areas, the replacement of hardscape with soft, permeable surfaces, such as native grasses, shrubs, and trees, will improve both the ecological and aesthetic environment.

When hardscapes are unavoidable, planners should minimize their extent. Reducing hardscapes in new development can save money for local governments, developers, and homeowners. Infrastructure—roads, sidewalks, sewer lines, curbs and gutters, and parking spaces—is expensive to build and maintain.

Remove Buildings

Removing buildings from the floodplain helps restore more natural river functions. From 1990 to 1992, the city of Boulder, Colorado, spent $3 million to lower the floodplain in a flood-hazard area downtown along Boulder Creek. The city bought 13 structures, relocated residents from 132 apartments, and then removed the buildings and regraded a 10-acre area next to the creek. By lowering the floodplain two to three feet, the project allows floodwater to spread out, which also protects a downstream section of the creek from higher velocities and deeper flows. The floodplain now includes a park, playing fields for a high school, and a greenway corridor (Taylor 2002).

Remove Paving

Even small urban spaces can be converted to reduce impervious cover and create wildlife habitat and places for people. In downtown Jonesborough, Tennessee, an unused town park and its paved parking lots have been transformed since 1992 through a landscape restoration. Spearheaded by the

As a partial but significant solution, riverfront designs should minimize the total impervious area and use permeable materials wherever possible, including on trail surfaces.

BETTER SITE DESIGN FOR SUBURBAN DEVELOPMENT

A collection of planning practices known as "better site design" can conserve natural areas, reduce watershed pollution, save money, and increase property values. Better site design is an approach fundamentally different from typical subdivision design for residential and commercial development. These practices seek to accomplish three goals: reduce impervious cover, conserve more natural lands, and use porous areas for effective stormwater treatment.

In 1996, the Center for Watershed Protection convened a national site-planning roundtable, which created 22 model development principles. The following 16 principles, based on the roundtable's work, are adapted with permission from CWP (2003b). They are intended to help local governments to modify their ordinances rather than to serve as national design standards.

Residential Streets and Parking Lots

1. Design residential streets to minimize pavement width. Design streets to support travel lanes, parking, and emergency, maintenance, and service vehicles. Base street widths on actual traffic volume.

2. Reduce the total length of residential streets with alternative street layouts that increase the number of homes per street.

3. Reduce residential street widths to the minimum needed for the travel-way, sidewalk, and vegetated swales. Locate utilities and storm drains within the right-of-way pavement section.

4. Reduce residential street cul-de-sacs to the minimum radius needed for emergency and maintenance vehicles. Include landscaped areas to reduce impervious cover.

5. Where density, topography, soils, and slope permit, use vegetated open channels (swales) in the street right-of-way to convey and treat stormwater runoff.

6. Review local parking ratios to see if they can be reduced.

7. Reduce parking requirements where mass transit is available or spaces can be shared.   *(continued)*

International Storytelling Center, the project converted a valley with steep walls into a three-acre terraced park that accommodates 12,000 people for an annual storytelling festival. The restoration removed two parking lots—one on top of a hill, and the other in the floodplain. Slopes were regraded and reforested with native trees; the top terrace next to Main Street features an "urban" park with a plaza and fountain. A ditch that ran straight down from the top of the site was rebuilt into a stream with rocks and plants. Water now meanders through swales and biofiltration ponds (Franklin and Franklin 2002).

Reduce Paving in New Development

Smart growth planning and design reduces the square footage of parking and other paved or hard surfaces. Reconfiguring streets, parking lots, and driveways to reduce unnecessary pavement turns more of a site over to soil and plants that filter rainwater. Cluster developments, as opposed to

**BETTER SITE DESIGN
FOR SUBURBAN DEVELOPMENT** *(continued)*

8. Reduce overall parking lot imperviousness by providing compact-car spaces, minimizing stall dimensions, and using efficient parking lanes and porous materials for spillover parking.

9. Provide economic incentives for parking garages and shared parking.

10. Provide stormwater treatment for parking lot runoff with naturalized retention ponds, swales, and other features that can be integrated into landscaped areas like medians and traffic islands.

Lot Development

1. Protect the watershed by advocating for open-space design subdivisions with smaller lot sizes that will minimize total impervious area, reduce construction costs, conserve natural areas, and provide recreation space.

2. Relax side-yard setbacks and allow narrower frontages to reduce total road length in the community and overall site imperviousness. Relax front setback requirements to minimize driveway lengths and reduce overall lot imperviousness.

3. Promote more flexible design standards for residential subdivision sidewalks. Consider locating sidewalks on only one side of the street and providing common walkways linking pedestrian areas.

4. Reduce overall imperviousness by promoting alternative driveway surfaces and shared driveways to two or more homes.

5. Specify how community open space will be managed and designate a sustainable legal entity to be responsible for managing natural and recreational open space.

6. Direct rooftop runoff to pervious areas such as yards, open channels, or vegetated areas, and avoid routing rooftop runoff to roadways or the stormwater system.

Source: Center for Watershed Protection (2003b)

standard cul-de-sac layouts, reduce site imperviousness 10 to 50 percent (Schueler 1995c).

Zoning ordinances that allow fewer parking spaces for commercial and residential development make sense for sites near public transportation, or when existing parking can be shared with other new development. Narrower roads—even four-foot reductions from the standard 26-foot width—create much less runoff.

On commercial and municipal sites, developers can reduce paving with alternative parking designs. Businesses with parking demands at different times, such as a medical practice and a restaurant, can share the same parking lot. Other alternatives include planning lot capacity for average rather than peak parking demands, placing parking beneath commercial buildings, and constructing multistory parking garages (Lehner et al. 2001).

Portland, Oregon, has reduced its parking lot standards. City regulations formerly required 24-foot-wide aisles and 9-by-19-foot stalls, with some smaller

SMART SITE PRACTICES FOR REDEVELOPMENT AND INFILL PROJECTS

Urban redevelopment and infill projects can help revitalize city centers and provide opportunities for environmentally friendly growth. Because of the potential impact of such projects on urban rivers and streams, however, planners should consider the site location and other factors such as stormwater runoff, water quality, air quality, and natural habitat, along with building and zoning codes and regulations.

The Center for Watershed Protection convened the Redevelopment Roundtable, a group of national and local stakeholders, to develop Smart Site Practices for redevelopment and infill sites. The group issued the following 11 practices, which are adapted with permission from the *Redevelopment Roundtable Consensus Agreement: Smart Site Practices for Redevelopment and Infill Projects* (CWP 2001b):

Practice 1: Redevelopment and infill planning should include environmental site assessments that protect existing natural resources and identify opportunities for restoration where feasible.

Brownfield and other legislation generally requires that infill and redevelopment sites be subjected to a site history, surface soil and water testing, and clean-up. Bank loans also often carry such requirements. Even when not required by law or loan terms, developers should prepare a thorough environmental site assessment. To address environmental constraints and highlight opportunities for restoration and reclamation at a site, this assessment should include a base map that outlines existing buildings, transportation networks, utilities, floodplains, wetlands, streams, and other natural features.

Practice 2: Design sites to use impervious cover efficiently and to minimize stormwater runoff. Where possible, the amount of impervious cover should be reduced or kept the same. In situations where impervious cover does increase, sites should be designed to improve the quality of stormwater runoff at the site or in the local watershed.

Impervious cover has a direct impact on annual runoff volume and increases pollutant loads, flooding frequency, and stream channel degradation. Some impacts can be mitigated by reducing or using existing impervious cover efficiently, and by managing stormwater runoff on site.

Practice 3: Plan and design sites to preserve naturally vegetated areas and to encourage revegetation and soil restoration. Sites should use native or noninvasive plants where feasible.

Natural urban areas often are found in small fragments that suffer from poor quality soils, invasive plant species, dumping, and extensive alteration by past development. Collecting and mapping natural features, preserving areas in a consolidated manner, and evaluating the site for potential stormwater management, revegetation, and recreational benefits can provide environmental, aesthetic, and economic benefits.

Practice 4: Establish plans to guarantee long-term management and maintenance of all vegetated areas.

Long-term management, financing, and maintenance plans ensure that vegetated areas continue to function and that the public can enjoy them. Conservation easements, land trust donations, and innovative partnerships can help landowners guarantee that intensively used vegetated urban areas are well maintained.

Practice 5: Manage rooftop runoff through storage, reuse, and/or redirection to pervious surfaces for stormwater management and other environmental benefits.

Reducing urban rooftop runoff can reduce pollutant loads, flooding, channel erosion, and other impacts on streams and rivers. Stormwater management techniques such as green roofs, rain barrels, and downspout disconnection, as well as the design, slope, and architecture of rooftops, can reduce the volume of rooftop runoff.   *(continued)*

**SMART SITE PRACTICES FOR REDEVELOPMENT
AND INFILL PROJECTS** *(continued)*

Practice 6: Parking lots, especially surface lots, should be minimized and designed to reduce, store, and treat stormwater runoff. Where site limitations or other constraints prevent full management of parking lot runoff, designers should target high-use areas first.
Parking lots are one of the greatest sources of stormwater runoff. Some runoff management techniques include making parking lots incrementally smaller, providing landscaping that substantially contributes to runoff management, and treating the quality of stormwater runoff.

Practice 7: Use a combination of "better site design" techniques with infill projects to minimize stormwater runoff and maximize vegetated areas.
Many single-lot or small multilot infill projects contribute to "impervious creep" through new structures, sidewalks, and paved areas. Better site design benchmarks are applicable to infill development that entails single-lot or small multilot infill (one to three lots) or larger infill subdivisions (10 to 30 lots). Although infill development typically occurs on smaller lot sizes (10,000 square feet or less), it is often still possible to cluster lots to provide more open space and reduce impervious cover.

Practice 8: Use proper storage, handling, and site design techniques to avoid the contact of pollutants with stormwater runoff.
Pollutants can be controlled on-site through source control measures, such as proper handling and storage of pollutants in outdoor areas, and site design practices, including loading docks designed to contain pollutants. Source control measures usually are the simplest and most cost-effective way to reduce stormwater pollution at many commercial sites.

Practice 9: Design the streetscapes to minimize, capture, and reuse stormwater runoff. Where possible, provide planting spaces to promote the growth of healthy street trees while capturing and treating stormwater runoff. In arid climates, xeriscapes should be used to achieve similar benefits.
The streetscape, or area between the street, sidewalk, and other structures, provides opportunities to manage stormwater runoff while providing many other environmental and aesthetic benefits.

Practice 10: Design courtyards, plazas, and amenity open space to store, filter, or treat rainfall.
Much of the open space in redevelopment and infill projects consists of hard surfaces that are impervious to rainfall. Using creative site plans, these courtyards, plazas, and other hard surfaces can be designed to store, filter, and treat rainfall through alternative pavers, bioretention areas, and planting boxes, among other examples.

Practice 11: Design sites to maximize transportation choices so as to reduce pollution and improve air and water quality.
Redevelopment and infill sites should be designed to increase nonautomotive connections between adjacent land uses, parks, and public spaces. Bike paths and pedestrian walkways offer residents alternative modes of transportation that can improve environmental quality. Sites should also provide links to mass transit and offer commuter amenities such as bus shelters and bike racks.

Source: Center for Watershed Protection (2001b)

Permeable paving surfaces can reduce erosion and help recharge groundwater.

stalls for compact cars. While SUVs are big, they actually are shorter and narrower than the vehicles driven when the standards were written decades ago. In 2002, the city unveiled standards for "hybrid" spaces that fit most vehicles. Developers now have the option of building narrower, 20-foot-wide aisles and smaller, 8.5-by-16-foot stalls. Developers like the code because it reduces construction costs. An added incentive is lower fees. Portland charges commercial and multifamily developers a stormwater management fee based on square footage of impervious surfaces. In 2005, the city will begin discounting this fee for reduced paving. The city intends to begin the discount in 2005, retroactive to a year to be determined (Liptan 2002, 2003).

Alternative Pavers

Alternative paving surfaces—also called alternative pavers—are permeable or semipermeable surfaces that allow varying degrees of water infiltration. Alternative paving materials are an important component of low-impact development that can achieve stormwater management conditions close to nature. They can be used to infiltrate rainwater on site and reduce runoff leaving the site, which in turn help decrease downstream flooding, the frequency of combined sewer overflow events, and the temperature of stream water.

Studies by William James at the University of Guelph, for example, found that pavers made of interlocking concrete blocks can significantly reduce the surface runoff loads of such contaminants as nitrite, nitrate, phosphate, phosphorous, metals, and ammonium. They also reduced runoff temperatures by two to four degrees Celsius compared to asphalt paving. The Low Impact Development Center (2003) summarizes the benefits of alternative pavers: they "can eliminate problems with standing water, provide for groundwater recharge, control erosion of streambeds and riverbanks, facilitate pollutant removal, and provide for a more aesthetically pleasing site." In some cases, they can eliminate the need for underground sewer pipes and conventional stormwater retention and detention systems.

Alternative pavers can replace asphalt and concrete in parking lots, fire access roads, driveways, and walkways. Paving blocks are one type of alternative paver: these blocks are cement or plastic grids with voids that can be filled with gravel or grass and used for parking and driveways. Gravel, cobbles, brick, or natural stone arranged in a loose configuration can also be used to construct driveways. Wood mulch is appropriate for walking paths. Traffic volume and type, access for the handicapped, and climate considerations like soil and snow removal may limit the use of some of these alternatives. For example, alternative pavers are best used for overflow parking but not in high-traffic parking areas. Similarly, paths that use mulch or similar pavers may require more maintenance, especially in frequently inundated areas.

Alternative pavers can replace asphalt and concrete in parking lots, fire access roads, driveways, and walkways.

Permeable Paving

Permeable paving is a sustainable-design solution that takes advantage of a site's natural features (such as a slope) to allow stormwater to infiltrate through the paved surface and recharge groundwater, thus reducing erosion and eliminating the need for conventional and costly stormwater drainage systems.

Twelve years ago, the Morris Arboretum near Philadelphia created a permeable parking lot for 80 cars. The surface is constructed of a special permeable asphalt that, because it lacks fine particles, resembles peanut brittle. This permeable surface allows water to flow to a recharge basin beneath the parking lot. The basin is lined with filter fabric and filled with ostrich-egg-size stones that allow water to percolate through, preventing the clogging that thwarts some porous-paving systems. Pollutants such as oil and antifreeze are removed by being filtered through the soil mantle.

Stormwater soaks into the ground and seeps into Papermill Run, a 20-foot-wide urban stream on the property (Franklin and Franklin 2002).

Permeable paving will not work in every situation, but must be matched to a site's geology, soil structure, and hydrology. Heavy clay soil, for example, does not allow water to infiltrate unless the clay level is punctured. These paving surfaces also require careful, continuous maintenance (Low Impact Development Center 2003).

DESIGN PRINCIPLE 6:
Manage stormwater on site and use nonstructural approaches

Ecologically designed riverfronts capture, store, and infiltrate or otherwise naturally treat and release stormwater. Systems with natural processes, such as wetlands and bioswales (small linear wetlands planted with riparian and water-tolerant trees), can provide wildlife habitat and aesthetic value as well. These natural systems can often replace stormwater pipes and other engineered structures, most of which send high volumes of untreated stormwater directly into rivers and streams.

Stormwater infrastructure that relies on drains, sewers, and hard engineering also sweeps large volumes of urban contaminants from roads and parking lots into rivers. These pollutants—oil, grease, combustion

COMBINED SEWER OVERFLOWS

Most urban communities have an aging sewage infrastructure that leaks, spills, and overflows into rivers and streams. The riverfront also is usually the final point of discharge of treated wastewater. These sources of river pollution affect the aesthetics and the use of the riverfront for recreation and relaxation, and they create negative public perceptions.

Combined sewer overflows (CSOs) remain a major challenge for urban water quality. Combined sewer systems convey stormwater, sewage, and industrial waste through the same system. Remnants of older urban infrastructure, combined sewer

systems serve about 40 million people in 772 U.S. communities, mostly in the Northeast, Great Lakes, and Pacific Northwest regions. During heavy rainfall, these communities often experience CSOs that spill raw sewage into rivers. About 43 percent of all CSOs spill into rivers, and 38 percent into streams. Some 12 percent flows, into canals and ditches, and the rest goes into oceans, estuaries, and bays (5 percent), and lakes and ponds (2 percent) (U.S. EPA 2001b, 2002b).

CSOs occur during and after storms, when the volume of stormwater entering a combined sewer system overwhelms collector pipes and sewage treatment plants. As a result, industrial wastes and sewage combine with storm runoff and flow directly into streams and rivers. Nationally, more than one trillion gallons of untreated sewage and stormwater overflow into streams and rivers every year. (U.S. EPA 2001b). In response, the U.S. Environmental Protection Agency has developed the Combined Sewer Overflow Control Policy.

CSOs pose a challenge for cities with a stormwater problem: should the riverfront zone, the last place to treat sewage before it enters the river, become the location for a sewage treatment plant, or should city officials reserve this area for other purposes such as recreation?

In Portland, Oregon, CSOs are the primary stormwater issue. Portland needs $1 billion to build tunnels, tanks, and pump stations to meet state water-quality standards by 2011. By mid-2003, Portland was constructing giant tunnels on the West Side to keep the combined sewer overflow from discharging into the Willamette River. The city has begun designing tunnels for the city's East Side (Liptan 2002, 2003). Portland is also aggressively promoting on-site and nonstructural stormwater approaches to minimize the amount of stormwater flowing into sewers.

byproducts, metals, herbicides, pesticides, pet wastes, and many others—can be toxic to aquatic organisms, and expensive to remove to meet water-quality and drinking-water standards.

In contrast, well-designed stormwater management alternatives—including green roofs, stormwater planters, and biofiltration basins, either individually or in combination—can treat almost all stormwater on site, except during an event like a 100-year storm (Liptan 2002).

Site-design measures such as natural drainages instead of storm pipes and culverts help delay the timing and reduce the peaks of stormwater runoff. Detention measures, such as constructed wetlands, ponds, and rainwater cisterns, as well as reforesting and preserving buffer zones, also filter stormwater before it enters stream and river channels (Riley 1998).

Nonstructural approaches can save money. These approaches can range from simple measures, such as providing inexpensive rain barrels for homeowners to catch downspout drainage for use in their gardens, to more complicated systems that store and treat water for part of a watershed.

The most successful stormwater practices are based on site conditions—the climate, soils, hydrology, degree of impervious materials, and how the buildings and the landscape work together. Stormwater strategies may also depend on the intensity and setting of new development. For example, infill and other urban development may not have enough land to construct wetlands for stormwater treatment. In such cases, stormwater control structures can be retrofitted to provide water treatment—in other words, the infrastructure both removes contaminants and controls water flow (Lehner et al. 2001).

Natural Stormwater Management

Naturalizing techniques can supplement infrastructure to cleanse and control stormwater, resulting in substantial savings for developers and local governments. These include detention ponds, bioretention ponds and swales, cisterns, stormwater planters, and infiltration ponds.

Bioretention ponds. Bioretention ponds capture runoff in constructed wetlands and allow water to infiltrate slowly into the ground. Placed two to six inches below grade, bioretention areas use layers of soil, sand, and mulch with native plants that filter pollutants and slow and cool the water. Bioretention areas can fit into small spaces such as parking-lot islands and infill sites. With no concentrated release point, they do not cause erosion.

North Carolina State University researchers are studying the effectiveness of bioretention ponds in preventing water pollution and the alteration of stream channels. In North Carolina, Carpenter Village has installed two dry ponds, each 800 square feet and six feet deep, in two pocket parks at the top and bottom of a hill. These bioretention areas have been filled with topsoil, native plants, and trees. Installed as permanent features, they share the open space with a path and benches. Researchers will monitor how the ponds, designed to drain within 24 hours, reduce the volume and velocity of stormwater (White 2002).

Smaller versions of bioretention areas are called rain gardens. They are designed to infiltrate water within four to six hours. Rain gardens remove pollutants at the rate of 60 to 80 percent for nutrients and 93 to 99 percent for heavy metals. Each lot at Somerset, a New Urbanist community in Maryland, features a rain garden of 300 to 400 square feet. Sited at topographic low points, the gardens are planted by the developer and maintained by homeowners. The developer estimates that substituting rain gardens for more conventional detention basins will reduce infrastructure and other costs by $300,000 (Russell 2000).

Infiltration basins and trenches. Infiltration basins resemble dry detention ponds but have no outlet, forcing water to infiltrate through the bottom

The most successful stormwater practices are based on site conditions—the climate, soils, hydrology, degree of impervious materials, and how the buildings and the landscape work together.

of the basin. Infiltration trenches, generally filled with rocks and gravel, create a reservoir for water that will be infiltrated to surrounding soil. French drains, another widely used infiltration technique, are small infiltration trenches at the bottom of gutter downspouts. These allow water to infiltrate on site rather than passing into the storm sewer system (Lehner et al. 2001).

Although less natural than bioretention ponds or swales, infiltration basins can still provide water-quality benefits. These basins temporarily store runoff until water percolates slowly into the soil. Infiltration basins reduce peak flow and recreate to some extent the natural pattern of water infiltration. They can handle up to 98 percent of stormwater and remove significant amounts of pollutants. They can cool stormwater significantly, to 55 degrees, as it infiltrates into the ground, and they thus reduce the damaging effects of heated stormwater on aquatic environments.

Successful projects require soil that is capable of infiltration. One study suggests such soil can contain no more than 30 percent clay. Yet other studies of infiltration basins suggest a high rate of failure, mostly due to clogging from sediments carried in by runoff. To prevent clogging, experts recommend a pretreatment settling pond or other sediment-removal device (MacElroy and Winterbottom 2000).

Biofiltration channels and swales. Biofiltration uses plants—generally grasses and wetland plants—to filter and treat stormwater runoff conveyed though open channels or swales. Whether natural or constructed, such wetland areas absorb excess nutrients and metals and help break down microbes. By slowing the flow of stormwater, biofiltration also allows contaminants to settle out.

An award-winning example is a stormwater treatment project at the Oregon Museum of Science and Industry (OMSI) in Portland, which restored natural processes to a former industrial site along the Willamette River. OMSI's 10-acre, 768-car parking lot incorporates about 2,300 lineal feet of bioswales—small linear wetlands planted with riparian and water-tolerant trees—instead of traditional landscaped islands. Unlike a rain garden, which allows water to infiltrate by holding it stationary, a bioswale allows infiltration as water moves along its length.

Curb cuts channel stormwater runoff into the bioswales, where check dams slow the water's speed to allow sediment to drop out while water infiltrates into the soil. Plants also filter out oils and other pollutants. Designed to fit a small space while also conforming as much as possible to standard design, construction, and maintenance for parking lots and storm drains, the bioswales are a pragmatic, aesthetically striking, and cost-effective solution. The bioswales cost $78,000 less to construct and require no more maintenance than conventional storm drain systems (Liptan 2003).

The OMSI project won a 1996 award in a stormwater design competition sponsored by public agencies in the Portland metropolitan area (Jerrick 1998). The example worked so well for the developer, the city, and the environment that the city now requires all new parking lots to follow OMSI's model. There are two complementary codes. The first is a planning code created 20 years ago and modified in 2002 that requires developers to install landscape areas to filter stormwater equivalent to 10 percent of the interior area of a parking lot. The second is a public works water-quality code that requires developers to use landscaping in parking lots as filters for stormwater management, rather than piped and engineered systems.

Combined with the new Portland code (mentioned above) that allows for narrower aisles and smaller stalls in parking lots, the city has experienced no net loss of parking spaces while it has improved on-site stormwater management and water quality in aesthetically pleasing ways (Liptan 2002, 2003).

The Oregon Museum of Science and Industry uses 2,300 linear feet of small wetlands to treat stormwater in its 768-car parking lot.

Unlike a rain garden, which allows water to infiltrate by holding it stationary, a bioswale allows infiltration as water moves along its length.

City of Chicago

This green roof rests on top of Chicago's City Hall.

Considering the savings associated with deferred maintenance and reduced energy consumption, green roofs compare in cost to conventional roofs.

Also in Portland, the Water Pollution Control Laboratory harvests rainwater directly from the lab's gutterless roof. Scuppers that extend from the roof shoot rainwater in a trajectory into a wide, rock-lined bioswale several feet from the edge of the building. Planted with ornamental wetlands grasses and other plants, the bioswale offers an artistic approach to stormwater management (Thompson 1999).

Green Roofs. Rooftop gardens are another solution that minimizes runoff volume by absorbing stormwater. Widely used in Europe, so-called green roofs are beginning to sprout in American cities. Green roofs are a lighter modern variant on sod roofs and can capture 15 to 90 percent of stormwater, depending on soil, rooftop cover, and weather conditions (Low Impact Development Center 2003).

Green roofs also can improve water quality by filtering pollutants such as nitrogen, which breaks down in soil and is absorbed by plants. Green roofs provide extra insulation that can reduce energy costs for heating and cooling, and can extend the roof's life span by preventing exposure to ultraviolet rays. Considering the savings associated with deferred maintenance and reduced energy consumption, green roofs compare in cost to conventional roofs (Low Impact Development Center 2003).

They also soften and beautify urban skylines with flowers and shrubs that draw birds and butterflies, which, beyond their aesthetic and ecological value, can raise property values. They can even produce vegetables and fruit.

Green roofs are not merely container gardens. They completely cover roofs with lightweight planting material and have an additional layer impenetrable to roots, sharp objects, and water seepage. Because urban rooftops in many regions can have a desert-like microclimate, they often do best with drought- and heat-tolerant plants with shallow roots. Designed and installed properly, with the help of engineers who specialize in green roofs, they pose little risk of collapse or water damage.

Green roofs come in two general types. An *extensive* garden—basically a meadow planted on a thin layer of planting medium—requires little or no irrigation or maintenance and usually is not accessible to the public. An *intensive* rooftop garden is landscaped with trees, water structures, walkways, and other elements of a traditional garden that may need frequent irrigation. Some green roofs rely on a simple plant palette, such as native grasses.

In 2001, the North American Premier Automotive Group, a division of Ford Motor Company, installed a 45,000-square-foot roof garden on one wing of its new 300,000-square-foot headquarters in Irvine, California.

The garden atop the one-story building features drought-tolerant groundcover plants. Ford hopes the roof will produce oxygen, create a habitat for bees and butterflies, reduce stormwater runoff, extend the roof's life, and help reduce interior heat. Although the rooftop is not being monitored formally, the property manager reports that air conditioning costs are lower compared to other buildings (Borghese 2003; Roofscapes, Inc. 2003).

Spanning 20,300 square feet atop an 11-story building, the green roof of Chicago City Hall includes walkways and 20,000 plants covering a range of landscape environments from native meadows to trees and shrubs. Completed in 2001, the design ranges from 3.5-inch-deep extensive areas to 24-inch-deep intensive areas. Rooftop weather-station monitoring indicates the gardens have lowered surface temperatures. For example, on one August afternoon in 2001, the air temperature was in the 90s. The roof garden registered between 91 and 119 degrees Fahrenheit, at least 50 degrees cooler than the black tar roof on the adjacent Cook County building. The green roof saves $3,600 per year in energy costs (City of Chicago 2003).

Cisterns. Cisterns are a less common but promising detention measure. A "green" house at Carpenter Village, a New Urbanist development in North Carolina, features two underground cisterns that supply irrigation water. The yard contains two in-ground pump tanks connected to gutters. Downspouts direct rainwater to the cisterns, which hold up to 1,250 gallons each. The cisterns work by pressure, pumping out water for irrigation, car washing, and other exterior uses. For $4,000 to install the system, the cisterns provide effective stormwater treatment. Ninety percent of rainwater is treated and reused on site; the cisterns also recharge the groundwater because the retained water is reapplied during a dry time (White 2002).

A system like this one requires substantial planning. A water budget must be developed and followed. Tanks must be big enough to store two to three months of rainwater for dry times. But the design has great promise. Rainwater collection systems like this might be used to irrigate larger sites and even whole developments.

Stormwater planters. Stormwater planters are a low-cost alternative for stormwater treatment and water conservation. Installed at-grade or raised, stormwater planters filter rainwater that has been drained from downspouts connected to gutters. In Portland, Oregon, planters varying from 5-by-10 feet to 10-by-50 feet are filled with several feet of soil and plants. Portland State University uses planters to store water that is pumped into buildings for use in toilets. Through filtering and evaporation, stormwater planters can manage nearly 100 percent of roof runoff (Liptan 2002).

DESIGN PRINCIPLE 7:
Balance recreational and public access goals with river protection

Riverfront communities should provide facilities for as many recreational uses as possible while balancing some conflicting uses (for example, between power boats and birdwatching platforms) and managing possible overuse of the river corridor.

Thanks to the Clean Water Act and other initiatives, Americans have returned to urban riverfronts and other waterways in large numbers. In 2000, more than 34 million Americans over age 16 went canoeing, rafting, or kayaking (Outdoor Recreation Coalition of America 2001). That same year, some 71 million people went bicycling, many on riverfront trails and greenways, which now exist in 500 communities. Some 35 million American anglers spend $38 billion on fishing every year. Another 14 million hunters spend $20 billion a year pursuing migratory waterfowl that rely on rivers and others bodies of water (U.S. EPA Office of Water 2000).

Cities and towns have also done much to encourage Americans to return to urban riverfronts over the past two decades. Following the economically successful (if ecologically sterile) example of the San Antonio Riverwalk, communities like Estes Park and Pueblo in Colorado developed their own riverwalks that linked parks, natural areas, festival areas, and shopping. In recent years, major new riverfront parks have been introduced in Denver; Louisville, Kentucky; and San Jose, California. These combine public gathering spaces and trails with natural flood control and naturalized infiltration swales.

Environment/User Conflicts

The popularity of urban riverfronts can create conflicts between users and the environment. A 10-foot-wide greenway trail, for example, introduces one acre of paving per mile into a floodplain (Searns 2002). Many greenways have proven so popular they are being widened or augmented with separate hiking or equestrian trails. While these accessory trails often feature a porous surface such as crushed stone, they still may usurp wildlife habitat.

Riverfront communities should provide facilities for as many recreational uses as possible while balancing some conflicting uses (for example, between power boats and birdwatching platforms) and managing possible overuse of the river corridor.

Motorized boating presents a more direct threat to habitat. Eighty-five percent of the 29 million gallons of oil dumped into America's waterways each year comes from the two-stroke engines used in many boats and personal watercraft (PWCs), often known by the brand names Waverunner or Jet Ski. Even small spills measured at parts per trillion are toxic to fish and aquatic plants (Committee on Oil in the Sea 2003).

PWCs also create noise pollution and pose safety challenges. Only 10 percent of the motorized boats registered in the United States are PWCs, yet they account for 30 percent of accidents, of which 80 percent are collisions. In recent years, some communities have banned or restricted PWCs. In 1995, San Juan County, Washington, which includes the San Juan Islands, became the first jurisdiction to ban PWCs outright. San Francisco County enforces a 1,200-foot setback from shorelines for PWCs, except for limited access to boat ramps. The National Park Service has restricted or banned PWCs on portions of the Colorado, Missouri, and Rio Grande Rivers (Smith 2002).

Powerboats and marinas also present user conflicts and environmental concerns. No-wake zones help canoeists and anglers coexist with powerboats. Yet, some communities have rejected proposed marinas because of concerns about disturbing wildlife habitat and threatening endangered marine mammals.

Human health issues are another access challenge. Some 300,000 miles of rivers and streams do not meet state water-quality guidelines. Even with advances since the Clean Water Act, many urban rivers are not clean enough for swimming or to produce edible fish. The EPA and other regulatory agencies are struggling to control such pollution sources as urban runoff and combined sewer overflows (U.S. EPA Office of Water 2000).

Supporting Access and the Environment

Greenways and river trails combine recreational access with environmental enhancements and can often be incorporated into other infrastructure projects. For example, near the resort community of Glenwood Springs, Colorado, the widening of I-70 through Glenwood Canyon in the 1980s was accompanied by construction of a 16-mile trail, whitewater boat ramps, and large-scale native revegetation. River access was improved through new highway exits convenient to Colorado River parks.

While providing access, properly designed greenways also protect the floodplain and provide wildlife migration corridors between otherwise isolated "patches" of native habitat (Smith and Hellmund 1993).

Louisville and Jefferson County, Kentucky, worked together to create a greenway master plan that brings citizens in touch with the waterfront.

GREENWAY AND RIVERWALK
PLANNING IN PUEBLO

A prairie steel town in southeastern Colorado, Pueblo had the Rust Belt blues 20 years ago. Pueblo's unemployment rate soared above 20 percent after the city's biggest steel mill laid off 5,000 employees before heading into bankruptcy. Then the city slowly climbed back. Pueblo diversified its economy by recruiting 40 companies in the high-tech manufacturing and warehousing industries, adding nearly 9,000 jobs. From 1984 to 1995, the city's population grew from 107,000 to 137,000 and median household income jumped more than 60 percent (McNulty 2000).

In October 2000, Pueblo threw a three-day riverfront party to celebrate a crowning touch in its renewal campaign. Live music, beach volleyball, and a raft race and regatta marked the dedication of the $24-million Historic Arkansas Riverwalk of Pueblo (HARP). The 26-acre riverwalk features waterfalls, public art, natural areas, and a water taxi system that links Pueblo's historic, business, and commercial districts. In addition to providing new park and recreation opportunities for residents, HARP is expected to generate $9 million a year in tourism revenues (Munch 2002). In 2000, Partners for Livable Communities cited the riverwalk as a feature that made Pueblo one of the nation's four most livable cities.

Pueblo launched its downtown riverwalk planning in 1991. The key challenge was to daylight one-third of a mile of the Arkansas River that had been diverted into two eight-foot-wide pipes and an underground culvert. The plan called for redirecting the river into a new channel in the historic riverbed without reintroducing a flood risk. At the west end of the proposed channel, the city wanted to beautify and naturalize Lake Elizabeth, an eyesore the city leased to the local power company as a cooling pond.

Initial funding for the project hinged on a 1995 vote for a $12.85 million bond issue. To help Pueblo voters grasp the project's scope, local architects made a $9,000 scale model that was displayed in Pueblo at the state fair, where 500,000 people viewed it. The bond issue was approved by a narrow margin and has since been augmented by $7 million in private and foundation grants and another $3 million in state and federal funds.

HARP now unifies downtown as the city's focal point and links city hall with civic, cultural, and educational institutions such as the Sangre de Cristo Arts Center, El Pueblo Museum, and the new Buell Children's Museum. Some 6,500 feet of walkways and bike paths connect people with water features. Water taxis and observation boats ply 2,760 linear feet of the channel. At the west end, Lake Elizabeth hosts an outdoor education and nature study area with wetlands and native-plant landscaping. The riverwalk also includes benches and fountains made from local stone by Colorado sculptor and landscape architect Richard Hansen (Brandes 2002). In 2003, the Riverwalk attracted the first mixed-use project to its banks .

Greenways and river trails provide a "green infrastructure" by incorporating flood control, river buffer zones for filtering stormwater, and transportation. In Boulder, Colorado, where a 60-mile greenway system links neighborhoods to schools, jobs, and shopping, about 12 percent of the population commutes by bike, or about 12 times the national average.

After a major flood, Louisville, Kentucky, in 1946 created the Metropolitan Sewer District (MSD) to build dams and levees, channel streams, manage sewers, and build wastewater plants. In the 1990s, MSD officials admitted that many of its engineering measures were ineffective. The river still flooded, and surging stormwater brought pollution into the river and its tributaries.

Regional support for protecting the river led to passage of an innovative 1997 floodplain ordinance that protects 12 percent of Jefferson County as floodplain. As part of the process of reclaiming the Ohio River and its tributaries, the MSD also created a 1999 greenway master plan to bring citizens in touch with the waterfront (Louisville and Jefferson County 1999). Several trails have been built. Plans include connecting Beargrass Creek, now one of the city's most polluted urban streams, to a new $90-million, 120-acre Waterfront Park, under construction in three phases since 1991. Waterfront Park was planned in conjunction with 1 million square feet of new riverfront housing, commercial development, and a minor league baseball stadium (Calkins 2001). The park is located entirely within the 100-year floodplain. The first 50-acre phase withstood a 1998 flood with no major damage (Croce 2002; Flink 2002). Since then the master plan for Waterfront Park has been updated to dovetail with Jefferson County's greenway master plan.

These riverfront and tributary improvements have enhanced nearby property values. In the Louisville region, real estate with visual and physical access to the new greenways and riverfront parks commands a 5 percent premium (Searns 2002).

Ecologically Sensitive Design and Construction

Greenways and riverfront parks can be designed to minimize or mitigate effects on the natural environment. For example, greenway planning can reclaim other floodplain lands to make up for lands consumed by trails. Rather than closely following rivers, trails can weave in and out of waterfront access points, steering visitors away from sensitive wetlands and meadows or easily eroded banks (Searns 2002).

To avoid natural areas as well as privately owned land, 12 miles of new trails being built along the Anacostia River in Washington, D.C., will crisscross the river on a series of new biker-pedestrian bridges. The bridges will reduce the amount of paved trail on land while allowing visitors to enjoy a more intimate, yet low-impact, experience of the river and its marshes (Bunster-Ossa 2002).

A successful riverway trail system may increase public support for river protection, tributary restoration, and trails. Well-designed trail systems attract users—especially those who live nearby—and encourage social use, which, in turn, can minimize vandalism and other crime. A study of Seattle's

---

KEYS TO BUILDING PUBLIC SUPPORT FOR GREENWAYS AND RIVER IMPROVEMENTS

- Identify allies in positions of authority. Meet individually with elected officials, city staff, and business executives.

- Build grassroots support among interest groups that benefit directly, such as cyclist organizations and kayak clubs.

- Build support among nonusers, including business groups that recognize the economic benefits of greenway development and taxpayers who may not use greenways but can be helped to understand the value of funding them.

- Contact landowners and tenants whose properties may be directly affected by the greenway. They can become powerful allies—or vociferous opponents.

- Contact utility companies who may control river rights-of-way and be concerned about possible vandalism, trespassing, or other public-safety issues. Explain how they may be able to reduce their own costs and win public relations benefits by, for example, combining storm conveyance with greenways, or converting high-maintenance ornamental landscapes to naturalized landscapes.

- Create a pilot project such as a trail section with interpretive signs that demonstrates the value of greenways to all community members.

Source: Adapted from Flink and Searns (1993, 49–63)

Burke-Gilman Trail found no difference in crime rates when the trail area was compared to the rest of the city. Property values for homes near the trail enjoyed a 6 percent premium (Little 1995).

Water Trails: A Growing Movement

A water trail is a stretch of river, shoreline, or ocean that has been designated to provide educational, scenic, and challenging nature-based experiences to recreational boaters. For communities across the country, water trails are a valuable tool for promoting a healthy economy and a high quality of life while preserving natural systems and cultural heritage. Water trail projects can inspire individuals, unify communities, provide hands-on experience for recreation and city planners, and serve as outdoor classrooms for students and educators.

Inaugurated in 1998, a 24-mile stretch of the Susquehanna River between Halifax and Harrisburg became Pennsylvania's first water trail. It incorporated four access sites and 10 river islands for day use and primitive camping. The trail is managed by a partnership of the Pennsylvania Fish and Boat Commission, Pennsylvania Department of Conservation and Natural Resources, the Pennsylvania Game Commission, the city of Harrisburg, and the Alliance for the Chesapeake Bay. Volunteer groups have already adopted islands and access sites. Members serve as trail stewards and are responsible for maintaining the trail, monitoring resource impacts, and analyzing public use. Today this trail is a part of the 51-mile Middle Susquehanna River Water Trail, which is one of Pennsylvania's 16 state-designated water trails (Pennsylvania Fish and Boat Commission 2003).

DESIGN PRINCIPLE 8:
Incorporate information about a river's natural resources and cultural history

Ecological interpretation and education are important along urban rivers because so many natural systems and references have been erased. The river's history and function may not be obvious to the public. An informed public that understands river ecology as well as the potential for regeneration will support efforts to improve and protect its river. Citizens also need to know how to use their river safely and should be informed about water-quality issues and hazards to swimming and boat navigation.

Riverfront wayfinding and other sign systems explain the river's unique characteristics and the region's natural assets. People of all ages, income levels, and ethnic backgrounds should be invited to participate in riverfront interpretation and activities. Public art initiatives, concerts, open-air movies, or other cultural events can draw people to explore the riverfront. So can sporting events, outdoor recreation activities, and festivals. Outreach efforts can include hiring river guides and interpretive experts from varied ethnic and economic backgrounds, interpreting riverfront cultural sites to various groups within the local population, and scheduling special activities and programs for community schools (Wilkinson 2000).

Interpretive Signs

Signs should contain clear and succinct information that tells stories or provides information about the river in language easily grasped by the layperson. Signs can be as simple as stenciled "Drains to creek" messages, such as those painted near stormwater drains in Sioux Falls, South Dakota, where stencils are designed through an art contest. The stencils alert residents that dumping motor oil or other wastes harms their own watershed.

Riverfront wayfinding systems should incorporate multiple languages and communication alternatives for people with disabilities. Trails and access points can feature universally accessible designs that avoid ungainly sepa-

CASE STUDY

River Issues. The Sammamish River in Redmond, Washington, is typical of many urban and suburban streams. The river lost much of its riparian area and native vegetation when the U.S. Army Corps of Engineers straightened and reconstructed the river into a deep trapezoidal channel in the 1960s. Straitjacketing the river destroyed habitat and dealt a blow to its once-abundant salmon.

Sammamish River, Redmond, Washington

What Has Been Accomplished. Rather than rely upon the Army Corps' traditional approach to controlling the river, project planners seek to let the river be a river. Using a multidisciplinary approach, groups have come together to revitalize Redmond's Waterfront. Among the groups involved are the project designers, Parametrix, the city of Redmond, King County, public agencies, and the citizens of Redmond.

Chinook salmon already have benefited from a pilot project on a 300-foot long stretch of riverbank. Additionally, since restoration of portions of the riparian corridor there has been a marked increase in species diversity and wildlife quantity. Among the animals benefiting are waterfowl, perching birds, and raptors including bald eagles. With the success of the pilot project, an additional 600-foot section was designed in 1998, with construction completed on the west bank in 2000. Current projects include restoring the east bank of the 600-foot section, which began in the summer of 2002, and restoration of an additional 600-foot section upstream.

rate ramps (PLAE, Inc. and USDA Forest Service 1993). Native-plant scent gardens and sound recordings can explain elements of the river to visually impaired visitors.

Signs and graphics are most effective when they use a consistent design with the same typography, graphics, colors, styles, sizes, materials, and construction techniques. While signs need to catch a visitor's eye, they should also blend into the landscape; they will blend in more effectively if they are constructed from natural materials found locally and employ colors that complement nearby geology and plant life.

Near Joliet, Illinois, at the Midewin National Tallgrass Prairie, two rivers and two prairie creeks are being interpreted through low signs incorporated into landforms. Designed to be durable and resistant to vandalism, the signs do not impede the sweeping prairie view. They are constructed from native dolomite limestone quarried from the nearby Des Plaines River. The stone is etched with information as well as images of the site's natural and cultural history, including prairie grasses, Native American motifs, symbols of farming, and images from the site's use as the Joliet Arsenal during and after World War II (OZ Architecture and USDA Forest Service 2000).

Behind city hall, engineers have recreated the river's meanders and curves, and added boulders, root wads, and gravel bars to the once-uniform channel. To the west of city hall, the bank was graded into a series of earth benches. The top of the bank was moved back from the river about 50 feet at its maximum point. These benches were planted with native vegetation and provide the potential for different habitat zones. They also are helping to maintain the river's flood-flow capacity.

Tying these restoration projects together is Redmond's new riverwalk, a thoroughfare for joggers, bikers, and shoppers. The Sammamish River Trail links the communities of the Sammamish Valley with the King County trail system. The county hired JGM-Landscape Architects to develop a master plan that includes trails, fishing opportunities, planting buffers, and wildlife habitat enhancement. Currently underway is a water conservation demonstration garden where local residents can learn low-water use and environmentally friendly gardening techniques as part of public stewardship of the river's ecology.

Benefits to the River and Community. Development of the master plan for the Sammamish River Trail includes a commitment to creating a more natural waterway that is accommodating to people and wildlife, and that includes systems of flood control.

For more information . . .
- See the Parametrix web site, www.parametrix.com, and the JGM-Landscape Architects web site, www.jgm-inc.com/sammamish.htm

Public Art and Special Events

Other forms of public art, sometimes quite whimsical, can attract private support and public funding to river improvement projects.

In 1999, an alliance of community interest groups in and around New York City organized the first journey of the Golden Ball. Paddling alongside or walking the shore, residents followed a floating 36-inch golden orb down the Bronx River to a festival at Starlight Park. Since then, the event has grown significantly. In September 2002, the Bronx River Alliance—composed of more than 65 community organizations and agencies—coordinated the fourth annual journey, which drew media attention to this polluted waterway, the city's only freshwater river (Wichert 2002). The event is aimed at building support for water-quality improvements, debris removal, and habitat restoration. The Alliance has also used more traditional approaches to bring attention to the river. For example, it has organized canoe trips and nature walks for residents from low-income neighborhoods that line the river.

In the Pacific Northwest, a group of artists spent two-and-a-half years creating the Soul Salmon project to celebrate the region's most famous wild fish and its habitat. The project

The New York City Bronx River Golden Ball Festival has helped build support for water-quality improvements, debris removal, and habitat restoration on the city's only freshwater river.

distributed eight-foot-long fiberglass salmon to dozens of artists, who then decorated the salmon for display at special events in Puget Sound communities over six months. Maps and other information about regional ecosystems were available at the events, whose aim, the organizers stated, was to "inspire local salmon culture and generate charity to save native salmon" (Soul Salmon 2002). After the event's completion in April 2002, an auction of 11 Soul Salmon raised $43,000 for daylighting a creek buried under a shopping mall.

Interpretive Programs

Along 72 miles of river in the Mississippi National River and Recreation Area in Minnesota, the National Park Service (NPS) hosts a pair of innovative interpretation programs, Big River Journey and the Birding Boat. Both bring people out on the river—many for the first time—in 300-passenger paddlewheel boats that NPS leases from local tour operators.

In the past several years, Big River Journey has hosted river trips for 4,500 public school students, whose curriculum requires study of the Mississippi. The boat contains learning stations where students explore such topics as aquatic insects, water quality, geology, ecosystems, river birds, history, and stewardship.

At a cost of $7.50 per student, with financial assistance available, the students are accompanied by ecologists, birders, and experts from the Science Museum of Minnesota. Xcel Energy plant managers have also joined the tour to explain a successful program of hosting peregrine falcon nests on 450-foot-tall smokestacks near the river.

The Birding Boat is open to both students and the general public. Each year in season, about 5,000 people take 90-minute paddle-wheel boat rides to explore Mississippi bird life with expert birders.

The Mississippi National River and Recreation Area also employs the Park Service's only authorized "singing ranger," Charlie Maguire, who serenades visitors with songs that celebrate river history. Maguire's performances have helped some cities rediscover waterfront spaces. For example, in South Saint Paul, a concert in a neighborhood park situated on Mississippi River bluffs led the city to improve the park's wiring and move special events to this venue. Concertgoers now enjoy a spectacular view of several miles of river (Maguire 2002).

CONCLUSION

When William Least Heat-Moon crossed America by 5,000 miles of waterways to research his book *River-Horse* (1999), he found an amazing diversity of river types and systems. Some rivers appeared largely natural, perhaps as natural as when explorers first laid eyes on them. Other rivers had become little more than concrete barge channels linking reservoirs or systems of locks.

This is the political reality faced by today's riverfront planner. Cities and industries located within river floodplains cannot be dislodged, nor should they be. Agencies and utilities that control the flow and use of water will be reluctant to cede their power, although they can be encouraged to take a broader view of river management that includes wildlife and recreation. As a result, riverfront planners may not be able to apply every principle described in this chapter to every project. In some cases, compromises may leave doors open for future river improvements.

For several generations, we abused and nearly destroyed our rivers. Now, slowly, we are learning to appreciate, restore, and live *with* them in the best possible sense.

Amy Souers

CHAPTER 4
The Economic Benefits of Restoring and Redeveloping Urban Riverfronts

In the past two decades, urban waterfronts have undergone a renaissance. Once relegated to manufacturing and transportation, riverfronts are being restored with clean water and natural areas. Urban riverfronts are being redeveloped with trails, plazas, parks, housing, restaurants, shops, offices, cultural and recreation attractions, and other amenities that draw residents, businesses, and visitors to the water. Many cities have shown that riverfront revival can improve residents' quality of life, encourage new economic vitality, and beautify downtowns.

Although restoring natural river systems and redeveloping riverfront sites might seem conflicting goals, pursuing both can benefit the health of urban rivers and their communities. Cleaning up and restoring the natural systems of urban rivers and the land that borders them can improve water quality and ecosystem functions, aesthetics, and wildlife habitat. These improvements in turn can attract tourism through such activities as fishing, boating, and wildlife watching. Sensitive redevelopment of riverfront sites using environmentally responsible design and construction practices—especially on once-degraded or polluted industrial sites—can improve the riverfront's natural environment.

FINANCING RIVERFRONT RENEWAL

For all the benefits of urban waterfront revitalization, it can be difficult to finance. Some harbor cities followed (with varying success) Boston's and Baltimore's formula for waterfront "entertainment" retail. Other river cities have failed to revitalize their riverfronts because of lack of funding, imagination, or connectivity. For example, a new riverfront aquarium or retail

THE SOUTH PLATTE RIVER GREENWAY AND CENTRAL PLATTE VALLEY

Redeveloping the South Platte River has cost the city and county of Denver more than $70 million since the mid-1970s. A $2-million initial investment to build a greenway with riverfront paths that connected the river to Denver neighborhoods has been parlayed many times over. Over the past three decades, the private nonprofit South Platte River Greenway Foundation has invested $25 million in federal, state, and local funds, as well as from private foundation grants and corporate and individual donations, to build some 150 miles of trails, boat launches, whitewater chutes, and parks in four counties and nine municipalities.

Through the South Platte River Initiative, a division of the Department of Parks and Recreation, Denver has provided an additional $45 million since the early 1990s to build public amenities such as parks and infrastructure, including streets, sewers, utilities, bridges, and flood-control measures along 10.5 miles of riverfront. This includes: $23 million from Denver revenues and capital funds, $1 million in state revenues, $7 million in federal revenues through the U.S. Army Corps of Engineers, $7 million from GOCO (Great Outdoors Colorado, a state agency that distributes lottery revenues to land preservation and recreation projects), $5 million from the Urban Drainage and Flood Control District, and $2 million in land donated by the Trillium Corporation. Denverites passed an additional $14-million bond issue to help build infrastructure. The city and developers now each pay half for roads, sewers, water lines, and other services in the Central Platte Valley Metropolitan District.

The jewel in Denver's crown is the $30-million Commons Park, which the city built on a 20-acre riverfront site that had been a rail yard. Commons Park and the greenway were a linchpin for attracting $1.24 billion in public and private investments in the Central Platte Valley. This includes $16 million for three new city parks, $35 million in residential development, $982 million in retail, cultural, and entertainment projects, and a $51-million light-rail line. To attract investment to the riverfront, the city also offered tax incentives. The Denver Urban Renewal Authority established a tax increment financing district that will be worth $6 million to $8 million in sales tax refunds over 15 years for the Denver flagship store for REI, the outdoor recreation retailer (Chadwick 2003; Welty 2003).

center that was intended to attract investments may languish if it is separated from transit and the downtown commercial district by a highway.

In many cases, considerable public sector investment is required to plan, design, build, and attract development to riverfronts. Municipal investments can include the provision of infrastructure, tax breaks, deferred taxes, special taxing districts, and other public subsidies.

Ecologically sensitive designs are not necessarily more expensive. In fact, they often cost less than traditional riverfront development techniques. But because ecological designs for river restoration and protection can differ significantly from traditional ones, like concrete floodwalls and straightened channels, they often face more resistance from planners, governments, and stakeholders who are unfamiliar with these techniques. Proponents of ecologically sensitive projects must make a strong case that public and private investment in river and stream revitalization will improve the riverfront environment and leverage new investment.

How then do we quantify the value of healthy urban rivers and streams? While it is impossible to specify the exact economic benefits of a stream, river, or watershed restoration, we can closely estimate those benefits in property values, real estate premiums, leasing rates, new business opportunities, construction costs, stormwater utility fees, recreational access, and volunteer hours donated. To some degree we can also quantify the benefits in terms of municipal service costs avoided.

THE BENEFITS OF RESTORATION AND REDEVELOPMENT

BENEFIT 1:
Improve water quality and reduce costs

Open-space conservation often is the most cost-effective way to protect drinking water and other environmental resources. Across the nation, communities face billions of dollars in costs to treat drinking water polluted by septic and sewer systems, lawn and garden chemicals, and highway runoff. The U.S. Environmental Protection Agency estimates that $140 billion is needed in the next two decades to make drinking water safe ("Economic Benefits" 2002).

Ecologically sensitive approaches, such as restoring wetlands and buffers that filter stormwater runoff, save money by reducing pollution before it enters streams and rivers. This is a cost-effective alternative to spending money to cleanse polluted waters. For example, wetlands can remove 20 to 60 percent of heavy metals in water, trap 80 to 90 percent of the runoff sediment, and eliminate 70 to 90 percent of entering nitrogen. Similarly, forests next to rivers can also filter out up to 90 percent of runoff's excess nitrogen and 50 percent of excess phosphorous (Ecological Society of America 2003b).

Nitrogen and phosphorous are byproducts of farming, golf courses, and fertilized lawns. Excessive loads of either pollutant can damage human health as well as rivers and fisheries. Even in an intensely urban setting, a vegetated buffer can have a positive effect on the quality of water that enters the river and thus reduce the need for water treatment.

Examples of the cost-effectiveness of preserving or restoring natural systems to improve water quality are described in the following subsections.

Watershed Protection
When agricultural and sewage runoff overwhelmed the Catskill Mountains watershed, New York City's water source, city officials looked at building a filtration plant. The estimated price was $6 billion to $8 billion, plus annual operating costs of $300 million (President's Committee of Advisors on Science and Technology 1998).

THE BENEFITS OF RESTORATION AND REDEVELOPMENT

It is not always possible to distinguish the economic benefit of restoring riverfronts from the value of restoring rivers themselves. Watershed protection and restoration activities upstream often may have a greater impact than ecological design practices along the riverfront itself. In some instances, however, riverfront restoration efforts can make a significant difference to overall river health.

Still, the experience of many cities has shown that river restoration and ecologically sensitive redevelopment can:

1. improve water quality and reduce costs associated with cleanup and drinking water treatment;

2. curb flood damage and lower the costs of flood control;

3. decrease stormwater management costs;

4. reduce sprawl and related infrastructure costs;

5. revitalize the downtown riverfront with new opportunities for housing, offices, and commercial services that attract new residents, businesses, and visitors;

6. provide jobs for residents in construction and commercial businesses;

7. offer recreational opportunities, open space, and park amenities;

8. raise property values and generate new tax revenues; and

9. attract state and federal funding, new volunteers, and broad financial support.

THE ROUGE RIVER   *Detroit, Michigan*

River Issues. The Rouge River, considered one of the most polluted rivers in the country in the 1980s, has improved significantly since it became the subject of a massive federally supported cleanup in the early 1990s. As the effects of years of dumping industrial waste and untreated sewage into the river are being addressed, dissolved oxygen levels have begun to rise in even some of

Sally Petrella, Friends of the Rouge

Friends of the Rouge promote restoration and stewardship of the river.

the most industrialized portions of the river. Stormwater runoff is now one of the biggest threats to the river because of the pollutants it carries and the erosion and subsequent sedimentation it causes.

The health of the Rouge River varies greatly along its four branches and many tributaries, which are spread across Southeastern Michigan. Industrial pollution is concentrated in the main stem of the river while development poses the biggest threat to the rest of the watershed. The heavily industrialized stem of the river, flows through the Ford Motor Company manufacturing complex in Dearborn, contains most of the river's industrial pollution, and has the largest concentration of pollutants from upstream. The healthiest portion of the river is Johnson Creek, a spring-fed tributary of the middle branch. It is cold and clean enough to support brown trout but is now threatened by development and the subsequent warming, erosion, sedimentation, and eutrophication of the creek. The many lakes in the northern headwaters region are fairly clean but are beginning to show the same signs of eutrophication and sedimentation that have plagued impoundments further downstream. Zebra mussels have entered the lakes and Johnson Creek, and likely will soon be widespread throughout the watershed.

What Has Been Accomplished. The Rouge Project began in 1992 with a focus on creating 10 new underground combined sewer overflow basins. Nine of those basins are currently complete. The historically contaminated Newburgh Lake has been dredged of its toxic sediments and reopened. Local government agencies, community leaders, and environmental organizations are working to implement additional projects that will improve water quality. Additionally, a massive public education effort is being undertaken to limit nonpoint sources of pollution, such as lawn fertilizer, pet waste, and other toxins, that reach the river through storm drains.

Improving the health of the most polluted section of the river is the goal of the Gateway Project, a partnership of 12 agencies formed in 1999. The partnership seeks to create an eight-mile greenway to serve as a buffer between the river and nonpermeable surfaces that are a source of polluted runoff. The greenway is a central element of the partnership's master plan, which established guidelines for the restoration of wetlands, riparian shoreline, and fish and wildlife, and identified more than 50 proposed projects.

The first project under the plan, an environmental interpretive center, opened in 2001. Ford Motor Company has begun work on a new factory that incoporates ecological measures such as a green roof covered with insulating and water-absorbing plants and wetlands intended to retain all stormwater on the property. The restoration of an historic oxbow that includes wildlife habitat improvements is partially completed. Several businesses located on the Rouge were convinced to reorient their buildings to face the river. Future projects include a trail system and the possible replacement of a concrete channel installed by the U.S. Army Corps of Engineers with a walkway and buffer zone of native plants.

Friends of the Rouge promotes restoration and stewardship of the river through public education and hands-on restoration and monitoring activities. Every year, on a river cleanup day called Rouge Rescue, this nonprofit organization sends thousands of volunteers out to sites on the river to remove debris and restore the riparian corridor. Students and adults are involved in monitoring the river for chemical and biological pollutants and indicator species. Workshops are held to teach residents practices they can use at home to improve the health of the river. Friends of the Rouge also works with other agencies to implement streambank stabilization projects on public and private property that utilize natural materials.

The Johnson Creek Protection Group is working to improve and maintain the health of the watershed's cleanest and most threatened creek. The group uses public meetings and volunteer events to raise awareness of the creek and works closely with developers to ensure the creek is protected.

Benefits to the River and Community. Since the federal Rouge cleanup effort began in 1992, research has shown an increase in oxygen levels in the Rouge River as well as a decline in bacteria levels. Thousands of students and adults have become more aware of the river and its issues through monitoring programs. Streambank stabilization projects have been implemented in several public parks and private properties. Twenty-two sites were cleared of debris in 2002 alone for Rouge Rescue. Communities within the seven subwatersheds of the Rouge worked together to write watershed management plans in 2001 that established goals for protection and restoration of the river. Forty-three communities have completed a Storm Water Pollution Prevention Initiative Plan, which details how each will manage its stormwater over the next three years. An oil spill at the mouth of the Rouge River also galvanized public outrage over illegal dumping into the river and resulted in a bill passed by the state legislature that doubled fines for illegal dumpers.

For more information . . .

- See The Friends of the Rouge River web site, www.therouge.org, and The Rouge River Project web site, www.rougeriver.com.

CASE
STUDY

River Issues. The pressures of urbanization, agriculture, and grazing in the central coast region of California have degraded the habitat of the Napa River's watershed and drastically increased the rates of erosion and sedimentation. Alterations to the river resulting from dikes, levees, and channelization have resulted in hardening banks and altered stream flows that have made the natural drainage system insufficient to prevent extensive flooding in the area. Prop-

The habitat of the Napa River in California has been degraded.

erty damage in Napa County since 1970 due to six major floods totaled $542 million. The following four paragraphs for this case study are taken verbatim from Krevet (2003). (See the References section at the end of this case study.)

What Is Being Planned. After years of repeated flooding, residents of Napa County voted to increase their taxes to pay for the removal of the Napa River's traditional flood control system. Under the leadership of Friends of the Napa River, the community joined forces to create a plan for an alternative approach to flood control. The Napa River Flood Protection Plan, winner of a 1998 American Society of Landscape Architects award, was designed to restore the river's natural characteristics, freeing it as much as possible from artificial controls such as levees, channelization, and dredging.

Implementation of the plan will be a closely watched test case for the benefits of such nontraditional approaches to flood control. Levees will be pulled back to give the river room to expand during floods, while many floodwalls and other structures will be removed from the floodplain. Trees and other vegetation will be restored to the riverbank, and marshy terraces and wetlands will be created rather than cement terraces.

Instead, New York City is investing $1 billion in restoring its natural capital. In 1997, the city issued an environmental bond to purchase land and halt development in the watershed. This created $310 million for land acquisition through purchase and conservation easements over 15 years.

By 2001, the city had acquired or purchased contracts to acquire over 26,000 acres from more than 360 landowners at a total cost of $73 million. The city also is investing $300 million on constructing or upgrading public and private septic systems and other wastewater infrastructure, $240 million on rehabilitating and upgrading dams and water supply facilities, $232 million on upgrading upstate sewage treatment plants, and $75 million on establishing the Catskill Fund for the Future, an economic development bank to support environmentally responsible development (U.S. EPA 2003a).

"What they are doing in Napa is right along the lines of what we would like to see—local citizens and local governments taking the initiative to make smart land-use decisions," said Michael J. Armstrong, associate director for mitigation for the Federal Emergency Management Agency. He hopes that Napa's example will "embolden other communities to consider other similar approaches."

Benefits to the River and Community. Benefits to the river include improved water quality and protection of thousands of acres of wildlife habitat. Restoration of native plants along the riverbanks in downtown, new marshes, and riparian habitat will provide safe stopping grounds for such waterfowl as herons, egrets, red-shouldered and red-tailed hawks, and kites and other raptors.

For more information . . .

- See Friends of the Napa River web site, www.friendsofthenapariver.org

REFERENCES

Krevet, Bernhard. 2003. "The Napa River Flood Protection Project: 'The Living River Strategy.'" *Napa River Focus*, Fall, p. 8. Also available at http://www.friendsofthenapariver.org/assets/fonr1003.pdf

"The Napa River Watershed: Managing Land Use and Development in a Riverine Estuary System." In *Watershed Success Stories: Applying the Principles and Spirit of the Clean Water Action Plan*, September 2000. [Accessed January 12, 2004]. Available at www.cleanwater.gov/success/napa.html.

Wheeler, Doug. 1998. "The Napa River Flood Management Effort." *California Biodiversity News* 5, no. 4. [Accessed January 12, 2004]. Available at www.ceres.ca.gov/biodiv/newsletter/v5n4/chair.html.

Natural Water Treatment

At its River Rouge complex in Dearborn, Michigan, the Ford Motor Company built shallow drainage canals and artificial wetlands seeded with native plants to soak up and cleanse rainwater that drains into the Rouge River. Ford estimates that implementation of this "green" approach will be $35 million less expensive than building a conventional water-treatment system (Schneider 2002).

Riparian Buffers

Home prices increased an average of 17 percent because of trees and buffers, according to an economic study in California (Chesapeake Bay Program 1998).

Erosion and Sediment Control

The cost of dredging and disposing of sediments to keep Baltimore Harbor navigable is $10 million to $11.5 million a year. Erosion and sediment control could reduce these costs significantly (Chesapeake Bay Program 1998).

BENEFIT 2:
Curb flood damage and lower the costs of flood control

Flood damages continue to wreak havoc in many riverside communities by taking lives and causing property damage, especially in places with no regulations on floodplain development. Since the early 1900s, flood damages have increased sixfold, and now are about $6 billion per year, according to the Association of State Floodplain Managers (2003).

Engineered flood control measures can be just as expensive as damages caused by flooding. They require massive investments in infrastructure and maintenance, while working against the river's beauty and ecology. Unintended side effects often include increased flood frequency and severity and degraded water quality and wildlife habitat.

Sustainable natural river systems produce benefits for property owners as well as the community. The benefits of preserving or refurbishing rivers and streams to a natural state include less damage from flooding and erosion—intact yards, minimal damage to trees, structures, and landscaping, and healthier streamside parks. Alternatives to engineered approaches can achieve more stable stream banks, enhanced wildlife habitats, and a more aesthetically pleasing ecosystem.

Compared with levees, natural floodplains are like sponges: they temporarily store floodwaters and then slowly release those waters.

Compared with levees, natural floodplains are like sponges: they temporarily store floodwaters and then slowly release those waters, reducing the velocity of the river and increasing the capacity of the river channel to move floodwaters downstream. Floodplains also reduce the heights of floods, filter pollutants, and recharge groundwater supplies. These effects reduce the costs of flood control and minimize flood damage. Preserved and restored natural river systems, therefore, can save money in the short and long term.

Examples of successful, ecologically sound flood control measures that have saved communities money are described in the following subsections.

Natural Flow

The Napa River in Napa County, California, has caused $542 million in property damage in six major floods since the 1960s. A flood in 1986 killed three people, destroyed 250 homes, and damaged 2,500 other homes. In 1995, a coalition of community groups in Napa County rejected a traditionally engineered U.S. Army Corps of Engineers flood control project, and instead created a river management plan that would allow the river to flow naturally. In 1998, voters approved a 20-year, half-cent county sales tax to fund the plan. The sales tax could raise between $8 million and $10 million a year, supplemented by federal grants and other sources.

By 2002, some 400 acres of the floodplain had been acquired and restored to a tidal marsh. The Napa County Flood Control and Water Conservation District purchased 50 parcels within the floodplain from which buildings have been removed, with plans to remove structures on another 45 properties.

The estimated $238 million project is expected to save $20.9 million annually in property damage, according to a cost/benefit calculation by the Corps. Further savings from reduced insurance, cleanup, and emergency services costs and from enhanced environmental improvements will bring the annual savings to $26 million for county residents (American Rivers 2003b; Malan 2002; Napa County Flood Control and Water Conservation District 2002).

Wetlands

Preserving and restoring natural areas along the upper watershed of the Charles River has saved money for the federal government and the Boston metropolitan region. Instead of spending $100 million on dams and levees, the U.S. Army Corps of Engineers spent $8.3 million to buy 8,103 acres of wetlands along the Charles capable of containing 50,000 acre-feet of water.

Conversely, the loss of wetlands costs the public money. The Minnesota Department of Natural Resources cites a cost of $300 an acre to replace wetlands that store one foot of water during a storm. Thus the cost to replace the 5,000 acres of wetlands Minnesota loses annually to development could be $1.5 million (Floodplain Management Association 1994).

Natural Flood Control

In the 1970s and 1980s, Tulsa, Oklahoma, was declared a federal disaster area 10 times and led the nation in flood disasters. Then Tulsa developed a system of greenways and trails linking permanent lakes for flood control along Mingo Creek. Using funds from the Federal Emergency Management Agency, a local revenue bond sale, and a stormwater utility fee, the city has acquired frequently flooded properties and moved 900 structures. As a result, Tulsa's flood insurance rates have dropped 25 percent and are now among the lowest in the nation (American Rivers 2003c).

Dam removal along the Baraboo River restored its natural functions. Such restoration is often more cost-effective than building flood-control measures that still may not work.

BENEFIT 3:
Decrease stormwater management costs

Healthy watersheds with vegetated buffers save money by reducing the need for engineered stormwater systems. Stormwater treatment systems that integrate natural processes cost less to construct than storm drain systems while producing better environmental results. Even with best management practices, engineered storm drain systems can cost as much as $50,000 per impervious acre (Schueler 1997a, 1997b). In contrast, stormwater management systems that preserve or restore natural systems can cost far less. The restoration of forested buffers, for example, can cost as little as $2,000 per acre (Center for Watershed Protection 2001a).

Stream Restoration vs. Riprap

Well-designed stream restorations that use a "soft" approach of grading, planting, and natural rock structures stabilize banks at least as well as—but at less cost than—"hard" engineered solutions such as riprap and concrete walls. Depending on the height and angle of banks and other factors, naturalized stream restoration projects can range from $150 per linear foot for grading to $350 per linear foot for more extensive natural stream design, including naturalistic grading, building a new stream channel with rock structures, and replanting banks and buffers (Rouhi 2003).

In 1999, the Northern Virginia Soil and Water Conservation District restored the degraded Kingstowne Stream in Fairfax County by raising the channel level to meet the floodplain, reconstructing meanders, and planting native plants to stabilize banks. The $200,000 project, completed in just two months, was funded equally by the state and county, and installed with help from trained community volunteers. The most degraded 1,000-foot section represented $150,000 of the budget. The county had been considering spending three-and-a-half times the project's amount ($700,000) to riprap or pipe the stream (Hoffman 2003).

Natural Stormwater Systems

Stormwater best management practices are less expensive to construct and provide better environmental results than enclosed drain systems. Natural systems remove pollutants, reduce the size and cost of conventional storm drains, and eliminate costly manholes, pipes, trenches, and catch basins.

The Village Homes in Davis, California, a 70-acre development of 240 homes clustered on one-third of the site, uses vegetated swales that channel stormwater from roofs and streets to a large detention pond. Compared to standard stormwater systems with piping, curbs, gutters, and catch basins, the natural stormwater system saved $800 per home, for a total of $192,000 in savings when the community was built in 1981 (Liptan and Brown 1996).

In Portland, Oregon, parking lots at the Oregon Museum of Science and Industry employ bioswales, landscaped medians that detain and filter stormwater with native wetlands plants. These features saved about $78,000 in construction costs over conventional stormwater management (Liptan and Brown 1996).

Naturalized Detention Basins

Naturalized detention basins with wetland plants and natural slopes have been proven more cost-effective than conventional riprap-lined detention basins. In one study, installation costs were about $7,000 for a 1.5-acre naturalized basin, nearly 70 percent lower than the $26,000 required for an engineered detention basin. Maintenance costs after 10 years were also lower because the naturalized basin did not need mowing or chemical applications. Native vegetation also cleanses stormwater, provides wildlife habitat, and beautifies the landscape (Milner 2001).

Stormwater ponds and wetlands create a "waterfront effect" that makes development more attractive.

Stormwater ponds and wetlands create a "waterfront effect" that makes development more attractive. In 1995, the U.S. EPA analyzed 20 real estate studies across the United States and found that developers could charge a premium of up to $10,000 per lot for homes next to well-designed stormwater ponds and wetlands. The EPA also found that office parks and apartments next to natural stormwater features could be leased or rented at a considerable premium, and often at a faster rate (U.S. EPA 1995a).

Tree Cover

A recent study by American Forests and the USDA Forest Service found that tree cover in the Willamette/Lower Columbia Region in Oregon and Washington provides billions of dollars of benefits in stormwater management, energy savings, and improved air quality. The total stormwater retention capacity of trees in the region, which spans 7 million acres from Vancouver, Washington, to Eugene, Oregon, is valued at $20.2 billion.

Residential summer energy savings resulting from tree shade was about $1.8 million annually. The tree canopy, covering an average of 24 percent of the land regionwide, removed 178 million pounds of pollutants annually, an environmental benefit worth $419 million. The study made the case for even greater tree coverage, which had declined from 46 percent of the region in 1972 to 24 percent in 2001 (American Forests and USDA Forest Service 2001).

BENEFIT 4:
Reduce sprawl and related infrastructure costs

Sprawl contributes to the degradation of urban rivers and streams by covering land with impermeable surfaces such as rooftops, streets, and parking lots. Smart growth alternatives save developers and municipalities money by reducing construction costs for infrastructure while protecting natural resources. Smart growth principles call for smaller lots, walkable neighborhoods, narrower streets, and infill and brownfield redevelopment.

One smart growth approach known as conservation design (i.e., cluster development) concentrates smaller lots in a compact developed portion of a site while preserving 40 to 80 percent of the land as open space. Concentrating the homes reduces the site's impervious cover by shortening the length of roads and sidewalks, which also reduces construction costs.

Because infrastructure constitutes more than half the total cost of subdivision development, municipalities and developers can save money by reducing the amount of impervious cover in subdivisions and parking lots, (CH2M Hill 1993).

Some benefits of smart growth development are illustrated by example in the following subsections.

Reduced Infrastructure Costs

A 1990 study for the city of Virginia Beach, Virginia, compared the costs and benefits of conventional and smart-growth development patterns. The study found the smart-growth pattern preserved 45 percent more land and reduced road surfaces by 50 percent, saving the city 45 percent in infrastructure costs (Siemon, Larsen & Purdy et al. 1990).

Using better site design principles, three proposed residential developments studied by the Virginia Department of Conservation and Recreation and the Center for Watershed Protection could save up to 49 percent on infrastructure costs. In all three cases, smart-growth development principles saved developers $200,000 in infrastructure costs, while producing the same number of homes (Center for Watershed Protection 2001c).

Better site design can reduce impervious cover from 10 percent to 50 percent, depending on the lot size and layout, which can reduce costs for stormwater conveyance and treatment. Costs to treat stormwater from a single impervious acre can range from $30,000 to $50,000 (Schueler 1997a, 1997b).

Developers of Prairie Crossing in Grayslake, Illinois, clustered 317 residences on 132 acres of the 667-acre site, leaving 80 percent as open space and agricultural land. The design saved as much as $2.7 million by using swales, prairie, and wetlands for stormwater conveyance and treatment, and eliminating curbs and gutters (Lehner et al. 2001).

By modifying codes, roadway surfaces can be reduced significantly, saving $150 per linear foot of road that is shortened and $25 to $50 per linear foot of roadway that is narrowed. Eliminating a commercial parking lot space can save $1,100 in construction costs and $5,000 to $7,000 over a lifetime for maintenance of the space (Schueler 1997a, 1997b).

Better site design can reduce impervious cover from 10 percent to 50 percent... which can reduce costs for stormwater conveyance and treatment.

Reduced Grading and Site Preparation Costs

Better site design reduces the need to clear and grade 35 to 60 percent of the total site area, which is typical for conventional development. The cost to clear, grade, and install erosion control devices at a development site can reach $5,000 per acre (Schueler 1995a).

Corporate Savings

Corporate landowners can save between $270 and $640 per acre in annual mowing and maintenance costs when open lands are managed as a natural buffer area rather than as lawn (Schueler 1997a, 1997b).

> **BENEFIT 5:**
> **Revitalize the downtown riverfront with new housing and business opportunities**

Restoring natural river features, creating riverfront parks, and redeveloping brownfields all improve a city's image and livability. Cities that have redeveloped downtown waterfronts to include attractive walkable areas with historic, cultural, commercial, and recreational amenities have

CASE STUDY

River Issues. Chattanooga's rise as a thriving industrial center exacted a significant toll on the health of the Tennessee River. The river's health has been severely threatened by polluted groundwater, illegal and legal dumping, the construction of dams to generate hydropower, and channelization to accommodate navigation. As riverfront industries went into decline after

RiverCity Company

Riverwalk in Chattanooga, Tennessee, is part of a regional plan for greenways in the southeast Tennessee River Valley.

the mid-twentieth centry, areas adjacent to the riverfront became eyesores that became emblematic of larger social and economic problems within the community. But since the 1980s, both the river and the city have made a significant comeback.

What Has Been Accomplished. The commitment to revitalize the areas adjacent to the Tennessee River in Chattanooga is among the better-known urban river and community revitalization success stories. Since completion of the plan Vision 2000 in 1987, Chattanooga and its citizens have built much of the downtown Tennessee Riverpark, a planned twenty-mile circuit of parks, trails, and historic landmarks in a greenway along the Tennessee. In downtown Chattanooga, picnic facilities, playgrounds, a rowing center, fishing piers, boat docks, a restored antique carousel, and the restoration of a 105-year-old bridge have helped make the Riverpark a community focal point. It has also rejuvenated the city's economy.

In the 1990s, advocacy groups such as the Trust For Public Land and the Rivers, Trails, and Conservation Assistance program of the National Park Service worked with local government agencies to complete a larger regional plan, *Greenways for the Southeast Tennessee River Valley.* As part of this plan, an additional 75 miles of greenway system have been proposed. This system will include the Riverwalk along the Tennessee River and connections to nearby trails along North and South Chickamauga Creeks, the 180-acre Greenway Farm, and Old Wauhatchie Pike on the side of Lookout Mountain. Additional proposed greenways include a trail along Chattanooga Creek and a "safewalk" along the streets of Chattanooga.

an edge in competition for new residents and businesses. Such amenities also attract visitors through tourism, conventions, and special events.

Riverfronts with parks, river access, open space, and natural areas can be a catalyst for downtown rejuvenation. Riverfronts redeveloped with recreational and other amenities also appeal to business owners. According to a 1995 National Park Service report, corporate CEOs say quality of life for employees is the third-most-important factor in locating a business, after access to domestic markets and availability of skilled labor. Likewise, a survey of small business owners ranked access to parks, recreation,

Benefits to the River and Community. Declared the dirtiest city in America by the U.S. EPA in 1969, Chattanooga's accomplishments in the 1980s and 1990s provide benchmarks for other communities seeking to revitalize their downtown riverfronts in terms of economic development, cultivating a sense of historic and cultural pride among community residents, and promoting a vibrant tourist industry.

For more information . . .

- See The Project for Public Spaces web pages about the Chattanooga Riverwalk at pps.org/topics/pubpriv/roles/success_chatanooga
- More information about Chattanooga and the city's relationship with its river is available from the RiverCity Corporation web site, www.rivercitycompany.com, and the Chattanooga Area Chamber of Commerce web page, www.chattanooga-chamber.com

REFERENCES

"Chattanooga, TN. Best Practice: Greenways." 1999. [Accessed May 29, 2003]. Available at www.bmpcoe.org/bestpractices/external/chatt/chatt_4.html.

Motavalli, Jim. 1998. "Chattanooga on a Roll: From America's Dirtiest City to Its Greenest." *E: The Environmental Magazine*, March-April.

National Park Service, Rivers, Trails, and Conservation Assistance Program. 2000. *Managing Greenways: A Look At Six Case Studies.* [Accessed May 29, 2003]. Available at www.nps.gov/phso/rtca/grnmgmt2.htm.

Sustainable Communities Network. 1996. "Chattanooga: A City Worth Watching." [Accessed May 29, 2003]. Available at www.sustainable.org/casestudies/tennessee/TN_af_chattanooga.html.

and open space as their first priority in choosing a new location for their business (Crompton, Love, and More 1997).

The South Platte River in Denver (see pp. 32–33) is a prime example of a successful riverfront revitalization. Other examples are described briefly here.

Tennessee River. The Tennessee Riverpark in Chattanooga has stimulated investment of more than $250 million in the waterfront, including two new hotels. Located near the river, the Tennessee Aquarium attracts more than 1 million visitors a year and contributed $133 million to the community in the first year after its 1992 completion (Florida Department of Environmental Protection 2000; Vaughen 2000).

Milwaukee River. The once-moribund Milwaukee River has been revived with new parks, walkways, plazas, and landings that have transformed downtown into a thriving scene. The design for the $12 million Milwaukee Riverwalk, which debuted in 1996, was inspired by Milwaukee's industrial and architectural heritage. Warehouses overlooking the water have been redeveloped as loft apartments, offices, and restaurants. The project has encouraged more than $35 million in investment, adding $22 million of assessed value downtown. It is being extended through the downtown's historic Third Ward to the Henry W. Maier Festival Park on Lake Michigan (Kay 2000).

Connecticut River. Hartford, Connecticut, has attracted visitors and new business since 1999, when Riverfront Plaza reunited downtown with the Connecticut River. Visits to riverfront parks have more than doubled. One redevelopment project of sites formerly occupied by parking lots is Adriaen's Landing, a new $770 million mixed-use project with a convention center, hotel, apartments, a retail/entertainment complex, and a science and technology center. At least two other mixed-use projects have been inspired by the riverfront rejuvenation: a $100 million office and apartment redevelopment of an old firearms factory, and a $50 million redevelopment of office buildings and public spaces at Constitution Plaza on the riverfront. In all, some 2,000 new housing units are being introduced along the riverfront in downtown Hartford (Marfuggi 2003).

Upper Mississippi River. In the 1990s, tourism in the Upper Mississippi River corridor was on the rise, and travel expenditures increased by 3 to 6 percent. According to a 1995 U.S. Army Corps of Engineers study, recreation pumps more than $216 million annually in direct revenue to businesses in counties along the river, with another $171 million spent on durable goods such as boats, fishing equipment, and camping gear. This economic activity created jobs for about 3,000 people. The full impact of recreational spending in the Upper Mississippi River corridor totaled $1.1 billion per year, supporting about 12,600 jobs.

BENEFIT 6:
Provide jobs for residents in construction and commercial businesses

River cleanup and riverfront revitalization are job-making enterprises. Job creation… can be targeted to low-income communities and inner-city residents.

River cleanup and riverfront revitalization are job-making enterprises. Ecologically sensitive redevelopment can stimulate job growth by creating restoration and construction jobs and by providing cities a sustainable economic engine. Developing "green jobs," in fields such as wildlife management, habitat restoration, ecotourism, and environmental education, offers urban residents opportunities to get training and experience in a new field or to start businesses. Job creation in the following areas can be targeted to low-income communities and inner-city residents.

Cleanup and construction. River cleanup and riverfront revitalization employ ecologists, engineers, hydrologists, planners, landscape architects, and other professionals. A river renewal project can stimulate new business development, including new housing, offices, shops, restaurants, greenways, parks, and recreation facilities, while sustaining existing industries. Redeveloping a riverfront site prompts surrounding properties to invest in expansions, remodeling, and landscaping. A study of the economic value of the Schuylkill River Park near Philadelphia estimated construction-related economic benefits of $20.1 million, as well as a boost to downtown revitalization and an estimated $9.3 million appreciation in residential property values (Pennsylvania Economy League 1997).

Service industries. Attracting people to the urban core can be a huge boon to downtown service industries. Hotels, restaurants, shops, and other visitor services can profit from an improved view, expanded range of activities, and renewed interest in downtown.

Outdoor recreation businesses. Outdoor recreation activities and related businesses depend on clean water and preserved habitat. A renewed waterfront offers possibilities for local businesses such as fishing, boating, and wildlife watching. Three-quarters of the nation's outdoor recreation is within a half-mile of streams or other water bodies. According to a 2001 Recreation Roundtable national survey, 57 percent of adults used natural open space and recreation areas for fitness walking, 29 percent for wildlife viewing including birdwatching, 28 percent for fishing, 22 percent for hiking, 21 percent for running and jogging, and 7 percent for canoeing and kayaking (McHugh 2003; Recreation Roundtable 2002).

Revitalized rivers, therefore, play an important role in spurring the development of outdoor recreation business. The following five brief case studies illustrate this point.

Kennebec River. The 1999 removal of the Edwards Dam from the Kennebec River north of Augusta, Maine, opened 17 miles of riverfront. The result was renewed wildlife habitat likely to draw fishing, boating, wildlife watching, and other recreational activities. Because freshwater fishing is already big business in Maine—almost $350 million was spent on the sport in 1996—expectations were high for the economic impact of the dam removal. A 1991 study estimated removing the dam would generate about $48 million in economic benefits through increased sport fishing alone (Bridgeo 2003).

Delaware River. In 1996, anglers fishing mostly for trout on the Delaware River spent about $18 million for lodging, meals, equipment, and services, according to a survey of local businesses located in the Delaware River Tailwaters of New York. This economic activity generated nearly $30 million for local economies, supporting about 348 local jobs and adding about $720,000 to local tax coffers (Maharaj, McGurrin, and Carpenter 1998).

Connecticut River. Riverfront Recapture, an organization that oversees Hartford's downtown riverfront redevelopment projects, attracts major sporting events that draw participants and spectators. Events such as professional bass fishing tournaments and triathlons have already generated about $15.6 million in economic activity for the region since 1999 (Marfuggi 2003).

Gauley River. Whitewater rafters along a 24-mile stretch of the Gauley River near Summersville, West Virginia, pump $20 million a year into the local economy. Elsewhere in West Virginia, rafting on the New River provides 1,000 seasonal jobs in Fayette County while contributing $50 million to local economies, mostly from the sale of food, lodging, videos, photos, T-shirts, and cookbooks (Lerner and Poole 1999).

Farmington River. River recreation for five towns along the West Branch of Connecticut's Farmington River generates about $3.6 million annually, with an estimated 63 jobs supported by river recreation, according to a 2001 study. This is a large amount relative to the size of these small, rural towns—Colebrook, Hartland, Barkhamsted, New Hartford, and Canton—where only 10 percent of visitors stay overnight. The total value of river recreation was $9.45 million for three river activities: angling, tubing, and boating (Moore and Siderelis 2003).

According to a national survey, three-quarters of U.S. recreation occurs within a half-mile of streams. Here, triathalon competitors ready themselves for the swim portion of their event.

BENEFIT 7:
Offer recreational opportunities, open space, and park amenities

Redeveloping urban riverfronts introduces new recreational opportunities, from walking and biking on greenways to boating on a newly revitalized river to bird-watching in open-space buffers. Easy access to parks and open space has become a measure of community wealth and an important way to attract businesses and residents by guaranteeing both a high quality of life and a vibrant economy.

River Issues. Over the past 150 years, the 410-mile-long Connecticut River has been dammed and polluted to such an extent that it was known in the mid-twentieth century as the nation's "best landscaped sewer." Though the river has benefited from regional efforts to restore its health in recent years, certain threats remain, including: combined sewer overflows, non-point source pollution, increasing numbers of

Dragonboat on the Connecticut River in Hartford/East Hartford. The fourth annual dragonboat races are scheduled for September 2004.

powerboats, and, especially as the river approaches Long Island Sound, riverfront development. But efforts in Hartford have successfully transformed the river and its banks from a sewer and scrap heap to an economic asset.

What Has Been Accomplished. Riverfront Recapture is a private, nonprofit organization created to reclaim, revive, and restore access to the Hartford riverfront. It has raised more than $57 million from public and private sources to create a network of public parks and recreational facilities along both banks of the Connecticut. The centerpiece of the organization's efforts, Riverfront Plaza—a landscaped plaza built over a section of an interstate highway—has reconnected downtown Hartford with the river and an emerging system of riverfront parks. Riverfront Recapture has also created a park south of downtown, Charter Oak Landing, and is restoring Riverside Park, north of downtown, that was designed by the Olmsted Brothers firm in the 1890s. In East Hartford, Riverfront Recapture has created Great River Park, which extends along the riverfront for nearly two miles. By 2005, paved and lighted riverwalks will connect all of the parks.

The four parks, which lie entirely within a floodplain, feature public boat launch facilities, picnic areas, and riverwalks along the water's edge. Great River Park includes an amphitheater that seats about 350 people, while Riverfront Plaza has a performance space that seats 2,000. Charter Oak Landing includes a wharf for tall ships and a dock for an excursion boat that offers daily cruises during the summer. A larger restaurant boat operates out of a new dock in downtown Hartford from late spring through fall. A Victorian-style boathouse in Riverside Park, completed in 2002, accommodates Riverfront Recapture's community rowing program. This program includes adult instruction but places heavy emphasis on teaching local teenagers. Students at all three Hartford high schools and East Hartford High School now participate in crew.

Programming for the city's youth is an important part of Riverfront Recapture's mission, and the organization provides a variety of opportunities for young people to benefit from the riverfront. Beyond rowing, other programs include "Get Hooked on Fishing—Not on Drugs," fishing clinics, sessions on the Riverfront Adventure Challenge Course (which includes high and low ropes), boat building, and a summer science camp.

In addition, Riverfront Recapture works to bring national and regional sporting events to the river. These events have generated nearly $16 million for the local economy at no threat to the environment because they are dependent upon a clean, healthy river. The organization produces a year-round calendar of activities—including festivals, fireworks, concerts, fishing tournaments, dragon boat races, and rowing regattas—that draw people of all ages and backgrounds to the riverfront.

In 1998, Riverfront Recapture took on the responsibility for managing and programming the park system for the two municipalities that own the land and reached a historic agreement with the Metropolitan District Commission (MDC), the regional organization that provides water and sewer services to the area. Under this agreement, the MDC maintains the parks with its own employees and equipment. Funds for maintenance are generated by an increase in the water rate, averaging $6 per household per year. This money also funds a park rangers program administered by Riverfront Recapture.

All of this positive activity on the riverfront has spawned significant interest in economic development, most notably Adriaen's Landing, a $770 million project on 35 acres of land next to the downtown Riverfront Plaza that had been used primarily as surface parking lots. Work on a convention center, with a hotel, housing, and a major retail and entertainment complex is scheduled for completion in 2005.

Benefits to the River and Community. As Riverfront Recapture has restored access to the Connecticut River, the community has placed much greater value on the river and its banks. When the organization began developing parks, annual cleanup days measured their success in tonnage—the weight of the junked cars, washing machines, refrigerators, and other refuse removed from the parks. That tonnage is no longer removed: residents and local businesses no longer use these parks as scrap heaps. In 1990, the MDC asked voters for an additional $80 million to expand its efforts to prevent sewage overflows. Voters approved the measure by four to one, and the work is now well underway. Riverfront Recapture's efforts have instilled in local residents a sense of stewardship for the Connecticut, and that stewardship is now amply expressed.

The Connecticut Department of Environmental Protection, the Connecticut River Watershed Council, and the MDC each have helped bring the river to the point at which Riverfront Recapture can sponsor triathlons that include swimming in the river. Herons, egrets, and bald eagles have returned, and the fish population is healthy and abundant—all signs of the remarkable recovery of the Connecticut River.

For more information . . .
- See the web site of Riverfront Recapture, Inc., www.riverfront.org.

REFERENCES

Dillon, David. 2000. "River Dancing." *Landscape Architecture*, August, 70–75, 88.

Marfuggi, Joseph R., and Rick Porth. 1999. "A Riverfront Runs Through It." [Accessed January 12, 2004]. Available at www.urbanparks.pps.org/topics/rivers/riverruns.

Brooklyn Bridge Coalition

The Brooklyn Bridge Park Summer Film Series brings 1,000 people out on movie nights to the East River. Look closely and you'll see that the film, appropriately, is On the Waterfront.

Recreation opportunities. In 2000, the South Platte River's clean-up and redesign in Denver enticed Seattle-based recreational retailer REI to spend $34 million to renovate a historic transit power station on the river. The 98,000-square-foot flagship store includes a 55-foot-high rock-climbing wall. The five-acre landscape features a trail for customers to test-ride mountain bikes. Paddle-product shoppers can try out the whitewater in the river's kayak chutes (Takesuye 2003).

Open space. Open space such as parks, farms, and privately owned buffers can subsidize local government by enhancing property values with little demand for the expensive services required by suburban-style development. A 1990 study by Scenic Hudson, Inc., found that residential land required $1.11 to $1.23 in services for every dollar it contributed to revenue, while open land's requirements ranged from only 17 to 74 cents for each dollar contributed (Land Trust Alliance 1994).

BENEFIT 8:
Raise property values and generate new tax revenues

Preserved and restored natural lands in watersheds and along rivers and streams boost the value of adjacent real estate, which in turn increases city tax revenues. Redeveloping the downtown riverfront also boosts the local tax base by attracting new development and higher real estate assessments for offices, restaurants, shops, and hotels.

Clean river economic benefits. In 1996, the U.S. Environmental Protection Agency estimated that a clean Charles River contributed more than $100 million to metropolitan Boston by boosting property values, promoting tourism, and supporting recreation. Premiums for sales and rentals of waterfront properties were more than $60 million. Another $40 million was attributed to hotel business along the Charles. Recreational use with economic benefits includes boat rentals, tours, moorings, and collegiate crew teams (U.S. EPA New England Region 1996).

Stormwater pond premiums. An EPA study of several Virginia developments showed real estate premiums for property fronting urban stormwater ponds averaged as much as $7,500 per unit for condominiums, $10,000 for townhomes, $49,000 for single-family homes, $10 per month for apartment rentals, and $1 per square foot for commercial rentals (U.S. EPA 1995a).

Increased property values. Property values can increase near healthy, naturalized riverfronts. For example, the Maryland Conservation Act encourages conservation of trees and buffers. Developers there receive 10 to 15 percent premiums for lots next to forests and other buffers (Chesapeake Bay Program 1998).

A study by the California Department of Water Resources found that property prices in areas with restored streams increased by 3 to 13 percent. The study proved the differential was related to property owners' perception of greater amenities. In areas of Colorado, property values near restored urban streams increased from $4,500 to $19,000 (Streiner and Loomis 1995).

Tax revenue advantage. A Boulder, Colorado, study of greenbelts and neighborhood property values found that the city's greenbelt increased the aggregate property value for one neighborhood by about $5.4 million, resulting in about $500,000 additional potential annual property tax revenue (Correll, Lillydahl, and Singell 1978).

Protected floodplains. Buffers containing the entire 100-year floodplain are an extremely cost-effective way to avoid flood damage. A national study of 10 programs that directed development away from flood-prone areas found that the land next to protected floodplains had increased in value by an average of $10,427 per acre (Burby et al. 1988).

BENEFIT 9:
Attract state and federal funding, volunteers, and broad financial support

Waterfront redevelopment often attracts state and federal funds to remove or circumvent interstate highways or railroad tracks. Funding for riverfront parks, greenways, and infrastructure also can come from municipal bonds, tax-increment-financing, and riverfront improvement districts. Other sources are donations from corporations and local businesses. Combined with the effects of construction activity, such as hiring local designers and crews and purchasing materials, this financial support benefits local economies.

State and federal funds. Hartford's Riverfront Recapture, which has lowered I-91 and is linking the city with the Connecticut River to provide recreation space and invite economic redevelopment, has attracted over $52 million in state and federal dollars since 1981 (not including I-91 reconstruction).

One project involves installing ramps, a patio, park benches, a new parking lot, and hundreds of trees and shrubs around a new Victorian-style boathouse. The project was funded with $3.65 million in Federal Intermodal State Transportation and Equity Act for the 21st Century (ISTEA-21) funds allocated by the Connecticut Department of Transportation and special state bond funds through the state's Department of Economic and Community Development (Marfuggi 2003; Riverfront Recapture 2003).

River stewards. Volunteers also add and attract value to riverfronts. As part of National River Cleanup Week 2002, volunteers conducted more than 350 river cleanups nationwide, removing trash such as washing machines, mattresses, truck and car bodies, and tons of cans, bottles, and paper trash. Since its inception in 1992, some 429,000 volunteers have participated in 4,738 cleanups covering 95,269 miles of waterways during National River Cleanup Week (America Outdoors 2003).

Preserved and restored natural lands in watersheds and along rivers and streams boost the value of adjacent real estate, which in turn increases city tax revenues.

In Virginia, the Mattaponi and Pamunkey River Association reported 3,000 volunteer hours annually for water-quality monitoring, trash cleanup, and community education. Assuming a $15 per hour wage for public works employees, these volunteer efforts saved public agencies more than $45,000 a year (Center for Watershed Protection 2001a).

Corporate sponsorship. The American public generally supports the idea of corporations providing financial support for parks and recreation areas and sponsoring of trails and visitor centers. Some 71 percent agree with the idea of corporate financial support, while 67 percent agree that businesses should adopt public parks and other facilities (Recreation Roundtable 1998).

CHAPTER 5
The Chicago River:
A Reversal of Fortunes

For many years, in the unofficial competition for most trashed U.S. river, the Chicago River—reversed, rearranged, past repository of waste of every kind—was always a top contender. But today, instead of the abuse it once received, the Chicago River is winning recognition and awards for its return to life. Citizens and government officials have made dramatic steps in helping this urban river back to ecological health.

Sections of the once-maligned river are gaining crown jewel status in the limited open space inventory of the Chicago metropolitan area, home to about 8 million people. Lining the river's Main Branch is some of the country's most significant architecture. Recreational traffic on the river is up dramatically, and bars, restaurants, and other amenities have flourished along its banks in and around downtown.

These photos illustrate the many faces and phases of the history of the Chicago River.

As it runs through 24 city neighborhoods, the river is more and more dotted with green havens, places within the city limits where you might find the toothmarks of a beaver on a river-edge cottonwood or the eggs of a snapping turtle. Or in spring you might spot a flock of brilliantly colored migrants, from scarlet tanagers to yellow-rumped warblers. Dozens of species of fish once again live in the river. As a measure of how much the river has recovered, the Illinois EPA is conducting a study to determine if the river's long-term prospects have improved sufficiently to upgrade designated uses and water-quality standards to allow for recreational contact.

Laurene von Klan, executive director of The Friends of the Chicago River, has seen how much has changed since she joined the river advocacy group in the early 1990s. Back then the idea of the Chicago River as an amenity or ecological asset often elicited a snort of derision. "Today," says von Klan, "the footage introducing the local evening TV news zooms in over the river, and the message is that the river is something we want—it's beautiful, and it defines us as a city. The river is our new icon. It has a new place in the local psyche."

A HARD-WORKING RIVER

Since its inception, Chicago has had a reputation as a hard-working town—from slaughterhouses to steel mills—and the river has been intimately connected with that work. Chicago grew up where it did because the location offered a strategic connection between the Great Lakes and the Mississippi.

Two hundred years ago the Chicago River was not what anyone would call a river. It was more of a directional wetland, a meandering channel through a vast expanse of wetlands. This swamp-river supported a rich diversity of plants and animals; early European visitors noted the wolves, beaver, bears, and other wildlife that could be found there.

European settlement quickly changed the river. Chicagoans saw ways to put the river to work moving people, goods, and waste. People deepened existing channels and dug new ones. They filled wetlands, reversed the flow of parts of the river, lined its banks with steel sheet piling and riprap, and built massive tunnel systems beneath it for transportation and stormwater management. But while the Chicago River was central to the city's founding and growth, it quickly became a victim of Chicago's success. People literally turned their backs on the waste-choked stream: they constructed their buildings to face away from the foul smells and sights of the waterway.

From this low point, how did the Chicago River rise to the status of one of the city's major natural assets? Higher environmental standards—embodied in the Clean Water Act of 1972 and the resultant improvements in sewage treatment and stormwater management—were a key factor. The resilience of nature also played a role. But the obstacles to bringing the river back to life were (and still are) numerous. They include:

- persistent concentrations of heavy metals and other contaminants in the sediments of portions of the river;

- memories of the river's toxic past, which still lingered in the late 1990s, when researchers with the United States Department of Agriculture Forest Service found that nearly half of all people who were asked what first comes to mind about the Chicago River replied that it was "dirty" or "polluted" (Gobster and Westphal 1998); and

- miles of hard river-edge—the concrete, riprap, and steel-sheet piling that line most of the river's banks.

Another challenge to river improvement is the very limited open space around the river, which stymies efforts to restore a natural floodplain area or reduce the steep riverbank slopes. In a ranking of the open space resources of 20 major cities, Chicago finished worse than New York and Los Angeles (City of Chicago Department of Planning and Development et al. 1998). Within the city limits, there is practically no undeveloped land on the river, according to Nelson Chueng, CitySpace project manager with the city of Chicago's Department of Planning and Development. At the same time, Chicago has been experiencing what Chueng refers to as "rampant economic growth," putting even greater pressure on what few open parcels of land remain.

Another major issue for the river is the number of jurisdictions that are responsible for aspects of its welfare or management. The Chicago River runs 156 miles through Chicago and 42 surrounding suburban communities that range from well-to-do to impoverished. The decisions, actions, and policies of park districts, forest preserve districts, flood management and sewer treatment agencies, and private landowners—residential, industrial, and commercial—all impact the river.

Yet another consideration is that the Chicago is still today a working river. Restoration has to fit within the framework of stormwater management and commercial shipping. Observes Chueng, "This is still a working-class river. New uses and restoration need to be compatible with a river that still earns a living."

Despite these formidable constraints, residents have long had visions for a better river, a river that is an asset for all Chicagoans. Legend has it that more than three decades ago, Mayor Richard J. Daley envisioned a day when a worker could take a break and fish lunch out of the Chicago River. When von Klan and others at Friends of the Chicago River started talking about the river as an ecological asset in the early 1990s, "visionary" was probably one of the milder reactions. But today, more and more, her—and thus Daley's—viewpoint is becoming commonplace.

YESTERDAY'S PIPE DREAMS ARE TODAY'S REALITY

Activities on and along the Chicago River that would have been unthinkable as recently as 10 or 15 years ago have become reality. New river-edge park facilities incorporate fishing stations and canoe and kayak access. For the past two years, the Chicago River Flatwater Classic and the Chicago Chase Regatta have attracted more than 250 boats. Riverside residential real estate has become highly desirable—and, accordingly, highly expensive. And residents continue to make hands-on efforts to improve the river's ecological health.

Chicago's river development plan divides the Chicago Ribert into nine reaches, each with specific development land-use and open space characteristics.

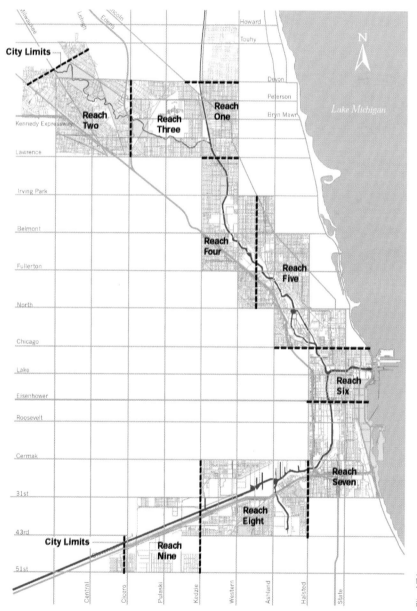

City of Chicago

Kathy Dickhut, assistant commissioner for the Chicago Department of Planning and Development, sees the move toward greater ecological focus on the river as "a progression of the possibilities. First it was just having people deal with the river at all. Before, people couldn't even get to the river." But investments in improved water quality and grassroots cleanup efforts made it more appealing for people to interact with the river. So a new stage emerged. "People started getting to the river," she explains, "and then they started looking at the possibilities of what could be done with it."

This progression meshed with changes in Chicago's economy. The city has seen strong growth in residential real estate in recent years. The industrial and commercial sector also expanded during the 1990s, but far fewer industries are river-dependent in the way they were in the past. This economic evolution has also helped open the door to new ways of treating the river.

Chicago's current mayor, Richard M. Daley, has been another factor in the river's renaissance. Daley's focus on a greener Chicago is evident in the city's now-ubiquitous flowers and landscaping in the medians of once dreary major thoroughfares; in efforts to make Chicago safer for migratory birds; in the installation of a "green roof" at City Hall; and in an aggressive commitment to open space acquisition.

Daley advocates thinking big when it comes to the possibilities of the river for people and wildlife. "People can use the river for fishing, relaxing, jogging, bike riding, and all that," he says. "You have to be a dreamer about these things."

Another catalyst for transforming seemingly far-fetched visions into reality has been The Friends of the Chicago River, formed in 1979. These days, the group has many partners, and the river has champions in high places. But the Friends remain the only organization dedicated exclusively to serving as the guardian of the Chicago River. The Friends' primary role has been to get the river on other people's and organizations' agendas. Especially in its early days as a small nonprofit, the group could not afford to take on major initiatives by itself. It instead communicated the potential of the river to a wide range of people and interests.

This approach has led to another notable feature of the Chicago River's rebirth: virtually all of the river's progress has grown out of partnerships and collaborations. Dozens of nonprofit agencies, units of government at every level, businesses, foundations, and individuals have been key partners in river improvement efforts.

The Chicago City Council established new river development regulations in 1998, including a requirement for a minimum 30-foot setback.

City of Chicago

PLANNING FOR A BETTER RIVER
The early efforts of The Friends of the Chicago River in the 1980s emphasized promoting the potential of the river downtown. The Friends spearheaded a successful joint effort by a variety of interests and groups to amend the city's zoning ordinance so as to make river-edge development take the river into consideration. In the same period, the Friends and the city of Chicago coauthored a set of river design guidelines for the river as it flowed through downtown Chicago. These guidelines urged turning riverfront building toward rather than away from the river and setting buildings back from

the river edge to allow pedestrian access to the river. These guidelines also envisioned a continuous walkway along the river. Aesthetics and access were heavily emphasized, though the guidelines also offered suggestions for reducing negative impacts on water quality.

Subsequent planning has built on these initial efforts in several ways. In 1998, Chicago's city council adopted a new river setback ordinance. All new development projects within 100 feet of the river are now required to provide a 30-foot setback from the river. In 1999, the City of Chicago River Corridor Development Plan was adopted. The plan's guidelines address the whole of the river within the city limits: it outlines provisions for public access, including a contiguous riverwalk, and for increased recreational opportunities. It also identifies a palette of native plants suitable for river-edge use and encourages development that fronts the river and incorporates softer and more naturalistic alternatives to steel-sheet piling and unadorned riprap.

The plan splits the river into nine reaches that have specific development and land-use characteristics and open space opportunities. The southern reaches are principally industrial, the central reach through

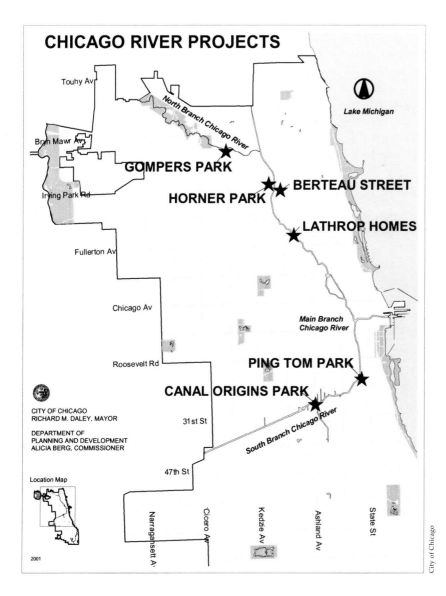

This map pinpoints just some of the projects described in the paragraphs below.

the central business district (the Loop) is commercially driven, and the parkland along the far northern reaches gives the river a more naturalistic character.

Despite the differences between these reaches, however, the Chicago Department of Planning and Development now urges developers to employ natural riverbank designs along all parts of the river wherever possible. All new riverfront development projects are processed as planned unit developments, which require Chicago Plan Commission and City Council approval. "With any new development," Chueng says, "the Plan Commission asks, How does it treat the river?"

To support developers in their efforts to treat the river well, the city, in cooperation with the Northeastern Illinois Planning Commission—the regional planning body for the six-county metropolitan area—and the Friends, gathered a panel of experts in design, planning, hydrology, engineering, and ecology to brainstorm ecologically sensitive techniques for restoring riverbanks practical for even the most industrial, built-up, and degraded sections of the Chicago and urban rivers like it. This design charette was summarized in "From Stockyards to Spawning Beds: A Handbook of Bank Restoration Designs for the Chicago River and Other Urban Streams" (Friends of the Chicago River et al. n.d.). Some of the concepts described in the handbook include: integration of vegetation into existing steel sheet piling, bioengineering techniques that rely on vegetation to stabilize riverbanks, and floating islands. The Chicago Park District's River Master Plan also establishes restoration and development guidelines for riverfront parks, including recommended riverbank and slope treatments for riparian wildlife habitat.

Architect Ted Wolff, a longtime member of the Friends and principal at Wolff, Clements and Associates, the firm that helped draft the details of the new plan, says the setback ordinance is critical to the success of Chicago River planning. "Setback is the key thing," he explains. "Staying 30 feet from the top of the bank keeps development from looming over the river and river trails. It leaves a corridor open for restoration." While a 30-foot setback may seem narrow, in a dense urban setting like Chicago it is significant. It creates room sufficient for a publicly accessible riverwalk, native landscape plantings, and riverbank improvements.

The city views as increasingly important that its riverbanks are aesthetically pleasing and good for wildlife habitat, but that they also provide erosion control and smart stormwater management.

The city's department of planning is currently seeking to expand the 30-foot setback ordinance to include the protection of the riverbank and to limit the proliferation of hard-edged sheet pile where possible. The city views as increasingly important that its riverbanks are aesthetically pleasing and good for wildlife habitat, but that they also provide erosion control and smart stormwater management (Chueng 2003).

PROJECTS AND GRASSROOTS CHANGE ON THE RIVER: PLANNING'S UNLIKELY DANCE PARTNER

There's another vital strand to this story. Progress on the Chicago River has long been a dance between planning and action. The new Chicago River Corridor Plan didn't grow out of abstract concern for the river. It grew from individuals' leadership and vision. People in Chicago didn't wait for plans to start making good things happen on the river.

By the mid-1990s, a wave of grassroots river activism was becoming evident, one based in neighborhoods and with an increasing focus on watersheds and the ecological health of the river. A number of restoration projects popped up throughout the Chicago River watershed. They varied from site to site, but they were all driven by grassroots involvement. They brought together many agencies as partners for the first time to oversee narrowly focused opportunities for river improvement.

Prairie Wolf Slough

One of the most ambitious projects to date within the Chicago River system has been the restoration of Prairie Wolf Slough. This effort brought together a wide array of partners. Though much of the Chicago River watershed is heavily urbanized, this project represented a rare opportunity to preserve open space and focus on ecological benefits at the watershed rather than the corridor level. Prairie Wolf Slough is a 42-acre former cornfield located along the Middle Fork of the Chicago River in Lake County, a growing suburban area 35 miles north of downtown Chicago. The site is thought to once have been a mixture of wetland, prairie, and savanna. Installation of drainage tiles by early settlers made the land suitable for farming but increased surface runoff to the river, aggravating flooding downstream.

Prairie Wolf Slough now contains 28 acres of restored wetland and wet prairie as well as 14 acres of restored forest, including rare oak savanna habitat. The area naturally stores rain and snowmelt and reduces flooding. It improves water quality by reducing stormwater runoff from nearby commercial and residential developments before reaching the river. The project also provides environmental education, recreational opportunities, and increased habitat for wildlife.

The Lake County Youth Conservation Corps cut brush, built walkways and bridges, and helped with planting. Volunteers helped to clear invasive vegetation and plant native wetland, prairie, and savanna plants. With additional training, volunteers are now taking on roles as long-term site stewards.

"This project was a huge amount of work, and it never would have succeeded without the contributions and leadership of volunteers," says the Friends' former watershed programs director David Ramsay of the 700 people who helped make the project possible. "We certainly wouldn't have got those 51,000 plant plugs in the ground without that effort."

Residents in Chicago's Ravenswood neighborhood have direct access to the Chicago River and have worked to stabilize eroding banks and to restore native vegetation.

Berteau Street, Ravenswood

Other successful ecologically oriented projects on the Chicago have been on a much smaller scale. For example, a group of neighbors in Ravenswood, a North Side city neighborhood, involved the Friends and other agencies in a bank restoration project. There were limited opportunities for large-scale runoff reduction or extensive habitat creation. But the community initiative managed to bring together neighbors and school children to provide safe neighborhood access to the river. It also stabilized eroding riverbanks and restored native vegetation along a small stretch of the river's North Branch.

City of Chicago

The initiative was first launched when a 30-foot section of riverbank collapsed near Berteau Street, creating a very steep and even more unstable river-edge. A group of neighbors asked the advice of local ecologists and civic organizations and then developed an informal plan to fix the bank and make the river a community asset.

Neighbors removed trash illegally dumped at the site. They cut back overgrown vegetation to allow needed sunlight for soil-holding groundcover and

If you want to interest people,

don't hand out a 60-page plan.

Have a cleanup.

—RICK MCANDLESS
NORTH COOK COUNTY SOIL AND
WATER CONSERVATION DISTRICT

other prairie plants, and built terraces from dead trees and other scrap wood to further reduce soil erosion.

Nearby Waters Elementary School developed an environmental education program tied to the project that introduced children to the plants and animals native to their area and allowed the children to study the ecology of urban river systems. The children also wrote poems and short stories about their experiences.

Today the riverfront habitat at Berteau Street is flourishing. It has recently expanded with the assistance from NeighborSpace, a not-for-profit land trust established by the city, the Chicago Park District, and the Cook County Forest Preserve District for the preservation of community gardens and other small-scale green spaces, which enabled a lease for riverbank land from the Metropolitan Water Reclamation District for bank improvements.

Betsy Otto

Lathrop Homes

As expertise in urban river restoration has grown, The Friends of the Chicago River and its partners have made river restoration possible on increasingly challenging sites. One such site is near the Julia C. Lathrop Homes, a Chicago Housing Authority development on the banks of the Chicago River. The area faces a former turning basin on a once heavily industrial section of the river at Diversey Avenue on Chicago's North Side.

The Friends have been working with members of the Lathrop Homes Local Advisory Council for several years. The first stage of the project, completed in 1999, was construction of the Jimmy Thomas Nature Trail. Before the trail was completed, Lathrop Homes residents avoided the river due to fears of a fall off the steep bank or a mug-

Local residents from Lathrop Homes, a Chicago Housing Authority development, restored the riverbank in their area, building a nature trail that is now a favorite spot for walkers and a source of community pride.

ging amid the overgrown vegetation. Many residents, including children and seniors, worked to remove weeds, reshape the bank, replant native vegetation, and create a woodchip path that meanders along the river. A flared wood staircase and a canoe launch and fishing platform were built as part of a post-prison job-retraining program. The river-edge park is now a favorite spot for residents and a source of community pride. The city is currently constructing a quarter-mile extension of the riverwalk trail and an under-bridge connection that will extend access from Lathrop Homes south to Fullerton Avenue.

David Jones

In October 2000, the Friends also created a floating wetlands garden in the turning basin, a first of its kind on the Chicago River. White lily, yellow lily, bur-reed, arrowhead, and pickerel weed were planted, species selected for their ability to withstand the tough conditions at the site. Some of those conditions include dramatic variations in water levels, high turbidity caused by carp activity, and significant levels of pollution and sedimentation. Carp mesh was installed to keep fish from rooting up the vegetation before it was fully established.

In addition to a core of committed adult residents who have helped make the project happen, a number of younger residents also come to workdays. "They love to be included," observes David Jones, community planner for the Friends. Between the trail and the wetland, these volunteers have planted 45 species of native plants on the two-acre site. The result, according to Jones, is "a marvelous improvement in plant diversity."

"Many things are being tried essentially for the first time on the site," says Jones of the wetland phase of the project. "We hope this will lead to wetlands being established up and down the Chicago River."

The City of Chicago is working on an extension of the Lathrop Homes riverwalk to connect neighborhoods along the river.

WOODS, WETLANDS, AND A GOLF COURSE

Lathrop Homes, Berteau Street in Ravenswood, and Prairie Wolf Slough are just a few of the projects now completed or underway on the Chicago River. A partial list of other projects follows.

Canal Origins Park

Canal Origins Park lies at the southwest corner of the South Branch Turning Basin where three of the most heavily industrial parts of the Chicago River come together on Chicago's South Side. It is historically important as the place where the Illinois and Michigan Canal was built to connect Lake Michigan with the Illinois and Mississippi Rivers.

Several years ago, before work began on the site, Andrew Hart of the Chicago Youth Centers Fellowship House, a local youth agency, described the site as an oasis. "The community is in an industrial neighborhood where kids don't have access to nature," he explained. "The Canal Origins site is an exception." Because it is home to a range of wildlife, he said, it provides "an opportunity to experience nature within an urban setting. Young people need places such as this to mature and to develop an appreciation for the environment" (Cohn 1998).

Spurred in part by cleanup and restoration efforts by Fellowship House, The Friends of the Chicago River, and other agencies, the site is now being developed as a city park. It is part of a master plan for open space acquisition by the city of Chicago that is focused on enhancing wildlife habitat, recreation (including fishing), and providing education on the historic importance of the site. The plan is a prime example of how separate sparks of interest in the river grew into a larger effort. Across the basin from the most complete section of the park, students from a local public school have become informal stewards of another river-edge site.

A canoe launch was created through a post-prison, job-retraining program.

Gompers Park Wetlands

Drained in the 1960s, a two-acre wetland and lagoon in a Chicago city park along the North Branch of the Chicago River has been restored by the Chicago Park District. The Gompers Park Wetlands project has become a living laboratory for environmental education for students from Chicago-area schools, including nearby Amundsen High School. The Park District also has

Query author

City of Chicago

The Gompers Wetlands project resulted in restoration of a two-acre lagoon by the Chicago Park District.

Ping Tom Park reflects the cultural heritage of Chicago's Chinatown as well as incorporating ecologically friendly design.

developed stewardship programs to assist native plant restoration.

North Side College Prep High School and Von Steuben High School
The Chicago Department of Environment partnered with the U.S. Army Corps of Engineers to rehabilitate the riverbank near these schools with native vegetation, a riverwalk, and an overlook for outdoor environmental school activities.

Ronan Park
The Chicago Park District has been working with The Friends of the Chicago River and local residents at Ronan Park along the river's North Branch to thin the bank of exotic woody vegetation and replant it with native woodland understory.

Ping Tom Park
A new riverfront park in Chicago's Chinatown neighborhood was built on former railroad company land and designed by architect Ernie Wong. Ping Tom Park's design reflects the neighborhood's cultural heritage and incorporates ecologically friendly design: preexisting steel-sheet piling along the river was lowered to create a softer river edge. The park is currently about five acres and will ultimately cover 12 acres.

Horner Park
Horner Park lies across the river from the Berteau Street project in Ravenswood. Numerous partners have come together to restore and improve access to the half-mile of riverbank that runs along the eastern edge of this existing city park. Plans include taking down a six-to-eight-foot-high chain link fence, opening up the dense thicket of green ash, buckthorn, and cottonwoods that line the bank, and regrading or terracing the existing steep slope to reduce erosion and provide easier access to the river.

Wilmette Golf Course
A project in the upper watershed brought together the Girl Scouts and the North Branch Watershed Project to make Wilmette Golf Course more river-friendly. The team restored ponds near the river to help reduce runoff. As part of the project, the golf course and other North Branch partners organized a seminar for other golf course managers on ecosystem-based golf course management.

RESTORATION OF THE SPIRIT: FOSTERING A CULTURE THAT CARES ABOUT THE RIVER

Coordination of these projects was not easy since the projects brought together jurisdictions and individuals unaccustomed to working with each other. But partnerships are now expected on the Chicago River. "Now it's accepted that we will do things together," says von Klan, head of the Friends. "It's not a surprise anymore. The more we do together, the easier it becomes. It's a process that builds on itself."

People's ability to connect to and care about the river has become a recurring theme in restoration projects along the Chicago River. The river's health depends on more than a list of guidelines for developers or a volunteer who spends one afternoon sticking plants in the mud; it requires citizens who show a sustained commitment to the river. As much work as has been put into the physical projects that brighten the banks of the river, the Friends and other river advocates emphasize that this intangible sense of stewardship is equally vital.

For example, since its founding, volunteers for the Friends have led walking tours to show residents their river. In the early 1990s, as water quality improved, the group added canoe trips. The Friends also developed a program called U-CAN, which annually recruits and trains a diverse group of young adults to lead canoe trips. The trainees learn canoe skills and gain awareness of river and watershed issues, which they then use to educate others. U-CAN is just one part of the Friends' extensive program of canoe trips, boat tours, and guided river walks.

Cleanups are also an outreach effort that have proven successful. In 1992, for instance, the Friends organized a cleanup at a single downtown site, Wolf Point, on the Chicago River. About 25 people helped. The next year the Friends generated enough interest to organize the first riverwide cleanup: River Rescue Day. Since then, the event has grown dramatically. It now draws dozens of partners, with almost 2,000 volunteers distributed over 40 sites. Says von Klan, "At some sites now we're going beyond trash hauling to more in-depth stewardship and restoration, like clearing brush and replanting vegetation."

Over time, the cleanups have attracted positive media attention to the river and have helped build a wider sense of stewardship. A cleanup brings people to the river and gives them something tangible to do to help make the river a better place. "We've built a connection, a sense of public ownership of the river," says von Klan. "It's important to recognize that putting people in touch with their river is also a kind of restoration."

FUNDING FOR PLANNING, PROJECTS, AND STEWARDSHIP

Funding for Chicago River projects has come from a broad base: special federal and state initiatives, foundations, corporations, city funding, and a great deal of in-kind time, services, and products.

Chicago's commitment to acquiring open space has made a significant difference for the riverfront. The city's planning budget annually includes several million dollars for riverfront public development. Since 1998, the city has also levied an open space impact fee on new residential development. "If you're bringing in more people to a neighborhood, you need to provide more open space," explains Kathy Dickhut of the city of Chicago. While the policy is not specifically geared toward the river, it has been used for riverfront open space in at least one case.

River advocates can't name the price of all that's being done and proposed on the Chicago River. It would be difficult to even guess at the total cost, says Jones, the Friends's community planner: "Consider the salaries and time of developers, city planning and environment staff, Streets and

---

CHICAGO RIVER DESIGN GUIDELINES

The Chicago River Corridor Design Guidelines and Standards, developed by the city's department of planning and development in 1999, regulates three zones regarding new development and redevelopment of riverfront sites:

1. *Riverbank zone:* Prohibits development next to the river between the water's edge and the top of the bank (except in cases of a vertical bulkhead or other structure where no riverbank exists). Exceptions are sometimes allowed to improve the aesthetics and natural function of the river and its use as a public waterway.

2. *Urban greenway zone:* Requires a 30-foot setback from the top of a bank. Development such as structures and parking lots are prohibited; exceptions are made for river-dependent uses, such as a building for a river-barge company, and for bicycle paths.

3. *Development zone:* Allows for renovation, redevelopment, or new development. Located beyond the urban greenway, this zone has the greatest potential for economic benefits and the least potential for ecological restoration or protection.

City of Chicago

While the river may not have reached Mayor Richard J. Daley's vision of fishing for one's lunch, citizens and the city have worked together to create a beautiful place to have lunch.

Sanitation, the Metropolitan Water Reclamation District. Then there are acquisition and construction costs. But everybody is in agreement that it's worthwhile and it pays off."

IMPACT

Ecologically oriented riverfront design in Chicago is still in its infancy. But what has been accomplished thus far should be an inspiration to advocates of even the most degraded urban river or stream. If revitalization can be accomplished on a river as devastated as the Chicago River once was, with enough vision and stubbornness, it can be done anywhere.

Some of the measurable results along the Chicago River include:

- Successful examples of new restoration techniques, such as naturalistic treatment of steel-sheet piling and floating urban wetlands in an old barge turning basin

- Increased recreational uses of the river, such as new canoe access points along the river, a motor boat launch, fishing tournaments, and a canoe race

- Three new planned city parks are underway along the river, joining the more than 30 acres of new park land that the city and park district developed between 1998 and 2001

- More than seven miles of landscaped riverwalk built as part of 36 private developments;

- Private sector developments with natural river-edge improvements in their site plans and riverfront amenities

Architect Ted Wolff says developers have changed how they do business. Turning developments toward the river and leaving a setback have "become routine and expected. The mayor's interest and emphasis on the river is so great. It's been insinuated into the culture."

Staff at the city's department of planning and development report that increased property values along the river have added to the city's tax base. The river is also becoming a draw for major corporations. Some have claimed that Boeing's relocation of its corporate headquarters in 2001 to the South Branch of the Chicago River is evidence that the river renaissance plays a role in the city's economy.

Extensive data on the ecological benefits of the river's restoration have not yet been collected, but early indications are promising. "Anecdotally, we see a lot more blue herons," says Jones. "We've seen soft-shelled turtle, black-crowned night herons." Jones also claims that more than 60 species of fish are currently living in the river system, which would mean that fish diversity has increased by at least 50 percent since the 1970s.

Despite these results, von Klan warns against complacency. "The job has just begun," she says. "We're doing a lot of tests, pushing the envelope, trying to get ideas on the ground and get them accepted. That's really the stage that everyone is at. We're shifting the dominant paradigm. The success is the process as much as the outcome."

LESSONS FROM THE RESTORATION OF THE CHICAGO RIVER
Collaboration

Getting a variety of partners involved and working together has been essential. The project focus in Chicago has been critical in this regard. Most of the projects highlighted here had at least five or more key partners. Small, hands-on projects up and down the watershed offered a critical opportunity for citizens, businesses, and nonprofit and government agencies to collaborate. That collaboration, in turn, made later, larger projects run more smoothly since the partners involved had already worked together.

Communication

Partnerships depend on communication: every partner needs to know what every other partner is doing. The most recent River Corridor Plan and accompanying guidelines incorporated the input of a broad range of stakeholders. Within the city government, a River Task Force Committee coordinates projects between departments. Communication is another area where the mayor has exerted leadership by setting the focus on results and interdepartmental coordination.

Connection

Members of The Friends of the Chicago River have a simple mantra: to love the river, you need to know the river. Connecting residents to their river has been an important element of the Friends' work. Projects and outreach a ctivities alike help foster a sense of stewardship and ownership in people.

Customization

Planning and projects should be in keeping with the scale and unique requirements of a site. "Make sure that the improvements are consistent with the scale of the neighborhood and the river," David Jones of the Friends advises. "The Chicago is a river you can shout across to a friend," he points out, which means that a riverfront project scaled for the mile-wide Mississippi River in Davenport, Iowa, is inappropriate for downtown Chicago. "Look to your own community," he insists. "Each and every river has its own scale, its own landscape, and its own political and economic setting."

Change

Changing minds is as important as changing the river itself. In a single generation, attitudes about the Chicago River have shifted dramatically. Allowing people to make a connection with their river and contribute to its improvement through grassroots projects has significantly changed how the river is treated.

RESOURCES

The Friends of the Chicago River
407 South Dearborn
Suite 1580
Chicago, IL 60605
www.chicagoriver.org

City of Chicago
Department of Planning
and Development
121 N. LaSalle St.
Room 1006
Chicago, IL 60602
www.ci.chi.il.us/plananddevelop

Chicago Park District
541 North Fairbanks
Chicago, IL 60610
www.chicagoparkdistrict.com

Northeastern Illinois
Planning Commission
222 South Riverside Plaza,
Suite 1800
Chicago, IL 60606
www.nipc.cog.il.us

CHAPTER 6

The Willamette River:
A Renaissance in the Making

alled Willampth, or "green water," by its first inhabit-
ants, the Willamette River in Oregon nourished surrounding wetlands, prairies, and forests. Its waters were home
to the salmon that provided physical as well as spiritual suste-
nance. It was the source of life. Today, the river remains a source
of life: millions rely on it for water, food, transportation, and
recreation. With 13 major tributaries, the river drains a watershed of approximately 12,000 square miles, almost one-eighth
of Oregon's total area. The Willamette flows 187 miles from the
river's source, south of Eugene, northward to the Columbia
River at Portland.

Over the past 200 years, the Willamette has been degraded,
cleaned up, and degraded again. For the people of Portland,
the river has alternately been a source of pride, shame, uncertainty,
and hope. Mayor Vera Katz has summed up its history best:
"The story of the Willamette reads like a potboiler romance—
one of love, abuse, neglect, partial redemption, and unrequited
promises" (Katz 2001).

Now Portland is embracing a massive effort known as River Renaissance that aims to end this cycle of ups and downs and set the river on a positive course for the future.

Two significant dates helped focus and galvanize the city and its citizens. The year 2001 marked the 150th anniversary of the city's founding on the banks of the Willamette. The year 2005 will mark the 200th anniversary of Lewis and Clark's arrival at the mouth of the Willamette as they floated down the Columbia. If the River Renaissance project succeeds, the city hopes that its completion will someday be the cause for another anniversary celebration—the year the Willamette became the centerpiece of the city's riverfront neighborhoods and its thriving economy.

CITY SNAPSHOT

Over the 17.5 miles that it flows through Portland, the Willamette River divides the city into east and west. Because the river is such an integral part of the city's identity, many Portlanders refer to their home as River City.

Portland's citizens have long been known for their environmental awareness and affinity for natural places.

Perhaps it is the influence of the river, or the surrounding forests, or the snow-capped volcanoes of Mt. Hood and Mt. Saint Helens in the distance, but Portland's citizens have long been known for their environmental awareness and affinity for natural places. One mayor in the early 1900s is said to have proposed ripping out the buildings on every other street and replacing them with rose beds.

Portland is nationally renowned for its high quality of life. Gil Kelley, director of the city's bureau of planning, describes Portland as "a city in nature, nature in the city" (Kelley 2002). More than 200 parks, an urban wildlife refuge, bicycle and pedestrian trails, and boat launches illustrate Kelley's characterization. Portland also offers an award-winning mass transit system and many urban amenities.

As Robin Cody, a travel columnist for the *Oregonian*, writes, "A great sustaining notion of this place is that salmon and steelhead still surge through the heart of a metro area of 1.6 million people. One of America's great fishing holes lies within view of a Merrill Lynch office. Here is a heron rookery within paddling distance of NBA basketball. I can dock the boat and stroll to the world's best bookstore" (Houck and Cody 2000).

Portland has received national praise for its planning efforts. According to *Governing* magazine, "It sometimes seems as if the whole country is looking to Portland as a role model for twenty-first century urban development" (Ehrenhalt 1997). In 1997, the *Utne Reader* named Portland one of the nation's "10 Most Enlightened Cities" (Walljasper 1997). Three years later, Portland made that magazine's top-10 list of most environmentally friendly cities (Utne 2000).

Trouble in River City

Over the past several decades, however, the key foundation for that "enlightened" reputation—a healthy natural environment—has been eroding. Local rivers and streams have been especially affected. As the Portland area has grown, roughly 388 miles of streams have been buried, according to a concept map study (Lowthian 2003). And as of 2002, 994 water bodies in Oregon had been declared "water quality impaired," including the entire length of the Willamette for temperature, pollutants, biological criteria, or a some combination thereof (Oregon Department of Environmental Quality 2003).

Portland's relationship to its river has been like that of many U.S. cities. For much of the last century, the Willamette was choked with waste and hidden behind seawalls, buildings, rail lines, and streets. While Portlanders prided themselves on their environmental stewardship, the river flowing through their lives was sick.

"It's time to look our history straight in the eye and admit the sad truth: a disfigured and sickly river still runs through Portland," said Katz in January 2001. "We have dammed it and diked it, filled it and diverted it, choked off its tributaries, and paved over much of its watershed, floodplains, and habitat. We've used it as a ditch, as a dumping ground, and a sewer and waste conveyor."

Population and Economy

The Willamette River basin is the fastest-growing region of the state. The Portland area alone is home to 44 percent of the state's population. Recent studies project the five-county region's population will increase by nearly 60 percent, to almost 3 million, by 2030 (Portland Metro Data Resource Center 2002).

The basin is also the state's most economically developed region. Agriculture, forestry, and business activity in the basin make up nearly three-quarters of Oregon's economic output. The largest employers in Portland include the service industry, wholesale and retail trade, manufacturing, and government.

The Port of Portland is a significant economic asset to the city and is the region's link to the global marketplace. The port exports more wheat than any other port in the country and is the fourth largest port on the west coast of the North America. In the Portland and Vancouver area, the maritime activity associated with the port generates over 21,000 jobs (Daly 2003; Martin Associates 2001).

The Port of Portland is a significant economic asset to the city and is the region's link to the global marketplace

HISTORY OF THE PORTLAND RIVERFRONT

People have lived along the Willamette's banks for approximately 10,000 years. But the major alteration and degradation of the river did not begin until European settlement.

Lewis and Clark came upon the Willamette in 1806 and camped where the University of Portland sits today. With news of great potential for timber, fur

Bureau of Planning, City of Portland, Oregon

In 1936, 4,000 schoolchildren joined a protest about the condition of the Willamette River.

trapping, and deep fertile soil for farming, European settlement began soon after. Thousands of settlers traveled the Oregon Trail to the Willamette Valley in the 1840s and 1850s. Kelley (2002) characterizes the first 100 years of European settlement and interaction with the river as years of "discovery and embrace."

Portland was incorporated as a city in 1851. Trees along the Willamette riverfront were clear-cut and a rectangular grid of buildings took their place. The grid's orientation—perpendicular and parallel to the river—demonstrates the mindset of the city founders: true north and south were not as important as the main source of their livelihood, the river.

The Thriving Seaport

Portland was ideally situated to become a thriving port. "Improvements" were necessary, however, to maintain a navigable shipping channel. Snag removal and riverbed dredging began in 1891. Dredging has continued ever since: today, the Port of Portland maintains a 40-foot deep navigation channel on the lower Columbia and Willamette rivers—and wants to increase it to 43 feet.

Portland's early harbor was soon crowded with wharves, warehouses, and cargo ships. The Willamette became a major conduit for transporting goods to California, Alaska, Asia, and beyond. Most of the early waterfront development took place on the west bank, where steeper banks allowed boats to dock and kept damaging floods to a minimum. Flooding was more of a concern on the east bank, where wetlands prevailed. It wasn't long, however, before the east bank's wetlands and farmland were overtaken by warehouses and mills built on pilings.

Toward the end of the 1800s, the bustling waterfront suffered several damaging blows. After two fires destroyed downtown buildings, a flood discouraged redevelopment. The downtown center was moved from the waterfront to a safer location several blocks away. The waterfront's transformation from a community center to a forgotten industrial district had begun.

The arrival of the railroad substantially changed the character of the riverbank. In order to make way for rail lines and other commercial development, the rail companies filled many of the ponds and marshes in the floodplain with material dredged from the riverbed. Guilds Lake was filled in, as was Mocks Bottom, a haven for waterfowl. Significant changes to the river continued as the port authority deepened the Willamette's channel west of Swan Island and joined the island to the east bank.

From "An Open Sewer" to "A River Restored"

Portland's early riverfront development, uncoordinated and controlled by individual commercial interests, would have its consequences. When Kelley speaks of the second 100 years of European settlement, from roughly 1900, he speaks of "growth and alienation."

As the riverfront was industrialized, water quality plummeted. In 1911, the Oregon Board of Health declared the Willamette's lower reaches "an open sewer" and said the fish were unsuitable for eating. Over the next decade, the river became too polluted for fishing, boating, or swimming. Raw sewage was discharged regularly into the river.

Public concern for the river grew and in 1936, 4,000 schoolchildren protested, begging polluters to clean up the river. Oregon soon had 48 separate laws relating to water pollution, but they were largely ineffective.

It wasn't until 1962 that a popular journalist named Tom McCall galvanized the public with the documentary *Pollution in Paradise*. McCall later became governor and spearheaded the initiative to clean up the Willamette.

The success of those efforts served as one of the models for the Clean Water Act, passed in 1972. That same year, a National Geographic cover story proclaimed the Willamette "a river restored" (Starbird 1972). But the story wouldn't end there.

PORTLAND'S PLANNING EFFORTS ON THE WILLAMETTE

The positive steps for the Willamette didn't begin with McCall. Portland's planning efforts and the acknowledgement of the need for natural areas began as early as 1903. That year landscape architect John Olmsted (whose stepfather, Frederick Law Olmsted, designed Central Park in New York City) was hired to create a Portland Park Plan.

Portland's early riverfront development, uncoordinated and controlled by individual commercial interests, would have its consequences.

The Port of Portland maintains a 40-foot-deep navigation channel and wants to increase that channel to 43 feet.

Olmsted laid the groundwork for the creation of Portland's 5,000-acre Forest Park, the largest wilderness park within any American city. Today, the park is home to more than 100 species of birds, 60 species of mammals, and 140 plant species.

Olmsted also proposed the creation of a system of parks linked by a network of trails and greenways. His plan was never completed, but his idea of "interconnected natural features" laid the groundwork for future efforts.

During the 1970s, the city took many of its first river-friendly planning steps. One of these steps was the decision in 1974 to demolish Harbor Drive, an expressway that dominated the waterfront, and replace it with a public park that would connect people to the river. The act generated national praise and became a source of civic pride. Today, the west bank's Tom McCall Waterfront Park is a popular place for picnickers, sunbathers, joggers, and concertgoers.

The 1970s also saw the creation of Portland's first urban wildlife refuge. Michael Houck, executive director of the Urban Greenspaces Institute and urban naturalist with the Portland Audubon Society, calls the Oaks Bottom Wildlife Refuge the city's "premier Willamette River natural area." He describes the fight to save Oaks Bottom from development as "the city's first serious foray into debates about the future management of the Portland Park system, and the larger question of the city's responsibility for retaining wildlife and wildlife habitat in the urban core" (Houck and Cody 2000).

Several factors led to the protection of Oaks Bottom. A film captured the story and helped galvanize additional public support. Changes in the Park Bureau, combined with growing political support for urban greenspaces, helped as well. Houck also tells the story of "sporadic guerilla activism," referring to handmade Wildlife Refuge signs that supporters placed throughout the area. It wasn't long before the local newspapers were referring to the area as the Oaks Bottom Wildlife Refuge. The Portland City Council finally made it official in 1988. Today, this 163-acre swath of wetlands within view of downtown Portland is home to more than 100 species of birds and is laced with several popular walking trails.

The development of the City Greenway Plan in 1979 was also a significant landmark in Portland's planning history. The plan's goals included restoration of the river as a "central axis and focus" for neighborhoods;

The development of the City Greenway Plan in 1979 was also a significant landmark in Portland's planning history.

increased public access; and conservation of natural riverbanks and habitat. The plan called for the establishment of greenway trails that would provide recreation and transportation along the length of the greenway.

The plan also established a greenway boundary, located at least 150 feet from the river's low-water line. Any new development within the boundary was—and still is—required to meet specific standards. In addition, a greenway setback was created, a minimum of 25 feet measured from the top of the bank. All new developments must dedicate a right-of-way or easement for a greenway trail within this setback.

Finally, the newly formed, four-county Metro Government established an urban growth boundary in 1980 in fulfillment of state land-use requirements. The boundary, adjusted more than 30 times since but expanded only about 2 percent, has had major consequences—some good, some bad—for Portland (Portland Metro 2003). While the growth boundary was designed to limit sprawl in the city's outlying rural areas, Gil Kelley of Portland's planning bureau feels it may have had an unintended consequence. He says some now have the perception that "all nature exists outside of the boundary, and there's nothing natural within." Combating that perception remains a challenge as planners and conservationists strive to preserve natural areas and create new ones within Portland's city limits.

A NEW VISION: RIVER RENAISSANCE

While Portland has taken steps over the past 40 years to establish parks, trails, and cleanup plans, they haven't been enough for the Willamette. Since the 1972 *National Geographic* cover story, Portland has faced continued issues with the river's water quality, primarily because of combined sewer overflows, runoff from urban areas, and lasting effects of industrial and other development practices. The problem has gotten so serious that Portland now faces a mandate from the state to clean up the river.

The city is under federal scrutiny as well: a six-mile stretch of the Willamette that flows through Portland harbor was declared a Superfund site in December 2000. A century of industrial and maritime activity has contaminated river sediments with toxics such as PCBs, dioxin, mercury, and several pesticides. Many Willamette River fish suffer from deformities, lesions, and tumors. The Oregon Department of Environmental Quality has warned residents against eating the fish because the toxics pose a cancer risk.

As if that weren't enough, in 1999 two species in the Willamette—the steelhead and the Chinook salmon—were listed as threatened under the Endangered Species Act. As these fish travel from the ocean, they use the Willamette to reach upstream spawning grounds. The river is also important to the juvenile fish, which need food and refuge as they migrate downstream. Portland is required by law to restore habitat for these species.

These factors have created the impetus that drives the River Renaissance project. As Kelley (2002) explains, these realities are "forcing us to deal with the issues that have been facing us for a long time [and] to step back and take a holistic look at what will fix it for the long term." The river's troubles indicate deeper problems in the city, he suggests. "For years, we've ignored our very reason for being—the soul of our city, the river," he says. Because "the river is so symbolic and meaningful in terms of its ability to focus us, it made sense to rotate the river up to the highest priority." When Kelley talks about River Renaissance and Portland's next 200 years, he says it should be a time of "rediscovering pieces of our past."

Kelley's sentiments are echoed by Portland's current mayor, Vera Katz, who is urging Portlanders to unite and "recapture the heart of our city." The mayor says she wants to make the river Portland's "front yard."

Imagine a vibrant city centered on a healthy Willamette River. Look to the future of Portland where a natural river system thrives and links together industry, habitat, business districts, and neighborhoods.

—Portland Mayor Vera Katz
January 2001

River Renaissance, led by the city's Bureau of Planning, encompasses new initiatives as well as efforts already underway. It unites Portland's Clean River Plan, the Endangered Species Act program, an update of the Willamette River Greenway plan, urban renewal plans, parks plans, and others.

The visioning process for River Renaissance began in the fall of 2000. More than 1,000 Portlanders participated in public workshops, guided tours, and classroom sessions in which they contributed to the River Renaissance Vision. Their ideas were refined as more public comments were gathered, and the Vision was endorsed by city council in March 2001. Components of the River Renaissance program have gone through the next stage of research and planning, with some nearing or beginning early implementation. A full action plan is currently being developed and is scheduled for adoption by the city council in April 2004.

Although the first three years of the program have seen some dramatic results, it is too soon to tell how much of the River Renaissance Vision can or will come to fruition. Many of the project specifics and funding sources have not yet been ironed out or identified. Kelley readily admits that some of the results may not be seen for 50 or 100 years. But he thinks it is wise to have given River Renaissance such a long timeframe. He explains that River Renaissance is about "planning for the future." Thinking long-term "helps people think out of the box. This way, big ambitious projects don't seem so impossible."

Another benefit of the long timeframe is that funding can be more easily secured for the project. Portland alone will not be able to provide all funding. Partnerships with state and federal agencies, private foundations, and landowners will be essential. Kelley highlights the Army Corps of Engineers as a promising potential partner. By February 2003, Portland had in place a cost share agreement with the Corps, which Kelley (2003) said could tap into hundreds of millions of dollars in Water Resources Development Act funds. He also plans to rely heavily on volunteer work by citizens and neighborhood groups.

Kelley agrees that even though the city's thinking and planning is long-term, it still must come up with tangible short-term victories in order to maintain public involvement and support. He laid out 10 early action items to the city council in early 2003, with a total budget of more than $5 million. He estimated that the projects would cost the city $2 million, with the remainder leveraged from federal and private funds.

A series of events in the summer of 2003 demonstrate the city's efforts to galvanize public interest and involvement. In July, a new three-mile section of the riverfront pedestrian trail called the Springbank Corridor was opened with much ceremony, with rides on a vintage steam train and other events. The Portland Development Commission adopted the Development Agreement for the South Waterfront district, and city council indicated it would adopt a revised version after addressing concerns that the plan does not require affordable housing at the level set by other city standards. A river ferry also began a one-month demonstration run between stops on both sides of the river, again relying on volunteer effort.

Portland has been on the cutting edge of planning, and Kelley wants to keep it that way. He says that in the next two years of this unprecedented effort, city planners will be "inventing, pushing the envelope of science and art. . . . We can't just import solutions." But the city's first attempt to revise zoning in protected areas near streams, called the Healthy Streams Initiative, demonstrated that citizens may push back. The first iteration of more stringent zoning requirements for protection, conservation, and transition zones received what Kelley (2003) termed "a tough reception" by landowners who objected to the new

Bureau of Planning, City of Portland, Oregon

Not all cities have an official bird, but Portland does. About 15 years ago, Michael Houck, the Audubon Society of Portland's urban naturalist, got the idea to make the great blue heron Portland's official city bird. The mayor agreed and an annual Great Blue Heron Week began. This bird, a symbol of the Willamette, is a constant reminder to Portlanders of their connection to the river.

requirements. City officials responded with 100 site visits to hear the landowners' concerns and are reevaluating their streamside property inventories before proposing new protective zones.

The Five Goals of River Renaissance

River Renaissance Goal 1: Make the river clean and healthy for fish, wildlife, and people by emphasizing riverbank restoration, elimination of combined sewer overflows, and better stormwater management. In order for the Willamette to be healthy, its watershed must be healthy as well. Portland recognizes it will have to coordinate with upstream and downstream communities and government agencies. Improving buffers along nearby creeks and tributaries will be part of the plan, and the type of restoration will vary by location. "While it's not realistic to expect native cottonwood forests along the Willamette in the heart of downtown Portland," says Houck (2003), of the Urban Greenspaces Institute and Audubon Society of Portland, "it's perfectly reasonable to demand ecologically meaningful restoration for fish and wildlife on the banks and within the Willamette River Greenway of a major redevelopment project like South Waterfront, where the city is providing millions of public dollars to redevelop a 140-acre brownfield site."

On the Willamette itself, streamside habitat and floodplain areas will be restored and protected to improve water quality, provide natural flood control, and improve conditions for fish and wildlife. The city's planning bureau has proposed increasing the mandatory 25-foot greenway setback along the Willamette to 100 feet. The South Waterfront development will be one of the larger projects to incorporate this new, wider buffer, but the city has already implemented it elsewhere, such as at a new police stable in the River District, a redevelopment zone in the city's northwest quadrant. Native vegetation will be planted and invasive species controlled along the greenway and elsewhere on the river.

Much of the Willamette's riverbank is lined with concrete and engineered structures. Fifty-one percent of the bank is armored with rocks and other riprap; 21 percent is covered by structures such as pilings; 26 percent is natural; and 2 percent is bioengineered. "The river right now is a canal with hard edges that runs through downtown. We need to open it up, to green the banks up," explains Kelley (2002).

Included in the River Renaissance Vision are plans for more natural banks and improved river conditions. The city's first step toward these goals was publication of a report, "Framework for Integrated Management of Watershed and River Health," released in draft form in November 2002. The report defines watershed health in terms of stream flow and hydrology, physical habitat, water quality and biological communities. It describes methods and tools for implementation and evaluation, with indicators and quantitative objectives for each area (City of Portland 2002).

Another important piece of the River Renaissance puzzle is the elimination of combined sewer overflows (CSOs). More than 50 CSOs enter the Willamette about 100 times a year, sending nearly 2.8 billion gallons of untreated waste into the river annually.

State-imposed deadlines commit the city to halting 94 percent of these overflows by 2011. Laying the new pipes and expanding the city's treatment plant to stop sewage, storm runoff, and other debris from overflowing into the river will cost the city approximately $1 billion over 20 years (City of Portland Bureau of Environmental Services 2003). It will be the largest construction project in the city's history. Portland's sewer ratepayers—who already pay among the highest urban bills in the nation—will bear the cost.

To tackle the stormwater problem at its source, the city will push new building and street designs that improve drainage flow. For example, a

Bureau of Planning, City of Portland, Oregon

development at Buckman Heights in southeast Portland was designed to allow 100 percent of its stormwater to infiltrate into the ground. As a result, thousands of gallons of runoff never entered Portland's combined sewer system. Rooftop gardens and other "green roof" designs already gaining popularity in Portland will likely become more prevalent. Several additional demonstration projects were completed by 2003, including the Multnomah County Building's ecoroof and a bioswale parking lot at the Oregon Natural Resource Council. The Portland Department of Transportation has also adopted best management practices in erosion control, pollution prevention, water quality, and runoff management.

The first goal of River Renaissance is to make the river clean and healthy for fish, wildlife, and people.

In addition, residents will be encouraged to plant native vegetation in their yards to conserve water and improve water quality. A more extensive tree canopy will help intercept and filter rainwater before it reaches the river. The underlying philosophy is, as Kelley says, that "green infrastructure needs to be as readable as the city streets and the built infrastructure. The 'green' needs to be the other grid."

The Superfund cleanup at Portland Harbor will be another massive undertaking. The Port of Portland and 72 potentially responsible parties will be part of the effort to remove or isolate pollutants in the harbor and at their source. The city has completed initial testing of fish and sediment for contamination. The timetable for cleanup envisions completion of a feasibility study containing cleanup alternatives by autumn 2005, with adoption of cleanup and contaminated sediment disposal options by autumn 2006 (U.S. EPA 2003b). The cleanup effort will be essential if fish populations in the Willamette are to become healthy and safe for consumption again.

All of the above efforts will also aid recovery of imperiled salmon populations. But the special habitat requirements for salmon may create new obstacles for riverfront developers. For example, a park slated for the east bank was to include paths, overlooks, a boathouse, and much-improved river access. But the National Marine Fisheries Service raised concerns that the park and associated activity would damage important shallow water salmon habitat. The city has modified its plans for Crescent Park to address habitat concerns (Lozovoy 2003). In early 2003, Portland also finalized an agreement with federal permitting agencies to streamline future project reviews.

The city's proposals for larger setbacks also concern some private landowners. In response to these concerns, the Clean Streams Initiative slowed down its implementation schedule to consult streamside landowners and revise its ecological inventory.

A city-sponsored design handbook published in 2001 gives guidance for projects that affect the riverfront. Its purpose is "to establish a common frame of reference and common goals for all who are concerned with development at the river's edge," and "to guide riverbank design in directions that have multiple natural resource and urban benefits." The design notebook summarizes current riverbank conditions that affect endangered species, lists scientific "pathways and indicators" toward species recovery, and recommends design objectives and a process to meet them (City of Portland 2001).

Despite the challenges posed by restoration plans and the need to balance the river's health with residents' interests, Houck hopes River Renaissance will combine "financing schemes with planning processes to make sure we treat places as interconnected. You can't look at one restoration project without thinking about the other one downstream."

River Renaissance Goal 2: Maintain and enhance the working harbor and its infrastructure. River Renaissance promises that the Port of Portland will remain a vital economic asset. To follow through on its pledge, the city will need to maintain this asset while it also restores river health. But the harbor and its users will also face challenges as they adapt to the river's expanded natural and recreational functions.

The city aims to explore and adopt new technologies, designs, and industrial practices that can exist in harmony with habitat and water-quality restoration. The Superfund designation will also be an opportunity to create new partnerships as well as new environmental cleanup industries and technologies.

"As we are doing cleanup to mitigate for the damage, we can identify great opportunities and help the city identify projects," explains Jim Middaugh, a Portland Endangered Species Act program leader. "We can take restoration work that is required and apply it to projects that would aid in salmon recovery."

Some of the freeways, cargo docks, and rail lines that currently dominate the riverfront will likely be redesigned and better integrated into the larger built and natural environment. Already, the Port of Portland took advantage of a Toyota distribution center's most recent lease renewal to redevelop the company's 100-acre property. More than 1,000 feet of pavement were pulled up, and the riverbank was replanted.

In addition, regional transportation objectives linked to the harbor are to be integrated into river protection activities. One possible project is the burial of the interstate that currently crowds the east bank, just as Harbor Drive was transformed to Waterfront Park in the 1970s. As mayor, Katz has appointed a steering committee to review possible improvements to Portland's expressway infrastructure in coming decades. The redevelopment plan for the South Waterfront district also includes extensive transportation upgrades, from a streetcar extension to new city streets to an overhead tram.

River Renaissance Goal 3: Embrace the river as Portland's front yard. While the river is already a city centerpiece, the River Renaissance Vision aims to make the river even more accessible to residents so that it becomes an integral part of everyday life.

More destinations and access points will be created along the river corridor. Ramps, boat slips, docks, and marinas will provide new opportunities for boating, fishing, swimming, and other activities. Trails, bike paths, and view corridors will connect new and existing neighborhoods to and across the river. An expanded trail network will encourage walking and biking and will thus reduce car traffic and the toxicity of street runoff that reaches the river. The Greenway Trail will connect accessible riverside segments, with the goal to create a continuous recreation and transportation corridor along both banks of the river.

Historically, most of the riverfront redevelopment has occurred on the west bank. But that changed in May 2001 when the Eastbank Esplanade officially opened. The Esplanade, which cost roughly $30 million to build, is a narrow linear trail for foot, bicycle, and other pedestrian traffic

The third goal of River Renaissance is to embrace the river as Portland's front yard.

Bureau of Planning, City of Portland, Oregon

that follows the riverbank. It gives residents more access to the river, but many feel the project fell short because it didn't include riverbank or habitat restoration. But residents concede that, even though the noisy interstate dominates the Esplanade, the trail is a first step toward east bank riverfront access.

A three-mile extension of the Esplanade called the Springwater Corridor opened in 2002. It follows a rail corridor and provides pedestrian access from the city's north side to Oaks Bottom, on the south side. At the July 2003 grand opening celebration, volunteers gave rides on historic steam engine trains while joggers, walkers, bicyclists, and others traveled the trail. The area also features restoration efforts to replace invasive Himalayan blackberry with native dogwood, elderberry, Indian plum, and willows. Along the path, an art installation depicts geological strata.

The city recognizes the need to acquire lands for parks and natural areas. In spring 1995, Portland metro-area voters approved a bond measure that created a one-time $135 million fund to acquire important natural areas. As of July 2003, Metro, the regional governing body, had acquired 7,935 acres of open space in 251 separate property transactions, incorporating the land into 14 regional natural areas and six regional trail and greenway projects throughout the four-county region. But acquisition can only go so far. As Houck says, "Acquisition alone is never going to cut it—there's never going to be enough money."

Travis Williams, executive director of the river advocacy group Willamette Riverkeeper, thinks existing parks, such as the city's popular Waterfront Park, could be improved. He would like to see the seawall that currently separates the park and downtown from the river torn down or at least reconfigured. Getting rid of the seawall—a project that may be incorporated into River Renaissance—would allow people to have closer contact with the water. "There are drawings of what a waterfront park would look like without the seawall. It would provide a much better experience for the people who go there. It's not a flooding issue, just a question of expense," Williams says.

Finally, art will also play an important role in connecting Portlanders to their river. The city already has a number of fountains, murals, and sculptures that reflect the river's importance in city life. At the south end of the Eastbank Esplanade, for example, is a bronze relief map of the Willamette oriented toward the river and its sources in the Cascades to the south and east and its confluence with the Columbia to the north. Portland's River Renaissance Vision provides for the construction of a "world-class monument in a prominent riverfront location." The monument will seek not only to connect civic life with the river, but could also reinforce the river's role in city history.

River Renaissance Goal 4: Create vibrant waterfront districts and neighborhoods. The river is to become the unifying feature of riverfront neighborhoods and a major contributor to the appeal and activity of these districts.

New development, such as 770 units of housing in the River District, will be oriented toward the river and will include greenway setbacks and river access. The River District is a high-density urban residential neighborhood that currently has 5,000 housing units under construction, including more than 2,000 affordable units, in vacant and underused land on the north edge of downtown Portland. The project also includes a connection to the Central City Streetcar system and the classical Chinese Garden in Portland's Chinatown, and has acquired 4.5 acres for park space (Portland Development Commission 2003).

More of the riverfront throughout the city will be dedicated to nature walks, urban promenades, playgrounds, marinas, cafes, museums, outdoor learning venues, Native American history, public art, and natural history

The fourth goal of River Renaissance encourages the orientation of new development toward the river with greenway setbacks and river access.

Bureau of Planning, City of Portland, Oregon

interpretation. Festivals, regattas, and sporting events will build awareness of and celebrate the river.

Existing riverfront developments, such as River Place, built in the 1980s,
feature a mix of marinas, shops, restaurants, outdoor seating, and art gal-
leries. What places like River Place lack are any benefits for the natural
river. The riverbank there is riprapped and offers no physical connection
to the river, except via the marina docks. River Renaissance plans to take
the proven, successful model of mixed-use development embodied by River
Place several steps further to incorporate ecosystem needs.

*Replacing hard edges with natural
vegetation brings people closer
to the river and provides habitat.*

*The North Macadam District
(now the South Waterfront District)
was natural (1867, above), then
a brownfield (1964, top right),
and now a site for extensive
redevelopment (2001, bottom right).*

One of these new opportunities exists in a place known as the South Waterfront District (formerly the North Macadam District), a privately owned 130-acre brownfield site immediately south of downtown Portland. Formerly used for barge and shipbuilding, the land is now slated for redevelopment with apartments, offices, a biotech research center, shops, and mass transit, including an extension of an existing streetcar line and a new aerial tram to the Oregon Health Sciences University. The city has negotiated an agreement with the developers of the South Waterfront's 30-acre central district to restore the riverbanks and allow for an average 100-foot vegetated greenway buffer, largely to improve salmon habitat. "It will be interesting to see the progression of something like River Place to what could be at North Macadam," says Travis Williams. "The city has a chance to really accomplish something good for the river there."

In addition to this residential and commercial development, new transportation options—such as river taxis, ferries, tour boats, and cruise ships—will also link waterfront neighborhoods. A river-ferry pilot project began operating for a month of weekends in July 2003 using an open-air yawboat, patterned after river transport from Portland's early years. Volunteers from RiversWest, a nonprofit that seeks to preserve maritime traditions, took passengers for free on hourly weekend runs from the West Side's River Place, across the river to the Oregon Museum of Science and Industry, and to two stops along the Eastbank Esplanade.

The South Waterfront Development Agreement, adopted by the city council in August 2003, provides one specific example of the potential economic boost provided by these new projects. The proposal for the area's 31-acre central district along the riverfront would drive $1.9 billion in total investment: $1.6 billion in private funds, $219 million in public investment, and $131 million in tax increment financing. The largest single development project in Portland history projects 1,000 construction jobs, 300 indirect jobs, and would include a biomedical research facility for the Oregon Health Sciences University, which will create 2,500 jobs (Mazziotti and Tweedy 2003).

River Renaissance Goal 5: Promote partnerships, leadership, and education. River Renaissance is not a single program; it is an umbrella for many programs. In that sense, it won't succeed without strong collaboration.

A group called the River Renaissance Partners—made up of government, tribal, business, neighborhood, and environmental leaders—has been assembled to advocate for implementation of the River Renaissance vision. In addition, a multijurisdictional organization called the River Trust was established to coordinate local river improvement efforts among 13 management agencies that have jurisdiction over the river, and with upstream and downstream communities. City officials say the River Trust was instrumental in devising an agreement with federal fisheries managers to streamline permitting of projects that are part of the city's Endangered Species Act response (Hart 2003; Reed 2003).

Educating and involving the community, especially through local schools, is also an important part of the city's plan to promote stewardship of the river. Even though the visioning process is over, Gil Kelley and others continue to talk with local groups and conduct informal slide shows and presentations about River Renaissance throughout the city. A second set of public meetings and reviews will accompany the development of the River Renaissance action plan in 2004. Kelley knows that building support and maintaining contact with the public will be essential to success.

River Renaissance is a remarkably ambitious river revitalization effort that may help ensure the health and beauty of the Willamette for future populations of Portlanders.

Bureau of Planning, City of Portland, Oregon

LOOKING FORWARD

River Renaissance is arguably the most ambitious river revitalization effort in recent U.S. history. It seeks to tackle the needs of a growing population as well as of endangered salmon. It encompasses restoration goals for streambanks, streets, and residential yards in downtown Portland as well as for distant watershed locations. It must serve as the umbrella for a variety of local, state, and federal programs. It requires the collaboration of diverse parties, from the industries that use the harbor to private landowners to conservationists.

But if any city is likely to succeed with such a task, it is Portland, a city known for its long history of planning and environmental stewardship. The Willamette was a model for restoration in the 1970s, and it can be again.

More Information on River Ecosystems

It is important for local communities to consider the specific functions, processes, and characteristics of their rivers so that restoration and management approaches that make sense in, for example, the coniferous forest watersheds of the Pacific Northwest are not applied to Midwestern prairie rivers without careful consideration of each river's special requirements. For more information about different river types, consult Cushing and Allan (2001) and Federal Interagency Stream Restoration Working Group (2001).

The first section of this appendix on geographically distinct river types, is adapted with permission from *Streams: Their Ecology and Life* by Colbert E. Cushing and J. David Allan (2001). The second section, "Habitats and River Ecosystems," is the work of American Rivers.

GEOGRAPHICALLY DISTINCT RIVER TYPES

There are several types of rivers that are characteristic of different regions and unique settings. The particular physical, chemical, and biological character of each will not be discussed here. Nor does this report address distinct river types with respect to how their urban riverfront challenges may vary. But it is important for local communities to consider the specific functions, processes, and characteristics of their rivers so that they can apply the most appropriate restoration and management approaches.

Desert Rivers of the Southwest

Major streams in arid regions receive their water from areas of high elevation, often many kilometers upslope, where precipitation is high and usually persistent. This precipitation is often seasonal and thus flows are usually timed to annual runoff events occurring far away. This is also characteristic of major tributaries and results in the distinctive flow regimes of desert rivers and streams.

Physical conditions can be very different from stream to stream and even within a single stream basin. Air temperatures are high and streams receive ample sunlight. The orientation of the streambed can cause local variations; if the bed is well shaded by cliffs, temperatures are ameliorated from those up- or down-stream where the full impact of the sun is felt.

Riparian vegetation is scant and usually is found only along the edges of the flood channel; the streambed itself is devoid of vegetation. When the streams contain water for any significant period of time, the water is usually clear and shallow; thus with the absence of shading riparian vegetation, the potential for high primary production is present, and this is usually found in these situations.

Southeastern Rivers

The southeastern region of the United States contains a wide diversity of streams. These range from high-gradient, clear-flowing headwater streams, which exhibit ecological characteristics in common with similar streams found elsewhere in the country, to the ecologically unique, blackwater streams found on the coastal plain region of several southeastern states.

The low gradient of blackwater streams results in a slow-flowing river with a sandy bottom. The sandy bottoms of these rivers would suggest that benthic invertebrate communities would be small and the streams unproductive. This is not the case. The sandy bottoms contain oligochaetes, several groups of dipteran larvae, and mollusks. Blackwater streams have an extensive floodplain that is inundated for several months each year, with important ecological consequences. As a result of these broad floodplains, little to no human development has occurred along these rivers.

Warm-Water Rivers of the Midwest

The small streams and rivers of America's heartland have fewer advocates and have received less study than cold-water streams with their highly valued salmonids. Most originate at low altitude and have low gradients. Long runs and pools predominate, but shallow, gravelly riffles can be found where the geology and gradient combine appropriately. Cascades, waterfalls, and boulders are rare. Substrate varies from place to place, of course, but often includes sand, silt, and mud. Water temperatures are cold in the north, then grade into cool and warm waters as one proceeds south.

In their pristine state, and where they have not been greatly altered, the streams and smaller rivers [are heavily shaded by] the broadleaf forests of the Midwest. . . .

Multiple glacial invasions over the past few million years shaped the northern half of this region and substantially influenced the southern half. The most recent glacial retreat profoundly affected the landscape and its drainage pattern. . . . In regions of deep glacial deposits, rainwater infiltrates easily, resulting in extensive groundwater aquifers. Hydrographs are very constant in these superstable groundwater streams. In regions with extensive lake deposits of clay, soils are very impermeable, and stream runoff is very responsive to rain events, or "flashy."

Large Rivers of the West

Several large rivers have headwaters in the western United States, including the Columbia, Colorado, Missouri, Yellowstone, Snake, Arkansas, and Rio Grande Rivers. The ecological history of these rivers can be summed up in a single word—abuse. This abuse largely has been due to the construction of large hydroelectric and storage dams to produce cheap and abundant electrical energy, to supply irrigation water to crops throughout the western United States, and to control floods.

Preimpoundment ecology. Most of the free-flowing reaches of the upper Colorado River remain relatively pristine, with a rich and diverse fauna and flora of fishes, macroinvertebrates, and algae. Little is known of the preimpoundment ecology of the lower Colorado River Basin, that region most severely impacted by the large dams.

Postimpoundment ecology. In general, the aquatic habitat of the postimpounded lower Colorado River is characterized by more constant thermal regimes (though waters immediately below dams usually are cooler), higher salinities, lower turbidity, and reduced scouring by bed sediments resulting in a more profuse benthic algal (periphyton) population. Macroinvertebrate fauna and fish populations remain diverse but are composed of species different from those found prior to extensive impoundment.

Cold-Desert Spring Streams

A group of unique spring streams occurs in the cold-desert, shrub-steppe region of the western United States, largely in western Utah, Nevada, southern Idaho, eastern Oregon, and southeastern Washington. These regions are characterized by low winter and high summer temperatures, low annual precipitation, and regional vegetation dominated by big sagebrush and an understory of perennial bunchgrasses; cheatgrass now occupies much of the area that has been disturbed. Research on these ecosystems has been largely limited to three sites in southeastern Washington and one in southeastern Idaho, yet several interesting features about their ecology have been discovered.

Generally, these spring streams are closed; they arise from seepage areas, flow for various distances, and disappear into the arid soils. Perennial flow is ordinarily present, but the stream terminus usually recedes as the summer season progresses.

Primary production is relatively high in these small spring streams. This would be expected given their openness to the sun, a rich population of algae, watercress, and other instream macrophytes, and adequate concentrations of nitrogen and phosphorus.

Alpine Streams

There are two types of streams that can be found flowing in alpine situations, essentially those regions above timberline. One type originates in seeps and bogs, lake outlets, small springs, or melt from snowfields. The second type originates as glacier melt.

Alpine streams are usually crystal clear, cold, and flow through a treeless area of scenic alpine tundra. Riparian vegetation can be fairly abundant, especially as the streams approach timberline. The growing season is usually quite short, limited to the brief period between the disappearance of the ice-cover in late spring and early summer, when water temperatures begin to warm up, to the onset of winter conditions in early fall. Despite this brief period of time, flourishing communities of algae, macroinvertebrates, and fishes can be found in many of these systems; Eurothocladius, a midge, is commonly found in cold, snow-fed high streams.

The second type of stream that can be found in alpine situations results from the melting of glaciers and [flows] from the glacier's terminus. These unique streams have special characteristics that shape their biological communities. As expected, the waters are extremely cold (at or near freezing) year round, and they are milk-white in color because of the heavy load of suspending silt resulting from the grinding action of the glacier on the rocks over which it flows. Given these two factors, cold temperatures and a heavy silt load, it is not surprising to find that the biological communities found in these streams are quite depleted and highly restricted in diversity.

HABITATS AND RIVER ECOSYSTEMS

Rivers provide habitat to many plants and animals. These habitats consist of benthic, aquatic, and terrestrial components. The *benthic zone* consists of the streambed and the plants and animals that live in, under, or close to it. In this zone, species generally are attached to or buried in the substrate and are accustomed to being submerged. The *aquatic zone* includes the flowing water and the animals in it, such as fish, insects, reptiles, amphibians, and some mammals. It also includes floating plants such as algae. The *terrestrial zone* comprises the adjacent upland and the plants and animals that live on the land that is seldom submerged. It is important to note that river corridors function as a single ecosystem with numerous connections and interactions among the benthic, aquatic, and terrestrial components (FISRWG 2001).

These three zones are the most important river habitats that should be considered when riverfront plans and development and restoration decisions are being made. River habitat zones and their importance for riverfront planning and design decisions are discussed in more detail in Chapter 3 of this report under Planning Principles and Design Principles.

Benthic Zone

Plants and animals found along and near the streambed vary significantly based on the type of substrate and other conditions (e.g., water temperature, oxygen and other nutrient levels) present at the bottom of streams and rivers. In the same way that different plants grow in different soil types on land, the composition and abundance of aquatic insects (macroinvertebrates) has been observed to be quite different in snags (fallen trees), sand, bedrock, and cobble along the bottom of a single stream reach of the same river (FISRWG 2001).

The importance of another component of the benthic zone has only recently become understood: the *hyporheic zone*. The hyporheic zone is the area that lies below the water and substrate at the bottom of the river. This transition zone provides habitat for aquatic insects, protozoa, and bacteria populations that are specially adapted to this environment, which is limited in food, oxygen, space, and light (Biksey and Brown 2001). It functions as the surface/groundwater boundary through which water, oxygen, and other nutrients seep into the river. This zone is a layer that surrounds the sides and bottom of a river channel, and it can extend a few inches from the channel, or it can reach a distance of nearly two miles. Its average depth can be up to 30 yards (Stanford and Ward 1988).

In urban settings, planners and other decision makers must be cognizant of the hyporheic zone and its importance for healthy rivers. The area beneath and surrounding the stream channel is often used for water and sewer pipes, transmission lines, and other infrastructure. Digging in these sensitive areas, removing hyporheic substrates to lay pipes and other infrastructure, and periodic maintenance activities can all cause severe damage.

FIGURE A-1. THE HYPORHEIC ZONE

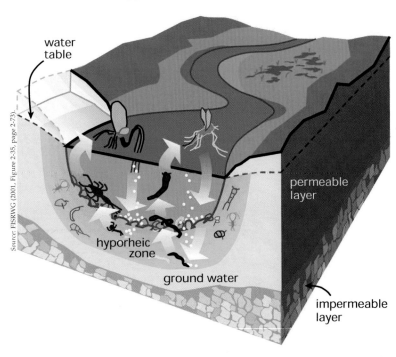

Members of the stream benthic community migrate by different means through the hyporheic zone.

Aquatic Zone

River habitats vary with local conditions. Animal and plant species will differ between a shaded, swift-flowing mountain stream and a deep, broad river with warm, slow-moving water. Ecosystems also vary along a river's length as it grows from small head-water streams to large floodplain rivers. The plants and animals within a river's aquatic zone, therefore, can vary significantly between headwaters and mouth.

This way of thinking about rivers is known as the river continuum concept. It helps to explain the unique connectivity of biological processes within rivers and streams: where organic matter comes from, how it moves, how it is stored, and how it is consumed by biological communities.

In its first, uppermost section, typical of headwaters streams, a stream receives organic material directly from the adjacent landscape through leaf-fall and woody debris. In the second, organic material is also produced within a stream's aquatic zone through the growth of plants and algae. In the third, the river contains all of the organic material and energy from the upper sections, and receives most of its organic material in the form of sediment from sources upstream and direct land runoff (FISRWG 2001). All of these sections of the aquatic zone can be rich in fungi and bacteria, microscopic animals like plankton, aquatic insects, algae and other aquatic plants, and fish. Amphibians, reptiles, small mammals, and birds are often also present (MacBroom 1998).

In urban landscapes, changes to vegetation along streams as well as dams and other in-stream and floodplain structures disrupt the normal flow of organic material and movement of aquatic life. These changes to a river's aquatic zone can have a significant impact on river health downstream.

Terrestrial Zone

The ecological integrity of river ecosystems is integrally tied to the ecological character-istics of the upland plant and animal communities that lie along the river, as well as to the entire watershed.

FIGURE A-2. THE RIVER CONTINUUM CONCEPT

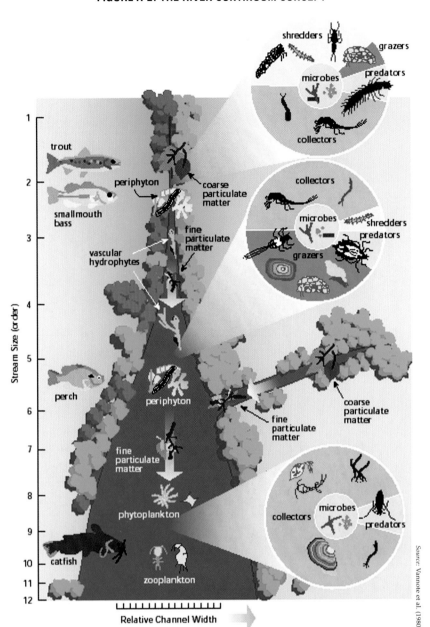

Source: Vannote et al. (1980)

The river continuum concept helps make clear the complex, changing environment that makes rivers different from lakes and ponds. It also helps to explain why human activities can have more drastic effects on water quality and animal life.

The *riparian zone* is the area immediately adjacent to a river. It is the transition between the stream and its upland. It may consist of wetlands, relatively level upland, or steep hillsides that slope to the water's edge. Even if riparian areas are relatively dry and are thus not strictly wetlands, they are critical to the entire river. Riparian vegetation is the main source of organic detritus for headwater streams, and is thus the basis of the food chain.

The riparian zone also helps shade the water, lowering temperatures and providing cover for fish and terrestrial animals. If it is healthy and of adequate width, the riparian zone provides important physical habitat for many mammals, birds, and other animals. It can also offer a connected corridor for animal movement, particularly in landscapes fragmented by human activity. Healthy riparian zones also slow and filter contaminants from upland runoff, and the roots of riparian vegetation help to stabilize riverbanks and thus prevent erosion (FISRWG 2001).

Wetlands are often found directly along rivers as well as in upland areas near the river. A wide variety of wetlands exists across the United States because of regional and local differences in hydrology, vegetation, water chemistry, soils, topography, climate, and other factors. Wetlands perform many critical functions: storing floodwaters, trapping excess sediment, recycling nutrients, providing wildlife habitat, recharging or discharging groundwater, and contributing to the beauty of the landscape (FISRWG 2001). Wetlands also serve as paths for seasonal migrations and may form the main link between large open space areas. Some animals spend their entire life in wetland or aquatic habitats; others use them as nursery grounds or as sources of food or cover.

List of References

"Additional Acreage for Wetlands in New State Park." 2003. *St. Louis Front Page*, January 12. Available at www.slfp.com/STC-News010803.htm.

Alaya, Ana M. 2000. "An Artist Adopts the River." *Newark Star-Ledger*, September 20.

Aldrich, Robert. 2003. Director of Information Services, Land Trust Alliance, Washington, D.C. Interview with authors, June 4.

Allen, Diana. 2002. Interpretive Specialist, National Park Service Rivers and Trails Program, St. Louis. Telephone interview with authors, June 28.

Alley, William M., Thomas E. Reilly, and O. Lehn Franke. 1999. *Sustainability of Ground-Water Resources*. U.S. Geological Survey Circular 1186. Denver: U.S. Geological Survey.

America Outdoors. 2003. "National River Cleanup Week: Interest Is High for 2003 Event!" Press release, February.

American Forests and USDA Forest Service. 2001. *Regional Ecosystem Analysis for the Willamette/Lower Columbia Region of Northwestern Oregon and Southwestern Washington State: Calculating the Value of Nature*. Washington, D.C.: American Forests.

American Rivers. 2003a. "10 Ways Dams Damage Rivers." [Accessed December 18]. Available at www.americanrivers.org/damremoval/tenreasons.htm.

_____. 1999. *In Harm's Way: The Costs of Floodplain Development*. [Accessed August 19, 2003]. Available at www.americanrivers.org/floodplainstoolkit/inharmsway.htm.

_____. 2003b. "Napa Makes Way for the River." [Accessed June 23]. Available at www.americanrivers.org/floodplainstoolkit/napa.htm.

_____. 2003c. "Reducing Flood Damage—Naturally—in Tulsa." [Accessed June 23]. Available at www.americanrivers.org/floodplainstoolkit/tulsa.htm.

American Rivers, Friends of the Earth, and Trout Unlimited. 1999. *Dam Removal Success Stories: Restoring Rivers through Selective Removal of Dams That Don't Make Sense*. Washington, D.C.: American Rivers.

American Rivers, National Resources Defense Council, and Smart Growth America. 2002. "Paving Our Way to Water Shortages: How Sprawl Aggravates the Effects of Drought." Research report, August. Also available at www.americanrivers.org/landuse/sprawldroughtreport.htm.

Anacostia Waterfront Initiative. 2002. *Anacostia Waterfront Initiative Framework Draft Recommendations*.

_____. 2003. *Anacostia Waterfront Initiative Framework Plan*. November. Also available at www.planning.dc.gov/planning/cwp view.asp?a=1285&q=582200&planningNav_GID=1647.

Asheville, City of. 1991. *The Asheville Riverfront Open Space Design Guidelines*. September 5–7.

_____. 1989. *The Riverfront Plan*. April 26–29.

Asheville.com. 1999. "RiverLink Announces Bus Tours for the Historic Riverside District." [Accessed May 29, 2003]. Available at www.asheville.com/news/riverlink.html.

Association of State Floodplain Managers. 2002. "ASFPM Fundamental Policy Change Recommendations." Press release, November.

_____. 2000. "National Flood Programs in Review 2000." [Accessed August 12, 2003]. Available at www.floods.org/PDF/2000-fpr.pdf.

_____. 2003. "What Is NAI?" [Accessed May 28]. Available at www.floods.org/No AdverseImpact/whitepaper.asp.

Atlanta Regional Commission. 2003. "The Chattahoochee: Lifeblood of the Region." [Accessed May 29]. Available at www.atlantaregional.com/water/chattahoochee.html.

BRW, Inc. et al. 1999. *Above the Falls: A Master Plan for the Upper Falls in Minneapolis.* [Accessed May 29, 2003]. Available at www.ci.minneapolis.mn.us/citywork/planning/planpubs/above-falls/report/index.html.

Bartsch, Charles, and Bridget Dorfman. 2001. "Proposals to Promote Brownfield Redevelopment in the 106th Congress: Final Legislative Report." Research report, Northeast-Midwest Institute. January 25. Also available at www.nemw.org/brownleg.pdf.

Bear River Resource Conservation and Development. 2003. "Project Description: Upper Bear River Stream Bank and Riparian Restoration—In-Stream Reconstruction." [Accessed May 29]. Available at www.bearriverrcd.org/bearriver/field/UB2b.html.

Berger, Gideon. 2003. "A New Vision for Near Southeast: Will Waterfront Project Bring Real Change or More of the Same?" *The Hill*, May 21.

Bioengineering Group, Inc. 2003. "Bronx River, New York: Preliminary Restoration Plan." [Accessed May 29]. Available at www.bioengineering.com/Projects/bronx_river.html.

Biksey, Thomas M., and Elisa Brown. 2001. "In the Hyporheic Zone." *Water Environment and Technology* 13, no. 6: 40–45.

Bonci, Frederick. 2001. Landscape Architect, LaQuatraBonci Associates, Pittsburgh. Telephone interview with authors, March 13.

_____. 2002. Landscape Architect, LaQuatraBonci Associates, Pittsburgh. Telephone interview with authors, June 5.

Borghese, Victor. 2003. Property Manager, Premier Automotive Group headquarters, Ford Motor Company, Irvine, Calif. Interview with authors, June 13.

Brandes, Donald. 2002. Landscape Architect, Design Studios West, Denver. Telephone interview with authors, June 11.

Breen, Ann, and Dick Rigby. 1996. *The New Waterfront: A Worldwide Urban Success Story.* New York: McGraw-Hill.

_____. 1994. *Waterfronts: Cities Reclaim Their Edge.* New York: McGraw-Hill.

Bridgeo, Bill. 2003. City Manager, Augusta, Maine. Interview with authors, June 11.

Brinckman, Jonathan. 2000. "River 'Renaissance' Planned." *Oregonian*, September 29, E1.

Broeker, Dick. 1997. "Revitalized Riverfront Helps Relink St. Paul with Its Soul." *Minneapolis-St. Paul Star Tribune*, September 19. Also available at www.startribune.com/stories/1655/1118744.html.

Bronx River Alliance. 2003. "Who We Are." [Accessed May 22]. Available at www.bronxriver.org/whoWeAre.cfm.

Brown, Ken. 2002. Ecologist, Center for Watershed Protection, Ellicott City, Md. Telephone interview with authors, June 21.

Bunster-Ossa, Ignacio. 2002. Landscape Architect, Wallace, Roberts, and Todd, Philadelphia. Telephone interview with authors, May 24.

Burby, Raymond J., Scott A. Bollens, James M. Holloway, Edward J. Kaiser, David Mullan, and John R. Sheaffer. 1988. *Cities Under Water: A Comparative Evaluation of Ten Cities' Efforts to Manage Floodplain Land Use.* Boulder, Colo.: Institute of Behavioral Science, University of Colorado.

CH2M Hill. 1993. *Costs of Providing Government Services to Alternative Residential Patterns.* Annapolis, Md.: Committee on Population Growth and Development, U.S. EPA Chesapeake Bay Program.

Calkins, Meg. 2001. "Return of the River." *Landscape Architecture*, July, 74–83.

Canada Mortgage and Housing Corporation. 2003. "Merchandise Lofts Building Green Roof Case Study." [Accessed December 22]. Available at www.cmhc-schl.gc.ca/en/imquaf/himu/buin_020.cfm.

Caputo, Darryl F. 1979a. *Open Space Pays: The Socioeconomics of Open Space Preservation.* Morristown, N.J.: New Jersey Conservation Foundation.

———. 1979b. *Open Space Pays: The Socioeconomics of Stormwater BMPs: An Update.* Morristown, N.J.: New Jersey Conservation Foundation.

Caraco, Deborah. 2000. "Dynamics of Urban Stream Channel Enlargement." *Watershed Protection Techniques* 3, no. 3: 729–734.

Center for Watershed Protection. 2001c. "The Economic Benefits of Better Site Design in Virginia." Technical paper, Virginia Department of Conservation and Recreation. December. Also available at www.dcr.state.va.us/sw/docs/swmecon.pdf.

———. 2001a. "The Economic Benefits of Protecting Virginia's Stream, Lakes, and Wetlands." Technical paper, Virginia Department of Conservation and Recreation. December. Also available at www.dcr.state.va.us/sw/docs/swmecon.pdf.

———. 2003a. *Impacts of Impervious Cover on Aquatic Ecosystems.* Ellicott City, Md.: Center for Watershed Protection.

———. 2001b. "Redevelopment Roundtable Consensus Agreement: Smart Site Practices for Redevelopment and Infill Projects." October. Also available at www.cwp.org/smartsites.pdf.

———. 2003b. "Site Planning Model Development Principles." [Accessed December 22]. Available at www.cwp.org/22_principles.htm.

Center for Watershed Protection and National Environmental Education and Training Foundations. 2002. "Small Streams: Your Link to the Bay." *Envirocast: Weather and Watershed Newsletter* 1, no. 1. [Accessed August 19, 2003]. Available at www.stormcenter.com/envirocast/2002-11-01/envirocast-feature.php.

Chadwick, Bar. 2003. Director, South Platte River Initiative, Department of Parks and Recreation, City and County of Denver. Telephone interview with authors, November 17.

"Chattanooga, TN. Best Practice: Greenways." 1999. [Accessed May 29, 2003]. Available at www.bmpcoe.org/bestpractices/external/chatt/chatt_4.html.

Chesapeake Bay Foundation. 1996. *A Dollars and Sense Partnership: Economic Development and Environmental Protection.* Annapolis, Md.: Chesapeake Bay Foundation.

Chesapeake Bay Program. 1998. "Economic Benefits of Riparian Forest Buffers." Ref. 600.613.1 Fact Sheet.

Chicago, City of. 2003. "City Hall Rooftop Garden." [Accessed May 6]. Available at www.ci.chi.il.us/Environment/html/RooftopGarden.html.

Chicago, City of, Department of Environment. 2003. "Fishing." [Accessed August 19]. Available at www.ci.chi.il.us/Environment/Rivertour/teen/info/fish.html.

Chicago, City of, Department of Planning and Development. 1999. *Chicago River Corridor Design Guidelines and Standards.*

Chicago, City of, Department of Planning and Development; Chicago Park District; and Forest Preserve District of Cook County. 1998. *CitySpace: An Open Space Plan for Chicago.*

Chueng, Nelson. 2003. Coordinating Planner, City of Chicago Department of Planning and Development. Interview with authors, June 10, and personal communication to authors, December 10.

Cityscape Institute. 1999. "Intercity Exchange: Reclaiming Riverfronts." *Cityscape News,* Fall, 2–6. Also available at www.elizabethbarlowrogers.com/pdf/cityscap/Fall 1999.pdf.

Clean Water Action Plan. 2000. *Watershed Success Stories, Applying the Principles and Spirit of the Clean Water Action Plan.* [Accessed May 29, 2003]. Available at www.cleanwater.gov/success/index.html.

Close Landscape Architecture et al. 2000. *Saint Paul River Corridor Urban Design Guidelines.* May.

Cohn, Naomi. 1996. *The Unofficial Paddling Guide to the Chicago River.* Chicago: Friends of the Chicago River.

——. 2001b. "Redevelopment Roundtable Consensus Agreement: Smart Site Practices for Redevelopment and Infill Projects." October. Also available at www.cwp.org/smartsites.pdf. 1998. *What's Working on Working Rivers: A Handbook for Improving Urban Rivers. Examples from Chicago Area Rivers.* Milwaukee, Wisc.: Rivers, Trails, and Conservation Assistance Program, National Park Service.

Committee on Oil in the Sea. 2003. *Oil in the Sea III: Inputs, Fates, and Effects.* Washington, D.C.: National Academies Press. Also available at www.nap.edu/books/0309084385/html/.

Committee on Riparian Zone Functioning and Strategies for Management, Water Science and Technology Board, et al. 2002. *Riparian Areas: Functions and Strategies for Management.* Washington, D.C.: National Academy Press. Also available at www.nap.edu/books/0309082951/html/.

Conservation Fund, Natural Lands Trust, and Patrick Center for Environmental Research of the Academy of Natural Sciences. 2001. *Schuykill Watershed Conservation Plan.* [Accessed April 23, 2003]. Available at www.schuylkillplan.org.

Conservation Law Foundation. 2003. "Interview with Robert Zimmerman: The October Floods." [Accessed May 29]. Available at www.clf.org/pubs/intervu.htm.

Correll, Mark R., Jane H. Lillydahl, and Larry D. Singell. 1978. "The Effects of Greenbelts on Residential Property Values: Some Findings on the Political Economy of Open Space." *Land Economics* 54, no. 2: 207–17.

Council on Environmental Quality. 1998. *Environmental Quality along the American River: The 1996 Report of the Council on Environmental Quality.* Washington, D.C.: GPO. Also available at http://ceq.eh.doe.gov/nepa/reports/1996/front.pdf.

Croce, Phyllis. 2002. Greenways Coordinator, Metropolitan Sewer District, Louisville, Ky. Telephone interview with authors, June 14.

Crompton, John L., Lisa L. Love, and Thomas A. More. 1997. "An Empirical Study of the Role of Recreation, Parks, and Open Space in Companies' (Re)Location Decisions." *Journal of Park and Recreation Administration* 15, no. 1: 37–58.

Cushing, Colbert E., and J. David Allan. 2001. *Streams: Their Ecology and Life.* San Diego: Academic Press.

Daly, Jim. 2003. Business Planning Manager, Port of Portland, Ore. Personal communication with authors, September 17.

Dickhut, Kathy. 2002. Assistant Commissioner, Department of Planning and Development, City of Chicago. Interview with authors.

Didisheim, Pete. 1999. *A River Reborn: Benefits for People and Wildlife of the Kennebec River Following the Removal of the Edwards Dam.* Augusta, Maine: Kennebec Coalition.

Dillon, David. 2000. "River Dancing: A Riverfront Plaza Reunites Hartford with Its History." *Landscape Architecture*, August, 70–75, 88.

Don Watershed Regeneration Council. 1994. "Forty Steps to a New Don: The Report of The Don Watershed Task Force." Research report, Metropolitan Toronto and Region Conservation Authority. May. Also available at www.trca.on.ca/water_protection/strategies/don/#forty_steps.

——. 2000. "A Time for Bold Steps: The Don Watershed Report Card 2000." Research report, Metropolitan Toronto and Region Conservation Authority. October. Also available at www.trca.on.ca/water_protection/strategies/don/#don_bold_steps.

Ecological Society of America. 2003a. "Ecosystem Services Fact Sheet." [Accessed June 3]. Available at www.esa.org/ecoservices/comm/body.comm.fact.ecos.html.

_____. 2003b. "Key Points." [Accessed June 3]. Available at www.esa.org/ecoservices/wate/body.wate.keyp.html.

"Economic Benefits of Open Space, The." 2002. [Accessed October 16 at www.openspace1.org/OpenSpace/ISSUES/economicbenefitopenspace.htm]. No longer available.

Ehrenhalt, Alan. 1997. "The Great Wall of Portland." *Governing*, May. Also available at www.governing.com/archive/1997/may/growth.txt.

Embrace Open Space. 2002. "St. Paul Receives Land for New Lowertown Park on Mississippi." [Accessed May 29, 2003]. Available at www.embraceopenspace.org/openspace/news/news_detail.asp?ItemID=316&CatID=90.

Environment News Service. 2000. "$11 Million Jumpstarts Bronx River Greenway." [Accessed October 17 at http://ens.lycos.com/ens/oct2000/200L-10-17-09.html]. No longer available.

Ermann, Lynn. 2003. "On Top of Mt. Slag, Homes Sprout." *New York Times*, March 6, F1.

Federal Interagency Stream Restoration Working Group (FISRWG). 2001. *Corridor Restoration: Principles, Processes, and Practices*. Rev. ed. [Accessed May 29, 2003]. Available at www.usda.gov/stream_restoration.

Ferguson, Bruce, et al. 2001. "Restorative Redevelopment: The Nine Mile Run Mode." *Stormwater*, July/August, 10–12.

Firehock, Karen, and Jacqueline Doherty. 1995. *A Citizen's Streambank Restoration Handbook*. Gaithersburg, Md.: Save Our Streams Program, Izaak Walton League of America.

Fishman, Paul. 2002. Ecologist, Fishman Environmental Service, Portland, Ore. Telephone interview with authors, May 20.

Flink, Charles A. 2002. Landscape Architect, Greenways, Inc., Cary, N.C. Telephone interview with authors, June 13.

Flink, Charles A., and Robert M. Searns. 1993. *Greenways: A Guide to Planning, Design, and Development*. Washington, D.C.: Island Press.

Floodplain Management Association. 1994. "Economic Benefits of Wetlands." *FMA News*, June.

Florida Department of Environmental Protection, Office of Greenways and Trails. 2000. "About Greenways." [Accessed June 25, 2003]. Available at www.geoplan.ufl.edu/projects/greenways/whatisagreenway.html.

Franklin, Carol, and Colin Franklin. 2002. Landscape Architects, Andropogon Associates, Philadelphia. Telephone interviews with authors, June 13.

Freeman, Adele. 2002. Don River Highland Specialist, Toronto and Region Conservation Authority, Downsview, Ont. Telephone interview with authors, June 24.

Friends of the Chicago River. 1999. *Voices of the Watershed: A Guide to Urban Watershed Management Planning*. Chicago: Friends of the Chicago River.

Friends of the Chicago River, Northeastern Illinois Planning Commission, and City of Chicago Department of Planning and Development. n.d. "From Stockyards to Spawning Beds: A Handbook of Bank Restoration Designs for the Chicago River and Other Urban Streams." Pamphlet.

Friends of the Mississippi River. 2003. "Regional Conservation Agencies Celebrate New Pine Bend Bluffs Scientific and Natural Area." Press release, March 11. Also available at www.fmr.org/pr03112003.html.

Galli, J., and R. Dubose. 1990. "Appendix C: Water Temperature and Freshwater Stream Biota: An Overview." In J. Galli, "Thermal Impacts Associated with Urbanization and Stormwater Management Best Management Practices." Research report, Metropolitan Washington Council of Governments. December.

Garton, Nicole. "River of Life." 1999. [Accessed June 3, 2003]. Available at www.redding.com/specials/River_of_Life/river_091399_02.shtml.

Garvin, Alexander. 1996. *The American City: What Works, What Doesn't*. New York: McGraw-Hill.

Georgia, University of, Institute of Ecology. 2003. "Tools for Quality Growth: Riparian Buffers." Fact sheet. [Accessed December 1]. Available at http://outreach.ecology.uga.edu/tools/fact_sheets/riparian%20buffers1.pdf.

Gobster, Paul H., and Lynne M. Westphal. 1998. *People and the River: Perception and Use of Chicago Waterways for Recreation*. Milwaukee, Wisc.: Rivers, Trails, and Conservation Assistance Program, National Park Service.

Government Finance Officers Association. 2003. "Issue Brief: Brownfields." May. Also available at www.gfoa.org/flc/briefs/112403/brownfields.5.03.pdf.

Grannemann, N.G., R.J. Hunt, J.R. Nicholas, T.E. Reilly, and T.C. Winter. 2000. *The Importance of Ground Water in the Great Lakes Region*. USGS Water Resources Investigations Report 00-4008. Lansing, Mich.: U.S. Geological Survey. Also available at http://water.usgs.gov/ogw/pubs/WRI004008/.

Grant, Peter. 2000. "This Plan Has a Catch." *Wall Street Journal*, October 18, B1.

Great River Greening. 2003. "Pine Bend Bluffs—Oak Savanna, Dry Prairie, and Mesic Prairie Restoration." [Accessed August 14]. Available at www.greatrivergreening.org/project_pinebend.asp.

Grillmayer, Rick. 2000. "Soil Bioengineering for Streambank Protection and Fish Habitat Enhancement, Collingwood, Ontario." In *Best Management Practices for Soft Engineering of Shorelines*, edited by Andrew D. Caulk, John E. Gannon, John R. Shaw, and John H. Hartig. Detroit: Greater Detroit American Heritage River Initiative, pp. 62–65.

Gustaitus, Rasa. 2001. "Los Angeles River Revivial." *Coast and Ocean*, Autumn, 2–14.

Hansen, Norma. 2001. "Participation Figures in Human-Powered Outdoor Recreation." *Outdoor Network Newsletter*, Summer, 16–17.

Hart, Barbara. 2003. Community Affairs Manager, River Renaissance Program, City of Portland, Ore. Personal communication with authors, July 21.

Hartig, John H., John K. Kerr, and Mark Breederland. 2001. "Promoting Soft Engineering along Detroit River Shorelines." *Land and Water*, November/December, 24–27.

Heat-Moon, William Least. 1999. *River-Horse: The Logbook of a Boat across America*. Boston: Houghton Mifflin.

Hellmund, Paul Cawood, and Daniel S. Smith, eds. 1993. *Ecology of Greenways: Design and Function of Linear Conservation Areas*. Minneapolis: University of Minnesota Press.

Herricks, Edwin E. 1995. *Stormwater Runoff and Receiving Systems: Impact, Monitoring, and Assessment*. Boca Raton, Fla.: CRD Lewis Publishers.

Hodge, Tiffany. 2002. Public Relations Specialist, Schuylkill River Development Council, Philadelphia. Telephone interview with authors, June 18.

Hoffman, Diane. 2003. District Administrator, Northern Virginia Soil and Water Conservation District, Fairfax County, Va. Interview with authors, June 17.

Holt, Gordy. 2002. "Redmond Helps Give Salmon a Little 'Re-leaf.'" *Seattle Post-Intelligencer*, September 9. Also available at http://seattlepi.nwsource.com/local/86121_sammamish09.shtml.

Houck, Michael. 2003. Executive Director, Urban Greenspaces Institute, and Urban Naturalist, Audubon Society of Portland, Ore. Personal communication with authors, July.

Houck, Michael C., and M.J. Cody, eds. 2000. *Wild in the City: A Guide to Portland's Natural Areas*. Portland: Oregon Historical Society.

Hough, Michael, Beth Benson, and Jeff Evenson. 1997. *Greening the Toronto Port Lands*. Toronto: Waterfront Regeneration Trust.

Jefferson, Jennifer. 2003. "New Center Celebrates Mississippi River." St. Paul Pioneer Press, August 4, B1.

Jerrick, Nancy. 1998. "Winning Projects: Stormwater Design Award Competition 1996 and 1997, Portland/Vancouver Metropolitan Area." Sponsored by Portland Metro Growth Management Services Department, City of Portland Bureau of Environmental Services, Unified Sewerage Agency of Washington County, Clark County Development Services Division, and Clackamas County Water Environment Services. July.

Johnson, Todd. 2002. Landscape Architect, Design Workshop, Inc., Denver. Telephone interview with authors, June 15.

Jones, David. 2002. Community Planner, Friends of the Chicago River, Chicago. Interview with authors.

Jones, Jonathan. 2002. Civil Engineer, Wright Water Engineers, Denver. Telephone interview with authors, June 11.

Kantner, Ananda M. 2000. "The West River Greenway: Toward a Citywide Greenways System for Providence, Rhode Island." Senior thesis, Brown University. [Accessed May 29, 2003]. Available at www.brown.edu/Research/EnvStudies_Theses/full9900/akanter/index.htm.

Karasov, Deborah. 2002. Landscape Planner, Great River Greening, St. Paul, Minn. Telephone interview with authors, June 12.

_____. 2003. Landscape Planner, Great River Greening, St. Paul, Minn. Telephone interview with authors, July.

Katz, Vera. 2001. "State of the City 2001: Our River Renaissance." Speech to Portland City Club, Portland, Ore., January 27.

Kay, Ken. 2000. Principal Landscape Architect, Ken Kay Associates, San Francisco. Telephone interview with authors, June 9.

Kelley, Gil. 2002. Director, Bureau of Planning, City of Portland, Ore. Public presentation on River Renaissance, August.

_____. 2003. Director, Bureau of Planning, City of Portland, Ore. Presentation to Portland City Council, February 18.

Klucas, Gillian. 2000. "Dreaming Big in Coffee Creek." *Conservation Voices*, December/January, 12–15.

Kratzer, Dave. 2000. "Interest in Developing River Assets Is the Latest Trend in Revitalization." *Wichita Business Journal,* May 22. Also available at http://wichita.bizjournals.com/wichita/stories/2000/05/22/story7.html.

Krevet, Bernhard. 2003. "The Napa River Flood Protection Project: 'The Living River Strategy.'" *Napa River Focus*, Fall, 8.

Land Trust Alliance. 2003a. "Conservation Options for Landowners." [Accessed August 14]. Available at www.lta.org/conserve/options.htm.

_____. 1994. *Economic Benefits of Land Protection*. Washington, D.C.: Land Trust Alliance.

_____. 2003b. "Voters Approve $2.9 Billion for Land Conservation." [Accessed August 13]. Available at www.lta.org/newsroom/pr_110602.htm.

Leccese, Michael, and Kathleen McCormick, eds. 2000. *Charter of the New Urbanism*. New York: McGraw-Hill.

Leeson, Fred. 2003. "Need to Cross the Willamette? Weekends, Try the Free Boat." *Oregonian*, July 21, E3.

Lehner, Peter H., George P. Aponte Clarke, Diane M. Cameron, and Andrew G. Frank. 2001. *Stormwater Strategies: Community Responses To Runoff Pollution*. New York: National Resources Defense Council.

Lerner, Steve, and William Poole. 1999. *The Economic Benefits of Parks and Open Space: How Land Conservation Helps Communities Grow Smart and Protect the Bottom Line*. San Francisco: Trust for Public Land.

Leopold, Luna B. 1994. *A View of the River*. Cambridge, Mass.: Harvard University Press.

Leopold, Luna B., M. Gordon Wolman, and John P. Miller. 1992. *Fluvial Processes in Geomorphology*. New York: Dover Press.

Liptan, Tom. 2002. Environmental Specialist, Bureau of Environmental Services, City of Portland, Ore. Telephone interview with authors, June 27.

_____. 2003. Environmental Specialist, Bureau of Environmental Services, City of Portland, Ore. Telephone interviews with authors, June 13 and July 25.

Liptan, Tom, and Carmel Kinsella Brown. 1996. "A Cost Comparison of Conventional and Water-Quality-Based Stormwater Designs." Unpublished manuscript.

Little, Charles E. 1995. *Greenways for America*. Baltimore: Johns Hopkins University Press.

Lloyd, Clayton. 2002. Director of Community and Economic Development, City of Davenport, Iowa. Telephone interview with authors, June 12.

Louisville, City of, and Jefferson County. 1999. *Multi-Objective Stream Corridor and Greenway Plan*.

Louisville and Jefferson County Metropolitan Sewer District. 2000. *Water Quality Report 2000: A Closer Look at Our Local Watersheds*. Louisville, Ky.: Louisville and Jefferson County Metropolitan Sewer District and Louisville Water Company.

Low Impact Development Center. 2003. "Introduction to Low Impact Development (LID)." [Accessed August 14]. Available at www.lid-stormwater.net/intro/background.htm.

Lowthian, Karen. 2003. Administrative Secretary, Metro Data Resource Center, Portland, Ore. Personal communication with authors, September 22.

Lozovoy, George. 2003. Project Manager, Portland Parks and Recreation, Portland, Ore. Personal communication with authors, July 29.

MacBroom, James. 2002. Civil Engineer, Milone and MacBroom, Inc., Cheshire, Conn. Telephone interview with authors, June 5.

_____. 1998. *The River Book: The Nature and Management of Streams in Glaciated Terranes*. Hartford: Connecticut Department of Environmental Protection Natural Resource Center.

MacElroy, William P., and Daniel Winterbottom. 2000. "Stormwater Ponds." *Landscape Architecture*, April, 48–54, 102–103.

Macy, Sydney S. 2002. Senior Vice President, Western Regional Office, The Conservation Fund, Boulder, Colo. Interview with authors, June 2.

Maguire, Charlie. 2002. Park Ranger, Mississippi National River and Recreation Area, St. Paul, Minn. Telephone interview with authors, July 3.

Maharaj, Vishwanie, and Janet E. Carpenter. 1996. *The 1996 Economic Impact of Sport Fishing in the United States*. Alexandria, Va.: American Sportfishing Association.

Maharaj, Vishwanie, Joseph McGurrin, and Janet Carpenter. 1998. *The Economic Impact of Trout Fishing on the Delaware River Tailwaters in New York*. Alexandria, Va.: American Sportfishing Association and Trout Unlimited.

Malan, Chris. 2002. Board Member, Friends of the Napa River, Napa, Calif. Telephone interview with authors, June 26.

Marfuggi, Joseph R. 2003. President and CEO, Riverfront Recapture, Hartford, Conn. Interview with authors, June 25.

Marfuggi, Joseph R., and Rick Porth. 1999. "A Riverfront Runs through It." *Parks and Recreation*, January, 48–55.

Martin Associates. 2001. "Local and Regional Economic Impacts of the Portland Harbor." Research report, Port of Portland, Ore. January 29.

Martin, Frank Edgerton. 2001. "Making the River Connection: Stewardship Marks the Projects of Saint Paul's Riverfront Restoration, Bringing Life Back to the Water's Edge." *Landscape Architecture*, February, 62–67, 88–91.

Massengill, Pat. 1998. "The 1965 Flood of the South Platte River." [Accessed August 13, 2003]. Available at www.littletongov.org/history/othertopics/flood.asp.

May, Christopher W., et al. 1997. "Effects of Urbanization on Small Streams in the Puget Sound Ecoregion." *Watershed Protection Techniques* 2, no. 4: 483–494.

Mazziotti, Don, and Cheryl Tweedy. 2003. Executive Director, Portland Development Commission, Portland, Ore., and Senior Development Manager, Portland Development Commission, Portland, Ore. Presentations to Portland City Council, July 10.

McCormick, Angela. 2002. Principal, Acadia Development, Boulder, Colo. Interview with authors, June 10.

McCormick, Kathleen. 1991. "We Don't 'Do' Wetlands." *Landscape Architecture*, October, 88–90.

McHugh, Erin. 2003. Administrative Assistant, American Recreation Coalition, Washington, D.C. Interview with authors, June 23.

McNulty, Robert. 2000. *The Livable City: Revitalizing Urban Communities*. New York: McGraw-Hill/Partners for Livable Communities.

Meyer, J.L., and J.B. Wallace. 2001. "Lost Linkages and Lotic Ecology: Rediscovering Small Streams." In *Ecology: Achievement and Challenge*, edited by M.C. Press, N.J. Huntly, and S. Levin. Oxford: Blackwell Science, pp. 295–317.

Meyer, J.L., R. Beilfuss, Q. Carpenter, L. Kaplan, D. Newbold, R.D. Semlitsch, D. Strayer, M. Watzin, C. Woltemade, J. Zelder, and P. Zelder. 2003. *Where Rivers Are Born: The Scientific Imperative for Defending Small Streams and Wetlands*. Washington, D.C.: American Rivers and Sierra Club.

Middaugh, Jim. 2001. Program Leader, Portland Endangered Species Act Response Program, Portland, Ore. Personal communication with authors.

Miller, Joe. 2001. "Whitewater Parks Offer Thrilling Twist and Turn in City Planning." *Raleigh News and Observer*, November 3, 1A.

Mills, Richard. 2002. Artist, Teaneck, N.J. Telephone interview with authors, July 2.

_____. 2000. *Hackensack River Stories: 16 Public Art Signworks for the Hackensack River Greenway through Teaneck, New Jersey*. Teaneck, N.J.: Return of the Bald Eagle Press.

Milner, George R. 2001. "Cost/Benefit Analysis: Conventional vs. Naturalized Detention Basin." *Land and Water*, November/December, 45.

Moore, Barbara J., John D. Rogner, and Drew Ullberg. 1998. *Nature and the River: A Natural Resources Report of the Chicago and Calumet Waterways*. Milwaukee, Wisc.: Rivers, Trails, and Conservation Assistance Program, National Park Service.

Moore, Roger L., and Christos Siderelis. 2003. "Use and Economic Importance of the West Branch of the Farmington River: Final Report." Research report, American Rivers and National Park Service. January. Also available at www.nps.gov/ncrc/portals/rivers/farm.pdf.doc.

Morrison, Patt. 2001. *Rio L.A.: Tales from the Los Angeles River*. Santa Monica, Calif.: Angel City Press.

Motavalli, Jim. 1998. "Chattanooga on a Roll: From America's Dirtiest City To Its Greenest." *E: The Environmental Magazine*, March-April. Also available at www.emagazine.com/march-april_1998/0398curr_chattanooga.html.

Muddy River Restoration Project. 2002. "Charlesgate Dredging: Boylston Street to Charles River." [Accessed May 22, 2003]. Available at www.muddyriverproject.org/Charlesgate_dredging.html.

Munch, Jim. 2002. City Planner, City of Pueblo, Colo. Interview with authors, June 12.

Myers, Mary. 2000. "Retrofitting Rocky Branch: Applying Natural Features in Urban Stream Design." *Landscape Architecture*, March, 44–49.

Napa County Flood Control and Water Conservation District. 2002. "The Napa River Flood Protection Project: Progress and Plan Summary." [Accessed August 13, 2003]. Available at www.napaflooddistrict.org/brochure.pdf.

"Napa River Watershed: Managing Land Use and Development in a Riverine Estuary System." 2000. In *Watershed Success Stories: Applying the Principles and Spirit of the Clean Water Action Plan*, September. [Accessed January 14, 2004]. Available at www.cleanwater.gov/success/napa.html.

National Park Service. 1995. *Economic Impacts of Protecting Rivers, Trails, and Greenway Corridors: A Resource Book*. 4th ed., revised. Washington, D.C.: National Park Service. Also available at www.nps.gov/pwro/rtca/econ_index.htm.

_____. 2003. Mississippi National River and Recreation Area website. [Accessed December 17]. Available at www.nps.gov/miss/.

National Park Service, Rivers, Trails, and Conservation Assistance Program. 2000. *Managing Greenways: A Look at Six Case Studies*. [Accessed May 29, 2003]. Available at www.nps.gov/phso/rtca/grnmgmt2.htm.

National Wildlife Federation. 1997. *Wet, Wild, and Profitable: A Report on the Economic Value of Water-Based Recreation in Vermont*. Montpelier, Vt.: Northeast Natural Resource Center.

National Wildlife Federation and Natural Resources Defense Council. 2002. "Wetlands Provide Tremendous Economic Benefits for People." Research report, National Wildlife Federation and Natural Resources Defense Council. July.

New York, State of, Office of the Governor. 2000. "Governor Pataki Announces State To Build Bronx River Greenway." Press release, October 15. Also available at www.state.ny.us/governor/press/year00/oct15_00.htm.

Northeast-Midwest Institute and Congress for the New Urbanism. 2001. *Strategies for Successful Infill Development*. Washington, D.C.: Northeast-Midwest Institute.

OZ Architecture and USDA Forest Service. 2000. *Midewin National Tallgrass Prairie Thematic Design Guidelines*. Denver: OZ Architecture.

O'Connell, Kim A. 2001. "Mending the Necklace." *Landscape Architecture*, July, 36–41, 90–93.

Ohio, State of, Environmental Protection Agency. 2001. "Clean Rivers Spring from Their Source: The Importance of Management of Headwater Streams." Fact sheet, August. Also available at www.epa.state.oh.us/dsw/wqs/headwaters/fact_sheet10_final.pdf.

Olmsted Brothers and Bartholomew and Associates. 1930. *Parks, Playgrounds, and Beaches for the Los Angeles Region*. Los Angeles: Citizens' Committee on Parks, Playgrounds, and Beaches.

Onaga, Lisa. 2000. "Project Aims To Revitalize Providence River Shoreline." *Brown Daily Herald*, April 10, n.p.

Oregon Department Of Environmental Quality. 2003. "Water Quality Limited Streams 303(d) List." [Accessed December 22]. Available at www.deq.state.or.us/wq/303dlist/303dpage.htm.

Outdoor Recreation Coalition of America. 2001. *Outdoor Recreation Participation Study*. 3d ed. Boulder, Colo.: Outdoor Recreation Coalition of America.

Overson, Susan. 2002. Landscape Architect and Park Planner, Mississippi National River and Recreation Area, St. Paul, Minn. Interview with authors, May 30.

Overton, Martin. 2002. Assistant Director of Public Works, Norwalk City Hall, Norwalk, Conn. Telephone interview with authors, June 7.

Owens-Viani, Lisa. 2000. "Nature as Landscape Architect: Plants and Plant Parts Help to Stabilize Riverbanks and Control Erosion." *Landscape Architecture*, February, 78–81, 92–95.

PLAE, Inc. and USDA Forest Service. 1993. *Universal Access to Outdoor Recreation: A Design Guide.* Berkeley, Calif.: PLAE, Inc., and MIG Communications.

Palone, Roxane S., and Albert H. Todd, eds. 1998. *Chesapeake Bay Riparian Handbook: A Guide for Establishing and Maintaining Riparian Forest Buffers.* Rev. ed. Radmar, Pa.: USDA Forest Service.

Patterson, Tim. 2000. "Comparison of Soil Bioengineering and Hard Structures for Shore Erosion Control: Costs and Effectiveness." In *Best Management Practices for Soft Engineering of Shorelines,* edited by Andrew D. Caulk, John E. Gannon, John R. Shaw, and John H. Hartig. Detroit: Greater Detroit American Heritage River Initiative, pp. 21–24.

Pennsylvania Fish and Boat Commission. 2003. Pennsylvania Fish and Boat Commission homepage. [Accessed August 14]. Available at http://sites.state.pa.us/PA_Exec/Fish_Boat/watertrails/trailindex.htm.

Pennsylvania Economy League, Inc. 1997. "Understanding the Economic Value of Schuylkill River Park." Report No. 689. [Accessed June 3, 2003]. Available at www.peleast.org/images/Schuylkill_River_Park.pdf.

Peterson, Bruce J., et al. 2001. "Control of Nitrogen Export from Watersheds by Headwater Streams." *Science,* April 6, 86–90.

Pinkham, Richard. 2000. *Daylighting: New Life for Buried Streams.* Snowmass, Colo.: Rocky Mountain Institute.

Pittsburgh, City of. 2003. *The Riverfront Development Plan: A Comprehensive Plan for the Three Rivers.* [Accessed May 29]. Available at www.city.pittsburgh.pa.us/rfp/.

Portland, City of. 2002. "Framework for Integrated Management of Watershed and River Health." Draft report, November. Also available at www.fish.ci.portland.or.us/pdf/FIMWRH_Doc.pdf.

Portland, City of. 2001. *Willamette Riverbank Design Notebook.* [Accessed June 3, 2003]. Available at www.pdc.us/pdf/dev_serv/pubs/willamette_riverbank_design_notebook.pdf.

Portland, City of, Bureau of Environmental Services. 2003. "Going Deep for a Cleaner River." Brochure, West Side Big Pipe project.

Portland, City of, Bureau of Planning. 2001. River Renaissance Vision website. [Accessed December 22, 2003]. Available at www.river.ci.portland.or.us/mainpages/vision/vision.htm.

Portland Development Commission. 2003. "River District." [Accessed July 25]. Available at www.pdc.us/ura/river.asp.

Portland Metro. 2003. "Urban Growth Boundary: Definition and Facts." [Accessed December 22]. Available at www.metro-region.org/article.cfm?articleid=277.

Portland Metro Data Resource Center. 2002. "Economic Report to the Metro Council: 2000–2030 Regional Forecast." Rev. ed., September.

President's Committee of Advisors on Science and Technology. 1998. "Teaming with Life: Investing in Science To Understand and Use America's Living Capital." March. Also available at www.ostp.gov/Environment/html/teamingcover.html.

Price, Jennifer. 2001. "Paradise Reclaimed: A Field Guide to the LA River: In the Beginning." *LA Weekly,* August 10–16. Also available at www.laweekly.com/ink/01/38/cover-price7.php.

Project for Public Spaces, Inc. 2000. *How to Turn a Place Around: A Handbook for Creating Successful Public Spaces.* New York: Project for Public Spaces, Inc.

Providence Plan. 2003. "The Woonasquatucket River Greenway Project." [Accessed May 29]. Available at www.provplan.org/html/projects/woon.html.

Ramsay, David. 2002. Watershed Programs Director, Friends of the Chicago River, Chicago. Interview with authors.

"Reclaiming The Willamette." 2000. *Oregonian,* September 29, E6.

Recreation Roundtable. 2003. "Key Findings of the 1996 Recreation Roundtable Survey: Outdoor Recreation in America." [Accessed June 3]. Available at www.funoutdoors.com/research.html.

———. 1998. "Outdoor Recreation in America 1998." [Accessed June 3, 2003]. Available at www.funoutdoors.com/roper98.html.

———. 2002. "Participation Increases for Most Recreational Activities." Press release, January 8. Also available at www.funoutdoors.com/news/news1_02.

Reed, Mike. 2003. Biologist, Portland Endangered Species Act Response Program, Portland, Ore. Personal communication with authors, July 25.

Return of the Natives. 2003. Return of the Natives Restoration Education Project homepage. [Accessed August 14]. Available at http://watershed.csumb.edu/ron/.

Riley, Ann L. 1985. *Riparian Restoration, A Timely New Mission for Federal Water Development Agencies.* Sacramento, Calif.: Department of Water Resources, Urban Stream Restoration Program.

———. 1998. *Restoring Streams in Cities: A Guide for Planners, Policymakers, and Citizens.* Washington, D.C.: Island Press.

Riverfront Recapture. 2002. *Boundless Energy and Optimism: 2001–2002 Annual Report.* Hartford, Conn.: Riverfront Recapture.

———. 2003. "Construction Update." [Accessed June 19]. Available at www.riverfront.org/construction.asp.

———. 2000a. "New Plaza To Reunite Downtown Hartford with Riverfront on Labor Day Weekend." Press release, n.d.

———. 2000b. *Take Me to the River! 1999–2000 Annual Report.* Hartford, Conn.: Riverfront Recapture.

Rivers, Trails, and Conservation Assistance Program. 1996. *Floods, Floodplains, and Folks: A Casebook in Managing Rivers for Multiple Uses.* Washington, D.C.: National Park Service.

Robbins, Bill. 2001. Environmental Historian, Oregon State University, Corvallis, Ore. Presentation during State of the City event, Portland City Club, January 27.

"Romancing the River." 2001. *Oregonian*, January 27, B6.

Roofscapes, Inc. 2003. "Premier Automotive Building." [Accessed June 2]. Available at www.roofmeadow.com/project4.html.

Rouhi, Asad. 2003. Urban Conservation Engineer, Northern Virginia Soil and Water Conservation District, Fairfax County, Va. Interview with authors, June 17.

Russell, Zolna. 2000. "Rain Gardens." *Landscape Architecture*, July, 24.

Saint Paul, City of, Department of Planning and Economic Development. 2003. "Bruce Vento Nature Sanctuary Project Overview." Press release, March 4. Also available at www.ci.stpaul.mn.us/depts/ped/news/ventosanctuary.html.

Saint Paul Riverfront Corporation. 2003. "History." [Accessed December 17]. Available at www.riverfrontcorporation.com/asp/page12.asp.

Sakrison, Rodney. 1997. "Water Use in Compact Communities: The Effect of New Urbanism, Growth Management, and Conservation Measures on Residential Water Demands." Department of Urban Design and Planning, College of Architecture and Planning, University of Washington.

Schneider, Keith. 2002. "Ford Gives River Rouge a Green Coat." *New York Times*, October 23, A30.

Schneider, Paul. 1997. "Clear Progress: 25 Years of the Clean Water Act." *Audubon*, September/October, 40.

Schueler, Thomas R. 2003. Director of Watershed Research and Practice, Center for Watershed Protection, Ellicott City, Md. Interview with authors, October 11.

_____. 1996."The Architecture of Urban Stream Buffers." *Watershed Protection Techniques* 1, no. 4: 155–163.

_____. 1997a. "The Economics of Stormwater Treatment: An Update." *Watershed Protection Techniques* 2, no. 4: 395–399.

_____. 1997b. "The Economics of Watershed Protection." *Watershed Protection Techniques* 2, no. 4: 469–481.

_____. 1995a. "The Importance of Imperviousness." *Watershed Protection Techniques* 1, no. 3: 100–111.

_____. 1995b. "The Peculiarities of Perviousness." *Watershed Protection Techniques* 2, no. 1: 233–238.

_____. 1995c. *Site Planning for Urban Stream Protection*. Washington, D.C.: Metropolitan Council of Governments.

Schueler, Thomas R., and Heather K. Holland, eds. 2000. *The Practice of Watershed Protection*. Ellicott City, Md.: Center for Watershed Protection.

Searns, Robert M. 2002. Greenway Planner, City of Denver. Telephone interview with authors, June 13.

_____. 1995. "The Evolution of Greenways as an Adaptive Urban Landscape Form." *Landscape and Urban Planning* 33, nos. 1–3: 65–80.

Siemon, Larsen & Purdy; Rogers, Golden & Halpern; and Hammer, Siler, George Associates. 1990. "Crossroads: Two Growth Alternatives for Virginia Beach." Research report, Office of Planning, City of Virginia Beach, Va. March.

Smart Growth Online. 2003. "About Smart Growth." [Accessed August 14]. Available at www.smartgrowth.org/about/default.asp.

Smith, Daniel S., and Paul C. Hellmund, eds. 1993. *Ecology of Greenways: Design and Function of Linear Conservation Areas*. Minneapolis: University of Minnesota Press.

Smith, Sean. 2002. Project Manager, Bluewater Network, San Francisco. Telephone interview with authors, June 27.

Sotir, Robbin B., and Nelson R. Nunnally. 1995. "Use of Riprap in Soil Bioengineering Streambank Protection." [Accessed May 29, 2003]. Available at www.sotir.com/pubs/publist/riprap/riprap.html.

Soul Salmon. 2002. "About the Soul Salmon Project." [Accessed May 8, 2003]. Available at www.soulsalmon.org/about.html.

Souers, Amy, and Betsy Otto. 2000. "Restoring Rivers Within City Limits." *Open Spaces* 3, no. 4: 24–29.

Stanford, J.A., and J.V. Ward. 1988. "The Hyporheic Habitat of River Ecosystems." *Nature* 355, no. 6185: 64–66.

Starbird, Ethel. 1972. "A River Restored: Oregon's Willamette." *National Geographic*, June, 817–835.

Stewart, Barbara. 2000. "A River Rises." *New York Times*, December 3, section 14, p. 1.

Stormwater Manager's Resource Center. 2003. "Buffers." [Accessed December 17]. Available at www.stormwatercenter.net/Model%20Ordinances/Buffers.htm.

Streiner, Carol F., and John B. Loomis. 1995. "Estimating the Benefits of Urban Stream Restoration Using the Hedonic Price Method." *Rivers* 5, no. 4: 267–278.

Sustainable Communities Network. 1996. "Chattanooga: A City Worth Watching." [Accessed May 29, 2003]. Available at www.sustainable.org/casestudies/tennessee/TN_af_chattanooga.html.

Sydell, Laura. 2000. "The Politics of Open Space Design." *Weekend All Things Considered*, National Public Radio, September 9. Available at www.npr.org/programs/specials/architecture/000909.html.

Takesuye, David. 2003. "REI Denver Flagship Store: A Reuse Example." *Urban Land*, October, 146–147.

Taylor, Alan. 2002. Floodplain Manager, City of Boulder, Colo. Interview with authors, October 2.

Thibodeau, F.R., and B.D. Ostro. 1981. "An Economic Analysis of Wetland Protection." *Journal of Environmental Management* 12, no. 1: 19–30.

Thompson, J. William. 1998. "Banking on a River." *Landscape Architecture*, September, 50–55.

Thompson, J. William. 1996. "Down by the Creekside." *Landscape Architecture*, October, 82–93.

_____. 2000. "Meadows Above." *Landscape Architecture,* September, 36–39.

_____. 1999. "The Poetics of Stormwater." *Landscape Architecture*, January, 58–63, 86–88.

Toronto, City of. 2003. "Restoration of the Mouth of the Don River." [Accessed August 14]. Available at www.city.toronto.on.ca/waterfront/don_river_mouth.htm.

Toronto Waterfront Revitalization Corporation. 2003. "Current Projects." [Accessed August 14]. Available at www.towaterfront.ca/topnavloader.php?first=3e9112548cd89.

Torres, Rene. 2003. Director of Trails and Landscape, Schuylkill River Development Council, Philadelphia. Interview with authors, May 28.

Trust for Public Land. 2003a. "About TPL." [Accessed August 14]. Available at www.tpl.org/tier2_sa.cfm?folder_id=170.

_____. 2000. "The Greening of Providence." [Accessed May 29, 2003]. Available at http://tpl.org/tier3_cdl.cfm?content_item_id=1243&folder_id=905.

_____. 2003b. "LandVote 2002." [Accessed August 13]. Available at www.tpl.org/tier2_rp2.cfm?folder_id=1666.

U.S. Army Corps of Engineers. 2002. "Civil Works Program Statistics." Information paper, February 28. Also available at www.usace.army.mil/inet/functions/cw/cecwb/GWiz02.htm.

U.S. Department of Agriculture et al. 2000. "The Bronx River Watershed: Community Cooperation in Urban Watershed Restoration." In *Watershed Success Stories: Applying the Principles and Spirit of the Clean Water Act*, September. [Accessed January 14, 2004]. Available at www.cleanwater.gov/success/bronx.html.

U.S. Environmental Protection Agency. 1998. "Brownfields Assessment Pilot Fact Sheet: Evanston, Wyoming." [Accessed May 29, 2003]. Available at www.epa.gov/brownfields/html-doc/evanston.htm.

_____. 2002f. "The Brownfields Program: Setting Change in Motion." Brochure, October. Also available at www.epa.gov/brownfields/pdf/bfglossy.pdf.

_____. 2002a. *The Clean Water and Drinking Water Infrastructure Gap Analysis*. Washington, D.C.: U.S. EPA. Also available at www.epa.gov/ogwdw/gapreport.pdf.

_____. 2002b. "Combined Sewer Overflows Demographics." [Accessed June 3, 2003]. Available at http://cfpub.epa.gov/npdes/cso/demo.cfm?program_id=5.

_____. 1995a. "Economic Benefits of Runoff Controls." EPA 841-S-95-002. [Accessed June 3, 2003]. Available at www.epa.gov/owow/nps/runoff.html.

_____. 1993. *Guidance Specifying Management Measures for Sources of Nonpoint Pollution in Coastal Waters*. Washington, D.C.: U.S. EPA. Also available at www.epa.gov/owow/nps/MMGI/.

_____. 2002c. "National Pollutant Discharge Elimination System." [Accessed May 6, 2003]. Available at http://cfpub.epa.gov/npdes/index.cfm.

_____. 2000. *National Water Quality Inventory: 1998 Report*. [Accessed August 19, 2003]. Available at www.epa.gov/305b/98report.

_____. 2002d. *National Water Quality Inventory: 2000 Report.* [Accessed August 19, 2003]. Available at www.epa.gov/305b/2000report.

_____. 2003a. "New York City and Seven Upstate New York Counties." [Accessed June 11]. Available at www.epa.gov/safewater/protect/casesty/newyorkcity.html.

_____. 2001a. "Nonpoint Source Pollution: The Nation's Largest Water Quality Problem." Pointer No. 1 (fact sheet), EPA841-F-96-004A. Also available at www.epa.gov/owow/nps/facts/point1.htm.

_____. 2003b. "Proposed Portland Harbor Superfund Site Timeline." Draft report, January 9.

_____. 2001b. *Report to Congress: Implementation and Enforcement of the Combined Sewer Overflow Control Policy.* Washington, D.C.: U.S. EPA. Also available at http://cfpub1.epa.gov/npdes/cso/cpolicy_report.cfm?%20program_id=5.

_____. 2002e. "Streambank Modification Successful in Utah." [Accessed May 29, 2003]. Available at www.epa.gov/OWOW/NPS/Success319/UT.html.

_____. 2001c. "Techniques for Tracking, Evaluating, and Reporting the Implementation of Nonpoint Source Control Measures: III. Urban." EPA 841-B-00-007. [Accessed December 1, 2003]. Available at www.epa.gov/owow/nps/urban.pdf.

_____. 1995b. "Wetlands Fact Sheets." EPA 843-F-95-001. Also available at www.epa.gov/owow/wetlands/facts/contents.html.

U.S. Environmental Protection Agency, New England Region. 1996. "A Healthy Charles River Contributes Over $100 Million To Local Economy." Press release #96-7-6, July 10.

_____. 2002. "Woonasquatucket River Overview: A River on the Rebound." [Accessed May 29, 2003]. Available at www.epa.gov/region01/ra/woonas/.

U.S. Environmental Protection Agency, Office of Water. 2000. *Liquid Assets 2000: America's Water Resources at a Turning Point.* Washington, D.C.: U.S. EPA. Also available at www.epa.gov/water/liquidassets.

_____. 2002. "Projects Funded By Five Star Restoration Program in FY00." [Accessed May 29, 2003]. Available at www.epa.gov/owow/wetlands/restore/5star/fy00grants.html.

U.S. Fish and Wildlife Service. 1998. "1996 National and State Economic Impacts of Wildlife Watching: Based on the 1996 National Survey of Fishing, Hunting, and Wildlife-Associated Recreation." April. Also available at http://fa.r9.fws.gov/info/publish/rpt_96-1.pdf.

_____. 2002. *2001 National Survey of Fishing, Hunting, and Wildlife-Associated Recreation.* Washington, D.C.: GPO. Also available at www.census.gov/prod/2002pubs/FHW01.pdf.

_____. 2001. *Status and Trends of Wetlands in the Conterminous United States 1986 to 1997.* Washington, D.C.: GPO. Also available at http://wetlands.fws.gov/bha/SandT/SandTReport.html.

U.S. Geological Survey. 2000. "A Tapestry of Time and Terrain: The Union of Two Maps—Geology and Topography." [Accessed August 19, 2003]. Available at http://tapestry.usgs.gov/features/14fallline.html.

Urban Design Strategies. 1997. *Saint Paul on the Mississippi Development Framework.* [Accessed December 1, 2003]. Available at www.riverfrontcorporation.com/asp/page4.asp.

Urban Land Institute. 2003. *Remaking the Urban Waterfront.* Washington, D.C.: Urban Land Institute.

Urbonas, Ben R., ed. 2001. *Linking Stormwater BMP Designs and Performance to Receive Water Impact Mitigation: Proceedings of an Engineering Foundation Conference.* Alexandria, Va.: American Society of Civil Engineers.

Utne, Leif. 2000. "Green Living: America's 10 Most Environmentally Friendly Cities." [Accessed December 1, 2003]. Available at www.utne.com/webwatch/2000_203/news/1498-1.html.

Van Metre, Peter C., Barbara J. Mahler, and Edward T. Furlong. 2000. "Urban Sprawl Leaves Its PAH Signature." *Environmental Science and Technology* 34, no. 19: 4064–70.

Vanden Brook, Tom. 2002. "Sewage Pouring into Lakes, Streams." *USA Today*, August 20. Also available at www.usatoday.com/news/nation/2002-08-19-sewage_x.htm.

Vannote, R.L.; G.W. Minshall; K.W. Cummins, Jr.; J.R. Sedell; and C. E. Cushing. 1980. "The River Continuum Concept." *Canadian Journal of Fisheries and Aquatic Sciences* 37, no. 1: 130-37.

Vaughen, Laurie Perry. 2000. "Take Me To the River." *Parks and Recreation*, January, 63–73.

Von Klan, Laurene. 2002. Executive Director, Friends of the Chicago River, Chicago. Interview with authors.

Waldie, D.J. 2002. "Notes from Los Angeles: Reclaiming a Lost River, Building a Community." *New York Times*, July 10, A21.

Walljasper, Jay. 1997. "America's 10 Most Enlightened Towns." *Utne Reader*, May/June, 43–57.

Washington County Soil and Water Conservation District. 1999. "Managing Streamside Areas with Buffers: Tips for Small Acreages in Oregon." Fact Sheet No. 5, January. Also available at www.or.nrcs.usda.gov/news/factsheets/fs5.pdf.

Watershed Professionals Network. 1999. "Watershed Fundamentals." In *Oregon Watershed Assessment Manual*. Governor's Watershed Enhancement Board. June. Also available at www.oweb.state.or.us/publications/wa_manual99.shtml.

Welty, Errin. 2003. Research Coordinator, Downtown Denver Partnership, Inc., Denver. Telephone interviews with authors, June 11, 26 and September 18.

Wenk, Bill. 2002. Landscape Architect, Wenk Associates, Denver. Telephone interviews with authors, April 20 and June 10.

Wheeler, Doug. 1998. "The Napa River Flood Management Effort." *California Diversity News* 5, no. 4. [Accessed January 14, 2004]. Available at www.ceres.ca.gov/biodiv/newsletter/v5n4/chair.html.

Whitaker, Barbara. 2001. "Visions of Parting a Sea of Concrete with a Unifying River Greenbelt." *New York Times*, January 27, A8.

White, Nancy. 2002. Associate Professor, School of Design, North Carolina State University, Raleigh, N.C. Telephone interview with authors, June 28.

Wichert, William. 2002. "Bronx River Golden Ball Makes Another Run." *Norwood News*, October 10–23. Also available at www.bronxmall.com/norwoodnews/past/101002/news/page5.html.

Wilkinson, Todd. 2000. "The Cultural Challenge." *National Parks*, January/February, 20–23.

Williams, Anthony A. 2002. Mayor, District of Columbia. Testimony on the Anacostia Waterfront Initiative to U.S. Senate Subcommittee on the District of Columbia, June 11.

Williams, Travis. 2001. Executive Director, Willamette Riverkeeper, Portland, Ore. Interview with authors.

Wine, Kathy. 2002. Director, River Action, Davenport, Iowa. Telephone interview with authors, June 26.

_____. 2003. Director, River Action, Davenport, Iowa. Telephone interview with authors, May 28.

Wolff, Ted. 2002. Principal, Wolff Clements and Associates, Chicago. Interview with authors.

Wrenn, Douglas. 1983. *Urban Waterfront Development*. Washington, D.C.: Urban Land Institute.

Zimmerman, Robert. 2003. Director, Charles River Watershed Association, Waltham, Mass. Interview with authors, June 16.

APPENDIX C

American Planning Association Policy Guide on Water Resources Management

INTRODUCTION AND FINDINGS

Water is a finite resource. Although three-quarters of the earth is covered with water, 97.6 percent our water is salty and 1.9 percent is frozen into the polar ice caps. This means that only about half a percent of our planet's water resources is fresh water. Of these fresh water resources, 0.02 percent is found in rivers, lakes, and streams while the rest, 0.48 percent, is groundwater. These water resources are used for water supply, ecological, recreational, navigational, and waste disposal purposes, and these diverse uses are currently managed under a large number of federal, state, and local laws.

The U.S. Geological Survey (USGS)—in its report, *Estimated Use of Water in the United States in 1995* (Circular 1200, 1998)—estimates that the total use of water (both fresh and saline) in the U.S. was around 402,000 million gallons per day (mgd) in 1995, about 2 percent less than the Survey's 1990 water-use estimate and 10 percent less than its 1980 estimate. This decline in water use occurred even though the nation's population increased 16 percent from 1980–95. Much of this water is used for thermoelectric power generation, which had declined from its 1980 peak use of 210,000 mgd to 190,000 mgd in 1995. Industrial water use (29.1 mgd in 1995) also declined 3 percent from 1990-95, a trend the USGS attributes to the more efficient production technologies used by new industries, more industrial water recycling, and changes in pollution laws.

Total irrigation withdrawals (134,000 mgd in 1995) increased from 1965 to 1980, but then gradually declined from 1980 to 1995, dropping 2 percent from 1990-95. Although the number of irrigated acres (around 58 million) remained fairly constant in the U.S. from 1980-95, irrigated acreage during this period declined in the 19 western states at the same time it increased in the more humid eastern states. On a per-acreage basis, average irrigation water use in 1995 was about 2.1 acre-feet, less than the 2.2 acre-feet average in 1985 and well below the 1975 and 1980 average of 2.5 acre-feet. Irrigation withdrawals vary not only by such factors as the amount of rainfall, energy costs, farm commodity prices, application technologies, and conservation practices, but they also vary by region.

The USGS notes that the only two water uses showing continual increases from 1950 to 1995 were the "Public Supply" and "Rural Domestic and Livestock" water-use categories. Although public supply withdrawals (40.2 mgd in 1995) increased 4 percent from 1990-95, the nation's population increased by 7 percent during this same five year-span, so per capita public supply water use actually declined from 184 gpd in 1990 to 179 gpd in 1995 (a trend that the USGS attributes to increased water conservation). The 13 percent increase in rural water use (8.89 mgd in 1995) is attributed to increases in livestock withdrawals; rural (self-supplied) domestic withdrawals were about the same in 1995 as they were in 1990.

It is often difficult to accurately assess and forecast the complex interrelationships between groundwater and surface water. This means the impacts that development will have on the quantity or quality of one water resource cannot be assessed without also assessing its impacts on all other water resources. For example, increased water demand may force aquifers to be overpumped, an action that not only leads to the drilling of deeper wells but one that may also impair groundwater quality (by increasing dissolved mineral concentrations when water is drawn deeper from the aquifer or by disrupting groundwater flow patterns and inducing saline or polluted surface water or brackish water from another aquifer to flow into the freshwater aquifer). The overpumping of alluvial or surficial aquifers may also reduce their base flow discharges to surface water bodies, thereby reducing stream flows and also indirectly affecting stream quality (as ambient pollutant concentrations increase).

Both groundwater and surface water resources can be disrupted by contamination. Pathogens, minerals, and organic and inorganic chemicals polluting the groundwater can cause surface water to become polluted and vice versa due to the interconnections between the two. Significant contaminant sources include agricultural chemical use, wastewater discharges from public sewer and on-site wastewater disposal systems, solid and hazardous waste landfills, storage tanks, and industrial materials spills and waste impoundments. Impervious surfaces can not only reduce aquifer recharge, but can also increase water pollution and flood hazards by increasing the amount of runoff. Aquifer penetrations, such as injection wells, oil and gas wells, or improperly abandoned wells, may also introduce contaminants directly into an aquifer. Atmospheric deposition of contaminants can also impair water quality. The minimal attenuation and the impracticality of remediation of contaminants in groundwater, and the high cost of water treatment make prevention of contamination the only really effective means of protecting aquifers and the most efficient means of protecting surface water resources.

Jurisdictional complexity often makes it difficult to comprehensively manage and protect our water resources. For example, while state and federal environmental protection statutes set water-quality standards for surface water and drinking water, other state laws may govern groundwater and surface water ownership and use, and still other state and local laws might regulate land-use activities generating water demand or posing threats to water quality. The needs of nonconsumptive in-stream uses of water—such as the protection of fish and wildlife habitats, the enhancement of recreational activities, the maintenance of navigation, and the need to maintain ambient water quality standards—are more and more coming into direct conflict with the needs of consumptive off-stream uses for the same surface water. Large-scale diversions of surface water and excessive pumping of groundwater diminish stream flows, further aggravating intense surface-water-use conflicts. Greater coordination is clearly needed between the state agencies, between the state and local agencies, and between the local agencies responsible for different aspects of water resources use and management.

Water resource issues need to be integrated better into the comprehensive land-use planning process. Urbanization increases runoff from impervious surfaces, causing stormwater flooding and nonpoint source pollution problems. As cities grow larger and water demand starts surpassing the amount of water found locally, people and businesses begin to look further and further from the community to meet their projected water needs—to drill wells in other aquifers, pipe water from large rivers and lakes hundreds of miles to their town, and to augmenting rainfall. As water supplies become even more constrained, even more complicated and expensive schemes to obtain adequate amounts of fresh water may be considered, such as desalination of seawater or brackish aquifers, towing large bladders of fresh water through the ocean to dry port cities, or hauling icebergs to coastal areas. These escalating water supply schemes represent the direct costs to a region of "mining" its water resources at unsustainable rates. But there are also indirect costs, in lost potential for development and in the potential disruption of the existing economic and social order in the receiving areas if they don't have the additional water and in the donating areas from loss of their water resource. Futhermore, dependency upon water resources derived from nonsustainable sources can create long-term economic uncertainty and instability for the dependent communities.

Conservation, each user using less water, is one way to create "new" and perhaps more sustainable sources of water. Water reuse is important. Returning treated effluent to a river where the next town takes out water for its potable supply has been going on for years. Wastewater can be treated and reused for irrigating golf courses, agriculture, parks and gardens, treated and released to surface waters for recreational, navigational, and ecological purposes, or even cleaned to drinking water standards and reused for aquifer recharge or water supply purposes. Similar strategies could also be used to manage stormwater.

Requiring water conservation, as the federal government did when it mandated water-conserving fixtures in the 1992 Energy Policy Act, is one approach to better managing our water resources. But, other strategies can also be employed—the conjunctive use of both groundwater and surface water resources, reducing water demand through Smart Growth initiatives and more sustainable land-use planning

GENERAL POLICY

Water should be treated as a collective public resource and managed in a sustainable manner.

1. Water should not be consumed to such an extent so as to:
   - interfere with its reasonable use by others;
   - impair the ability of a water resource to be naturally replenished; and
   - impair its ecological, recreational, or navigational functions.

2. Water should not be discharged in such a manner so as to:
   - interfere with its reasonable use by others;
   - create hazardous conditions (e.g., erosion, sedimentation, flooding and subsidence); and
   - impair its ecological, recreational, or navigational functions.

3. Pollution and other manmade threats to water resources should be minimized.

Commentary: This general policy is intended to articulate a "Golden Rule" of water resources management. By considering water both a "collective" and " public" resource, APA recognizes that, despite differing state water laws, any private or individual "right" to use water remains only contingent and is therefore always subject to whatever governmental oversight as may be necessary to protect and further the greater general welfare. By requiring that water resources be used "sustainably," APA recognizes that there is a duty to manage water resources in such a way so as not to impair their present and future utility and value. Sound water policy must address the contemporary and long-term needs of humans as well as the ecological community. These management responsibilities, which become an ethical obligation because of the centrality of water to life itself, are expressed in greater detail in the specific policies listed below.

SPECIFIC POLICIES FOR WATER USE

Policy 1. APA and its Chapters support legislation and funding to establish state comprehensive water resource and supply planning (conducted jointly by appropriate federal agencies, states, appropriate regional authorities, water utilities, and local governments), based upon watersheds and other natural hydrological boundaries (such as aquifer recharge and discharge areas) to the greatest extent possible. Ideally, such water resources planning should be undertaken within the context of comprehensive state planning.

The water resource and supply plans should include at least:
- a 20-year projection of water supply needs and service areas based on sound comprehensive planning principles;
- sources of surface and groundwater supply to meet needs;
- protection of watershed and evaluation of surface and groundwater resource impacts, and actions necessary to maintain or improve water quantity and quality to meet projected needs and to maintain the ecological, recreation, and navigational functions of the water resources;
- plan for water conservation and reuse, and, as appropriate, drought management and emergency contingency plans;
- a stormwater and floodplain management element addressing the on-site prevention, retention, and treatment of stormwater runoff;
- evaluation of alternatives to proposed plan including policies for resource and habitat restoration;

- environmental impacts and mitigating factors;
- analysis of existing and required legal and institutional arrangements, and roles and responsibilities of appropriate levels of government in carrying out the plan, including the use of intergovernmental or interstate agreements;
- a land-use framework for land located near sensitive water resources; and
- financing strategies for needed improvements, along with a system for monitoring or evaluating the attainment of plan objectives.

Commentary: Responsible water resource use and management requires careful planning. The first policy establishes a planning process that integrates projected water demand and resource characteristics with an impact assessment process to ensure considerations of longer-term sustainability. This policy sets forth the specific elements of such a planning process that promote a more rigorous governmental consideration of water resource use and interaction.

A minimum 20-year planning horizon is proposed to enable capital investments in water-related infrastructure to be recovered through financing mechanisms while ensuring a planning period that would allow for reasonably accurate demographic and other projections affecting water demand. The need for water users to repay bonds for water supply capital improvements or to repay state loans within a time period long enough to stabilize water utility rates suggests the need for longer-range rather than shorter-term water resource management planning. Although some states (e.g., Arizona, under its 1983 Water Use Act) may require that water for urban uses be secured for a century as a precondition of assessing water transfers, a 20-year planning horizon allows for more accurate longer-term need projections prior to making infrastructure investments.

Policy 2. APA and its Chapters support legislation to establish requirements for state comprehensive water-use permits issued pursuant to policies and criteria set forth in state comprehensive water resources and supply plans. State (and/or regional, in those states where multijurisdictional water districts exist) permit reviews should incorporate thorough environmental and socioeconomic review of applications for new or increased use of surface water and groundwater resources for consumptive and nonconsumptive uses prior to state approval or denial. State (and/or regional) requirements should be made pursuant to a public hearing process that involves all appropriate levels of government and allows public input to the decision-making process.

Commentary: The withdrawal of waters for public, industrial, agricultural, and power generation uses should not be undertaken without a full understanding of the impacts of such withdrawals upon the quantity and quality of groundwater and surface waters, and without regard to the interests of competing users. This analysis should also address ecological and recreational values of the water resources. State and/or regional overview is essential to the full consideration of the hydrological, ecological, and growth impacts of interbasin transfers, downstream quality and quantity impacts of upstream users, and the groundwater/surface water interrelationships of withdrawals and diversions. States need to consider comprehensively managing the consumptive use of all of their water resources—groundwater as well as surface water withdrawals — through a comprehensive permit system administered at the state or the regional level. The permit process should be designed to maximize public participation to ensure that all interests are represented in water-use permit decisions.

Policy 3. APA and Chapters support legislation requiring land-use and health regulations for source water protection in order to protect the existing water quality and capacity of aquifers and surface water resources.

Commentary: Because of the high costs of water treatment and aquifer remediation, source water protection for drinking water supplies remains a policy priority.

Policy 4. Water conservation must remain an important water resource and supply plan objective. APA and its Chapters support state legislation requiring the metering and leak detection of all significant private or public community drinking water system service connections as well as all major industrial, commercial, or agricultural users to promote and monitor water conservation.

Commentary: Water conservation remains an important component of any water supply plan. Metering provides an incentive for users to conserve water and the evaluation of leakage and other unaccounted for flow is essential in promoting and monitoring the success of water conservation efforts. Other measures, such as using reclaimed water or higher-efficiency systems for irrigation or employing drought-resistent or natural landscaping, can also be effective in reducing water use.

Policy 5. APA and its Chapters support appropriate state legislation establishing standards and permits for construction, operation, and abandonment of all wells. These standards should be based on the long-term sustainable yield of the water resources.

Commentary: Improperly constructed or abandoned wells can provide opportunities for water supply contamination and aquifer interconnection, especially for larger wells (10,000 gpd and larger) used for public water supply, industrial, and irrigation purposes. The impacts of all new major wells and existing wells that are abandoned should be assessed through a permit system requiring preconstruction and postclosure review. Operation guidelines for major wells, including controls on pumping rates, can also help manage well interference problems and stream baseflow reductions, while backflow valve requirements can protect against groundwater contamination by agricultural chemicals. Well permits issued by local permitting officers, boards of health or State environmental agencies should also be required for smaller noncommunity onsite domestic water supply wells.

Policy 6. APA and its Chapters should support legislative action and policy to manage stormwater runoff and its attendant water pollution risks. These policies include recognizing EPA-approved Nonpoint Source Management Plans (as established by Section 319 of the Clean Water Act) as an appropriate vehicle for allocating coastal, agricultural, urban, and other nonpoint source management program efforts and funds, and implementing plans and programs promoting best management practices to better control municipal and industrial stormwater runoff and discharges. APA and its Chapters emphasize the value of encouraging appropriate land uses in areas of sensitive water resources, and also support the establishment of local development standards that incorporate best management practices for managing postconstruction impacts on surface and groundwater resources. APA National and its Chapters continue to emphasize the importance of local comprehensive planning in legislation that is proposed for the management of stormwater runoff and nonpoint sources.

Commentary: Approved Nonpoint Source Management Plans establish uniform, state-specific blueprints for the nationwide effort to remediate all nonpoint sources of groundwater and surface water pollution through state land-use-related water quality management programs. Stormwater management remains a priority issue in many urban areas, where runoff and discharges from construction activity, small municipal separate stormwater systems, industrial stormwater systems, and combined sewer overflows threaten surface water and groundwater quality. Best management practices, many employing land-use controls, offer an important strategy for controlling these risks. Stormwater should be considered a water resource instead of a waste product, with natural attenuation, infiltration, and recharge promoted over collection, transport, storage, treatment, and discharge. This policy also encourages Smart Growth by promoting land-use patterns that minimize the generation of nonpoint source pollution and site planning that uses established best management practices to control pollution, especially with respect to stormwater runoff that can be treated onsite.

POLICY 7. APA and its Chapters should encourage legislation, with adequate federal funding, to require periodic comprehensive updating of Wastewater Facility Plans, consistent with local comprehensive plans, as a condition for receipt of state revolving loans or grants. The process for updating facility plans should be coordinated with revisions to community comprehensive plans and the integration of Smart Growth policies to focus new development in those areas served by existing wastewater infrastructure.

Commentary: The facility plans in the 1970s are approaching their design years. The current federal rules do not encourage comprehensive updating of these plans, but rather spot changes, often in conjunction with individual development proposals. Local plan consistency should be addressed as a requirement for the receipt of federal funds. Although this policy was initially adopted in APA's earlier Surface Water PIP, this is still an important policy to promote, especially since some states using revolving loan funds may propose phasing out facility plan requirements in order to reduce their administrative burdens.

Policy 8. APA and its Chapters promote aquatic biodiversity and habitat recovery by supporting programs that reduce hydrological alterations, the deterioration of habitat quality, and the deterioration of water quality. APA and its Chapters should promote regulatory development that emulates the natural hydrologic and ecologic regimes in an increasingly robust fashion, including the restoration of degraded stream reaches and their riparian areas, including associated wetlands.

Commentary: Waterways and their riparian areas are critical habitats for a variety of wildlife. Straightening, cementing over, and otherwise altering stream channels and wetlands remove the opportunities for biodiversity and also impact important ecological processes that remove pollutants and improve water quality. Health of riparian areas is an important indicator of ecosystem health and consequently of the sustainability of human activities within a watershed.

Policy 9. APA and its Chapters should support federal and state environmental protection agencies in implementing the Total Maximum Daily Load (TMDL) program of the Clean Water Act and the development of baseline, reference TMDLs associated with specific land uses.

Commentary: The Total Maximum Daily Load (TMDL) program of the Clean Water Act requires a comprehensive inventory and assessment of impaired waters in order to determine the amounts of pollutants being discharged into a waterway from all potential sources. Without this information, it is impossible to take the next step, which is to devise a plan to allocate the amount of pollutants each source may discharge (through regulations or by market-based mechanisms) and thereby clean up the waterway to the point it meets the fishable and swimmable standard. Watershed plans that support agreements between local entities will be needed in order to achieve regional strategies that truly move towards meeting TMDL compliance.

Policy 10. APA and its Chapters should support legislation to reauthorize and expand federal funding under the Clean Water and Safe Drinking Water Acts for water infrastructure (including funding authorized to support State Revolving Loan Funds) and to reauthorize the Coastal Zone Management Act. These legislative initiatives would provide continuing funding for nationally important water quality, infrastructure, and resource protection programs, while addressing the critical issues of controlling nonpoint sources, enhancing coastal resources, and protecting national estuaries and outstanding waters.

Commentary: EPA and the federal government need to maintain and strengthen their partnership with state and local governments in funding water quality improvement and infrastructure programs. State revolving loan funds offer new opportunities to consider state land-use and "smart growth" objectives within integrated priority ranking systems by incorporating such considerations into the ranking system in addition to the more traditional public health and environmental criteria. Infrastructure investments can also be tied better to land use by the use of various economic incentives (e.g., lower interest rates or alternative repayment structures) for projects supporting state and regional land-use policies. Given the large population growth projected within our coastal areas, supporting the reauthorization of and expanded funding for the Coastal Zone Management Act remains a critical legislative priority for APA and its Chapters.

Policy 11. APA and its Chapters should support legislation establishing interstate or regional compacts to limit drawdowns of shared aquifers and the use of common surface waters. APA and its Chapters and key water policy decision makers should actively encourage states, tribes, and interstate and basin authorities to seek negotiated agreements, ratified by appropriate legislation, to resolve issues regarding water allocations and to develop water resource management systems on an aquifer or watershed basis, to the greatest extent possible.

Commentary: Adjudication can be an effective, but complex, lengthy and expensive means of resolving water rights. Adjudications can act to bring parties to the negotiating table, but negotiated settlements are far more likely to result in long-term, constructive relationships — especially since the U.S. Supreme Court's ruling in Kansas v. Colorado, *handed down in June 2001, allowed damages to be imposed on a state for violating the Arkansas River compact. In the wake of this decision, federal courts may be more willing to enforce interstate (and, by implication, state/tribal) water agreements and compacts and to both impose and uphold sanctions against entities violating these agreements.*

Policy 12. APA and its Chapters support legislation providing opportunities for the integrated management of groundwater and surface water supplies, and funding for research on strategies for the integrated management, monitoring, and use of surface and groundwater. Whenever possible and appropriate, the planning area of such management programs should be based on natural hydrologic features, such as watersheds and aquifers. APA and its Chapters also support and encourage the development of land-use variables within water resource models.

Commentary: There is much we still need to learn about the interrelationships of surface and ground water. Monitoring of these resources is a complex and costly venture, but necessary if we are to assess their status and be alerted to new sources and instances of contamination. APA and its Chapters should support increased funding of federal and state programs that monitor, model, assess, and map our nation's groundwater and surface water resources.

MAKING GREAT COMMUNITIES HAPPEN

The American Planning Association provides leadership in the development of vital communities by advocating excellence in community planning, promoting education and citizen empowerment, and providing the tools and support necessary to effect positive change.

466. Planning for Hillside Development. Robert B. Olshansky. November 1996. 50pp.

467. A Planners Guide to Sustainable Development. Kevin J. Krizek and Joe Power. December 1996. 66pp.

468. Creating Transit-Supportive Land-Use Regulations. Marya Morris, ed. December 1996. 76pp.

469. Gambling, Economic Development, and Historic Preservation. Christopher Chadbourne, Philip Walker, and Mark Wolfe. March 1997. 56pp.

470/471. Habitat Protection Planning: Where the Wild Things Are. Christopher J. Duerksen, Donald L. Elliott, N. Thompson Hobbs, Erin Johnson, and James R. Miller. May 1997. 82pp.

472. Converting Storefronts to Housing: An Illustrated Guide. July 1997. 88pp.

473. Subdivision Design in Flood Hazard Areas. Marya Morris. September 1997. 62pp.

474/475. Online Resources for Planners. Sanjay Jeer. November 1997. 126pp.

476. Nonpoint Source Pollution: A Handbook for Local Governments. Sanjay Jeer, Megan Lewis, Stuart Meck, Jon Witten, and Michelle Zimet. December 1997. 127pp.

477. Transportation Demand Management. Erik Ferguson. March 1998. 68pp.

478. Manufactured Housing: Regulation, Design Innovations, and Development Options. Welford Sanders. July 1998. 120pp.

479. The Principles of Smart Development. September 1998. 113pp.

480/481. Modernizing State Planning Statutes: The Growing Smart℠ Working Papers. Volume 2. September 1998. 269pp.

482. Planning and Zoning for Concentrated Animal Feeding Operations. Jim Schwab. December 1998. 44pp.

483/484. Planning for Post-Disaster Recovery and Reconstruction. Jim Schwab, et al. December 1998. 346pp.

485. Traffic Sheds, Rural Highway Capacity, and Growth Management. Lane Kendig with Stephen Tocknell. March 1999. 24pp.

486. Youth Participation in Community Planning. Ramona Mullahey, Yve Susskind, and Barry Checkoway. June 1999. 70pp.

489/490. Aesthetics, Community Character, and the Law. Christopher J. Duerksen and R. Matthew Goebel. December 1999. 154pp.

493. Transportation Impact Fees and Excise Taxes: A Survey of 16 Jurisdictions. Connie Cooper. July 2000. 62pp.

494. Incentive Zoning: Meeting Urban Design and Affordable Housing Objectives. Marya Morris. September 2000. 64pp.

495/496. Everything You Always Wanted To Know About Regulating Sex Businesses. Eric Damian Kelly and Connie Cooper. December 2000. 168pp.

497/498. Parks, Recreation, and Open Spaces: An Agenda for the 21st Century. Alexander Garvin. December 2000. 72pp.

499. Regulating Home-Based Businesses in the Twenty-First Century. Charles Wunder. December 2000. 37pp.

500/501. Lights, Camera, Community Video. Cabot Orton, Keith Spiegel, and Eddie Gale. April 2001. 76pp.

502. Parks and Economic Development. John L. Crompton. November 2001. 74pp.

503/504. Saving Face: How Corporate Franchise Design Can Respect Community Identity (revised edition). Ronald Lee Fleming. February 2002. 118pp.

505. Telecom Hotels: A Planners Guide. Jennifer Evans-Crowley. March 2002. 31pp.

506/507. Old Cities/Green Cities: Communities Transform Unmanaged Land. J. Blaine Bonham, Jr., Gerri Spilka, and Darl Rastorfer. March 2002. 123pp.

508. Performance Guarantees for Government Permit Granting Authorities. Wayne Feiden and Raymond Burby. July 2002. 80pp.

509. Street Vending: A Survey of Ideas and Lessons for Planners. Jennifer Ball. August 2002. 44pp.

510/511. Parking Standards. Edited by Michael Davidson and Fay Dolnick. November 2002. 181pp.

512. Smart Growth Audits. Jerry Weitz and Leora Susan Waldner. November 2002. 56pp.

513/514. Regional Approaches to Affordable Housing. Stuart Meck, Rebecca Retzlaff, and James Schwab. February 2003. 271pp.

515. Planning for Street Connectivity: Getting from Here to There. Susan Handy, Robert G. Paterson, and Kent Butler. May 2003. 95pp.

516. Jobs-Housing Balance. Jerry Weitz. November 2003. 41pp.

517. Community Indicators. Rhonda Phillips. December 2003. 46pp.

518/519. Ecological Riverfront Design. Betsy Otto, Kathleen McCormick, and Michael Leccese. March 2004. 177pp.